PHILOSOPHY OF EDUCATION

PHILOSOPHY OF EDUCATION

Premchand Jogi

CRESCENT
PUBLISHING CORPORATION

Philosophy of Education

Edition 2026

ISBN 978-81-8342-130-0

Published by
CRESCENT PUBLISHING CORPORATION
4806/24, Mathur Lane,
Ansari Road, Darya Ganj,
New Delhi - 110 002
Ph.: 011 - 23244131
Mob.: + 91 - 9711991838, 9999021668
E-mail: crescentbook@gmail.com
Website: www.crescentpublishingcorp.weebly.com

Printed at:
Balaji Digital
Delhi

Preface

Enabling people to become productive beings of society, stretching their capabilities to the utmost, helping them respond creatively to the world they live in and satisfy their curiosity and their aesthetic impulses, education has been viewed throughout history as an optimistic endeavour. Societies have always viewed educational as crucial to their development, and have always sought to educate their people. Today, as the social, economic and political contexts of our world become increasingly complex, education has become indispensable for everyone. So even as many developing nations strive to make their people literate, most developed nations fulfil to continuously improve their standards of education.

Even though the objectives of imparting education have remained constant through time, the methods and ways of imparting education have been numerous through societies and milieus, depending upon the philosophy they subscribe to. This book in the series of books on educational philosophy undertakes the task of delineating exploring the history and evolution of educational philosophy, with an incisive insight into current modes of thinking contextualising the major educational philosophers of the world in their contemporary social needs and epoch, it present forth a lucid and detailed account of the important schools of thought in philosophy. In addition, it evaluates the impact of these philosophies, making a review of them as they have been adapted in different societies. Further, it also explores contemporary philosophies in education.

It is hoped that the comprehensiveness, information and lucidity of the book serve well for the readers.

Premchand Jogi

Contents

1

Philosophy of Education

Philosophy cannot be defined simply from the side of subject matter. For this reason, the definition of such conceptions as generality, totality, and ultimateness is most readily reached from the side of the disposition toward the world which they connote. In any literal and quantitative sense, these terms do not apply to the subject matter of knowledge, for completeness and finality are out of the question. The very nature of experience as an ongoing, changing process forbids.

In a less rigid sense, they apply to science rather than to philosophy. For obviously it is to mathematics, physics, chemistry, biology, anthropology, history, etc. that we must go, not to philosophy, to find out the facts of the world. It is for the sciences to say what generalisations are tenable about the world and what they specifically are. But when we ask what sort of permanent disposition of action toward the world the scientific disclosures exact of us we are raising a philosophic question.

From this point of view, "totality" does not mean the hopeless task of a quantitative summation. It means rather consistency of mode of response in reference to the plurality of events which occur. Consistency does not mean literal identity; for since the same thing does not happen twice, an exact repetition of a reaction involves some maladjustment. Totality means continuity — the carrying on of a former habit of action with the readaptation necessary to keep it alive and growing. Instead of signifying a ready-made complete scheme of action, it means keeping the balance in a multitude of diverse actions, so that each borrows and gives significance to every other. Any person who is open-minded and sensitive to new perceptions, and who has concentration and responsibility in connecting them has, in so far, a philosophic disposition.

One of the popular senses of philosophy is calm and endurance in the face of difficulty and loss; it is even supposed to be a power to bear pain without complaint. This meaning is a tribute to the influence of the Stoic philosophy rather than an attribute of philosophy in general. But in so far as it suggests that the wholeness characteristic of philosophy is a power to learn, or to extract meaning, from even the unpleasant vicissitudes of experience and to embody what is learned in an ability to go on learning, it is justified in any scheme.

An analogous interpretation applies to the generality and ultimateness of philosophy. Taken literally, they are absurd pretensions; they indicate insanity. Finality does not mean, however, that experience is ended and exhausted, but means the disposition to penetrate to deeper levels of meaning — to go below the surface and find out the connections of any event or object, and to keep at it. In like manner the philosophic attitude is general in the sense that it is averse to taking anything as isolated; it tries to place an act in its context — which constitutes its significance.

It is of assistance to connect philosophy with thinking in its distinction from knowledge. Knowledge, grounded knowledge, is science; it represents objects which have been settled, ordered, disposed of rationally. Thinking, on the other hand, is prospective in reference. It is occasioned by an unsettlement and it aims at overcoming a disturbance. Philosophy is thinking what the known demands of us — what responsive attitude it exacts. It is an idea of what is possible, not a record of accomplished fact. Hence it is hypothetical, like all thinking. It presents an assignment of something to be done — something to be tried. Its value lies not in furnishing solutions (which can be achieved only in action) but in defining difficulties and suggesting methods for dealing with them. Philosophy might almost be described as thinking which has become conscious of itself — which has generalised its place, function, and value in experience.

More specifically, the demand for a "total" attitude arises because there is the need of integration in action of the conflicting various interests in life. Where interests are so superficial that they glide readily into one another, or where they are not sufficiently organised to come into conflict with one another, the need for philosophy is not perceptible. But when the scientific interest conflicts with, say, the religious, or the economic with the scientific or aesthetic, or when the conservative concern for order is at odds with the progressive interest in freedom, or when institutionalism clashes with individuality, there is a stimulus to discover some more comprehensive point of view from which the divergencies may be brought together, and consistency or continuity of experience recovered.

Often these clashes may be settled by an individual for himself; the area of the struggle of aims is limited and a person works out his own rough accommodations. Such homespun philosophies are genuine and often adequate. But they do not result in systems of philosophy. These arise when the discrepant claims of different ideals of conduct affect the community as a whole, and the need for readjustment is general.

These traits explain some things which are often brought as objections against philosophies, such as the part played in them by individual speculation, and their controversial diversity, as well as the fact that philosophy seems to be repeatedly occupied with much the same questions differently stated. Without doubt, all these things characterise historic philosophies more or less. But they are not objections to philosophy so much as they are to human nature, and even to the world in which human nature is set. If there are genuine uncertainties in life, philosophies must reflect that uncertainty.

If there are different diagnoses of the cause of a difficulty, and different proposals for dealing with it; if, that is, the conflict of interests is more or less embodied in different sets of persons, there must be divergent competing philosophies. With respect to what has happened, sufficient evidence is all that is needed to bring agreement and certainty. The thing itself is sure. But with reference to what it is wise to do in a complicated situation, discussion is inevitable precisely because the thing itself is still indeterminate.

One would not expect a ruling class living at ease to have the same philosophy of life as those who were having a hard struggle for existence. If the possessing and the dispossessed had the same fundamental disposition toward the world, it would argue either insincerity or lack of seriousness. A community devoted to industrial pursuits, active in business and commerce, is not likely to see the needs and possibilities of life in the same way as a country with high aesthetic culture and little enterprise in turning the energies of nature to mechanical account.

A social group with a fairly continuous history will respond mentally to a crisis in a very different way from one which has felt the shock of abrupt breaks. Even if the same data were present, they would be evaluated differently. But the different sorts of experience attending different types of life prevent just the same data from presenting themselves, as well as lead to a different scheme of values. As for the similarity of problems, this is often more a matter of appearance than of fact, due to old discussions being translated into the terms of contemporary perplexities. But in certain fundamental respects the same predicaments of life recur from time to time with only such changes as are due to change of social context, including the growth of the sciences.

The fact that philosophic problems arise because of widespread and widely felt difficulties in social practice is disguised because philosophers become a specialised class which uses a technical language, unlike the vocabulary in which the direct difficulties are stated. But where a system becomes influential, its connection with a conflict of interests calling for some programme of social adjustment may always be discovered. At this point, the intimate connection between philosophy and education appears. In fact, education offers a vantage ground from which to penetrate to the human, as distinct from the technical, significance of philosophic discussions.

The student of philosophy "in itself' is always in danger of taking it as so much nimble or severe intellectual exercise — as something said by philosophers and concerning them alone. But when philosophic issues are approached from the side of the kind of mental disposition to which they correspond, or the differences in educational practice they make when acted upon, the life-situations which they formulate can never be far from view. If a theory makes no difference in educational endeavour, it must be artificial. The educational point of view enables one to envisage the philosophic problems where they arise and thrive, where they are at home, and where acceptance or rejection makes a difference in practice.

If we are willing to conceive education as the process of forming fundamental dispositions, intellectual and emotional, toward nature and fellow men, philosophy may even be defined as the general theory of education. Unless a philosophy is to remain symbolic — or verbal — or a sentimental indulgence for a few, or else mere arbitrary dogma, its auditing of past experience and its programme of values must take effect in conduct.

Public agitation, propaganda, legislative and administrative action are effective in producing the change of disposition which a philosophy indicates as desirable, but only in the degree in which they are educative — that is to say, in the degree in which they modify mental and moral attitudes. And at the best, such methods are compromised by the fact they are used with those whose habits are already largely set, while education of youth has a fairer and freer field of operation. On the other side, the business of schooling tends to become a routine empirical affair unless its aims and methods are animated by such a broad and sympathetic survey of its place in contemporary life as it is the business of philosophy to provide.

Positive science always implies practically the ends which the community is concerned to achieve. Isolated from such ends, it is matter of indifference whether its disclosures are used to cure disease or to spread it; to increase the means of sustenance of life or to manufacture war material to wipe life out. If society is interested in one of these things rather than another, science shows the way of attainment.

Philosophy thus has a double task: that of criticising existing aims with respect to the existing state of science, pointing out values which have become obsolete with the command of new resources, showing what values are merely sentimental because there are no means for their realisation; and also that of interpreting the results of specialised science in their bearing on future social endeavour. It is impossible that it should have any success in these tasks without educational equivalents as to what to do and what not to do.

For philosophic theory has no Aladdin's lamp to summon into immediate existence the values which it intellectually constructs. In the mechanical arts, the sciences become methods of managing things so as to utilise their energies for recognised aims. By the educative arts philosophy may generate methods of utilising the energies of human beings in accord with serious and thoughtful conceptions of life. Education is the laboratory in which philosophic distinctions become concrete and are tested.

It is suggestive that European philosophy originated (among the Athenians) under the direct pressure of educational questions. The earlier history of philosophy, developed by the Greeks in Asia Minor and Italy, so far as its range of topics is concerned. It had nature for its subject, and speculated as to how things are made and changed. Later the travelling teachers, known as the Sophists, began to apply the results and the methods of the natural philosophers to human conduct.

When the Sophists, the first body of professional educators in Europe, instructed the youth in virtue, the political arts, and the management of city and household, philosophy began to deal with the relation of the individual to the universal, to some comprehensive class, or to some group; the relation of man and nature, of tradition and reflection, of knowledge and action.

Can virtue, approved excellence in any line, be learned, they asked? What is learning? It has to do with knowledge. What, then, is knowledge? How is it achieved? Through the senses, or by apprenticeship in some form of doing, or by reason that has undergone a preliminary logical discipline? Since learning is coming to know, it involves a passage from ignorance to wisdom, from privation to fullness from defect to perfection, from non-being to being, in the Greek way of putting it. How is such a transition possible? Is change, becoming, development really possible and if so, how? And supposing such questions answered, what is the relation of instruction, of knowledge, to virtue?

This last question led to opening the problem of the relation of reason to action, of theory to practice, since virtue clearly dwelt in action. Was not knowing, the activity of reason, the noblest attribute of man? And consequently was not purely intellectual activity itself the highest of all excellences, compared with which the virtues of neighbourliness and the citizen's life were secondary? Or, on the other hand, was the vaunted intellectual knowledge more than empty and vain pretense, demoralising to character and destructive of the social ties that bound men together in their community life? Was not the only true, because the only moral, life gained through obedient habituation to the customary practices of the community? And was not the new education an enemy to good citizenship, because it set up a rival standard to the established traditions of the community?

In the course of two or three generations such questions were cut loose from their original practical bearing upon education and were discussed on their own account; that is, as matters of philosophy as an independent branch of inquiry. But the fact that the stream of European philosophical thought arose as a theory of educational procedure remains an eloquent witness to the intimate connection of philosophy and education. "Philosophy of education" is not an external application of ready-made ideas to a system of practice having a radically different origin and purpose: it is only an explicit formulation of the problems of the formation of right mental and moral habitudes in respect to the difficulties of contemporary social life. The most penetrating definition of philosophy which can be given is, then, that it is the theory of education in its most general phases.

The reconstruction of philosophy, of education, and of social ideals and methods thus go hand in hand. If there is especial need of educational reconstruction at the present time, if this need makes urgent a reconsideration of the basic ideas of traditional philosophic systems, it is because of the thoroughgoing change in social life accompanying the advance of science, the industrial revolution, and the development of democracy. Such practical changes cannot take place without demanding an educational reformation to meet them, and without leading men to ask what ideas and ideals are implicit in these social changes, and what revisions they require of the ideas and ideals which are inherited from older and unlike cultures. Incidentally throughout the whole book, we have been dealing with just these questions as they affect the relationship of mind and body, theory and practice, man and nature, the individual and social, etc.

Theories of Knowledge

Continuity *versus* Dualism.

The latter assumes continuity; the former state or imply certain basic divisions, separations, or antitheses, technically called dualisms. The origin of these divisions we have found in the hard and fast walls which mark off social groups and classes within a group: like those between rich and poor, men and women, noble and baseborn, ruler and ruled. These barriers mean absence of fluent and free intercourse. This absence is equivalent to the setting up of different types of life-experience, each with isolated subject matter, aim, and standard of values.

Every such social condition must be formulated in a dualistic philosophy, if philosophy is to be a sincere account of experience. When it gets beyond dualism — as many philosophies do in form — it can only be by appeal to something higher than anything found in experience, by a flight to some transcendental realm. And in denying duality in name such theories restore it in fact, for they end in a division between things of this world as mere appearances and an inaccessible essence of reality.

So far as these divisions persist and others are added to them, each leaves its mark upon the educational system, until the scheme of education, taken as a whole, is a deposit of various purposes and procedures. The outcome is that kind of check and balance of segregated factors and values which has been described. The present discussion is simply a formulation, in the terminology of philosophy, of various antithetical conceptions involved in the theory of knowing.

In the first place, there is the opposition of empirical and higher rational knowing. The first is connected with everyday affairs, serves the purposes of the ordinary individual who has no specialised intellectual pursuit, and brings his wants into some kind of working connection with the immediate environment. Such knowing is depreciated, if not despised, as purely utilitarian, lacking in cultural significance. Rational knowledge is supposed to be something which touches reality in ultimate, intellectual fashion; to be pursued for its own sake and properly to terminate in purely theoretical insight, not debased by application in behaviour. Socially, the distinction corresponds to that of the intelligence used by the working classes and that used by a learned class remote from concern with the means of living.

Philosophically, the difference turns about the distinction of the particular and universal. Experience is an aggregate of more or less isolated particulars, acquaintance with each of which must be separately made. Reason deals with universals, with general principles, with laws, which lie above the welter of concrete details. In the educational precipitate, the pupil is supposed to have to learn, on one hand, a lot of items of specific information, each standing by itself, and upon the other hand, to become familiar with a certain number of laws and general relationships. Geography, as often taught, illustrates the former; mathematics, beyond the rudiments of figuring, the latter. For all practical purposes, they represent two independent worlds.

Another antithesis is suggested by the two senses of the word "learning." On the one hand, learning is the sum total of what is known, as that is handed down by books and learned men. It is something external, an accumulation of cognitions as one might store material commodities in a warehouse. Truth exists ready-made somewhere. Study is then the process by which an individual draws on what is in storage.

On the other hand, learning means something which the individual does when he studies. It is an active, personally conducted affair. The dualism here is between knowledge as something external, or, as it is often called, objective, and knowing as something purely internal, subjective, psychical. There is, on one side, a body of truth, ready-made, and, on the other, a ready-made mind equipped with a faculty of knowing — if it only wills to exercise it, which it is often strangely loath to do. The separation, often touched upon, between subject matter and method is the educational equivalent of this dualism. Socially the distinction has to do with the part of life which is dependent upon authority and that where individuals are free to advance.

Another dualism is that of activity and passivity in knowing. Purely empirical and physical things are often supposed to be known by receiving impressions. Physical things somehow stamp themselves upon the mind or convey themselves into consciousness by means of the sense organs. Rational knowledge and knowledge of spiritual things is supposed, on the contrary, to spring from activity initiated within the mind, an activity carried on better if it is kept remote from all sullying touch of the senses and external objects. The distinction between sense training and object lessons and laboratory exercises, and pure ideas contained in books, and appropriated — so it is thought — by some miraculous output of mental energy, is a fair expression in education of this distinction. Socially, it reflects a division between those who are controlled by direct concern with things and those who are free to cultivate. themselves.

Another current opposition is that said to exist between the intellect and the emotions. The emotions are conceived to be purely private and personal, having nothing to do with the work of pure intelligence in apprehending facts and truths, — except perhaps the single emotion of intellectual curiosity. The intellect is a pure light; the emotions are a disturbing heat. The mind turns outward to truth; the emotions turn inward to considerations of personal advantage and loss. Thus in education we have that systematic depreciation of interest which has been noted, plus the necessity in practice, with most pupils, of recourse to extraneous and irrelevant rewards and penalties in order to induce the person who has a mind to apply that mind to the truths to be known. Thus we have the spectacle of professional educators decrying appeal to interest while they uphold with great dignity the need of reliance upon examinations, marks, promotions and emotions, prizes, and the time-honored paraphernalia of rewards and punishments. The effect of this situation in crippling the teacher's sense of humour has not received the attention which it deserves.

All of these separations culminate in one between knowing and doing, theory and practice, between mind as the end and spirit of action and the body as its organ and means. We shall not repeat what has been said about the source of this dualism in the division of society into a class labouring with their muscles for material sustenance and a class which, relieved from economic pressure, devotes itself to the arts of expression and social direction. Nor is it necessary to speak again of the educational evils which spring from the separation.

The forces which tend to make the untenability of this conception obvious and to replace it by the idea of continuity. *(i)* The advance of physiology and the psychology associated with it have shown the connection of mental activity with that of the nervous system. Too often recognition of connection has stopped short at this point; the older dualism of soul and body has been replaced by that of the brain and the rest of the body. But in fact the nervous system is only a specialised mechanism for keeping all bodily activities working together. Instead of being isolated from them, as an organ of knowing from organs of motor response, it is the organ by which they interact responsively with one another.

The brain is essentially an organ for effecting the reciprocal adjustment to each other of the stimuli received from the environment and responses directed upon it. Note that the adjusting is reciprocal; the brain not only enables organic activity to be brought to bear upon any object of the environment in response to a sensory stimulation, but this response also determines what the next stimulus will be.

While each motor response is adjusted to the state of affairs indicated through the sense organs, that motor response shapes the next sensory stimulus. Generalising this illustration, the brain is the machinery for a constant reorganising of activity so as to maintain its continuity; that is to say, to make such modifications in future action as are required because of what has already been done.

The continuity of the work of the carpenter distinguishes it from a routine repetition of identically the same motion, and from a random activity where there is nothing cumulative. What makes it continuous, consecutive, or concentrated is that each earlier act prepares the way for later acts, while these take account of or reckon with the results already attained — the basis of all responsibility. No one who has realised the full force of the facts of the connection of knowing with the nervous system and of the nervous system with the readjusting of activity continuously to meet new conditions, will doubt that knowing has to do with reorganising activity, instead of being something isolated from all activity, complete on its own account.

(ii) The development of biology clinches this lesson, with its discovery of evolution. For the philosophic significance of the doctrine of evolution lies precisely in its emphasis upon continuity of simpler and more complex organic forms until we reach man. The development of organic forms begins with structures where the adjustment of environment and organism is obvious, and where anything which can be called mind is at a minimum. As activity becomes more complex, coordinating a greater number of factors in space and time, intelligence plays a more and more marked role, for it has a larger span of the future to forecast and plan for.

The effect upon the theory of knowing is to displace the notion that it is the activity of a mere onlooker or spectator of the world, the notion which goes with the idea of knowing as something complete in itself. For the doctrine of organic development means that the living creature is a part of the world, sharing its vicissitudes and fortunes, and making itself secure in its precarious dependence only as it intellectually identifies itself with the things about it, and, forecasting the future consequences of what is going on, shapes its own activities accordingly. If the living, experiencing being is an intimate participant in the activities of the world to which it belongs, then knowledge is a mode of participation, valuable in the degree in which it is effective. It cannot be the idle view of an unconcerned spectator.

(iii) The development of the experimental method as the method of getting knowledge and of making sure it is knowledge, and not mere opinion — the method of both discovery and proof — is the remaining great force in bringing about a transformation in the theory of knowledge. The experimental method has two sides. *(i)* On one hand, it means that we have no right to call anything knowledge except where our activity has actually produced certain physical changes in things, which agree with and confirm the conception entertained. Short of such specific changes, our beliefs are only hypotheses, theories, suggestions, guesses, and are to be entertained tentatively and to be utilised as indications of experiments to be tried. *(ii)* On the other hand, the experimental method of thinking signifies that thinking is of avail; that it is of avail in just the degree in which the anticipation of future consequences is made on the basis of thorough observation of present conditions. Experimentation, in other words, is not equivalent to blind reacting.

Such surplus activity — a surplus with reference to what has been observed and is now anticipated — is indeed an unescapable factor in all our behaviour, but it is not experiment save as consequences are noted and are used to make predictions and plans in similar situations in the future. The more the meaning of the experimental method is perceived, the more our trying out of a certain way of treating the material resources and obstacles which confront us embodies a prior use of intelligence. What we call magic was with respect to many things the experimental method of the savage; but for him to try was to try his luck, not his ideas. The scientific experimental method is, on the contrary, a trial of ideas; hence even when practically — or immediately — unsuccessful, it is intellectual, fruitful; for we learn from our failures when our endeavours are seriously thoughtful.

The experimental method is new as a scientific resource — as a systematised means of making knowledge, though as old as life as a practical device. Hence it is not surprising that men have not recognised its full scope. For the most part, its significance is regarded as belonging to certain technical and merely physical matters. It will doubtless take a long time to secure the perception that it holds equally as to the forming and testing of ideas in social and moral matters. Men still want the crutch of dogma, of beliefs fixed by authority, to relieve them of the trouble of thinking and the responsibility of directing their activity by thought. They tend to confine their own thinking to a consideration of which one among the rival systems of dogma they will accept.

Hence the schools are better adapted, as John Stuart Mill said, to make disciples than inquirers. But every advance in the influence of the experimental method is sure to aid in outlawing the literary, dialectic, and authoritative methods of forming beliefs which have governed the schools of the past, and to transfer their prestige to methods which will procure an active concern with things and persons, directed by aims of increasing temporal reach and deploying greater range of things in space. In time the theory of knowing must be derived from the practice which is most successful in making knowledge; and then that theory will be employed to improve the methods which are less successful.

Schools of Method

There are various systems of philosophy with characteristically different conceptions of the method of knowing. Some of them are named scholasticism, sensationalism, rationalism, idealism, realism, empiricism, transcendentalism, pragmatism, etc. Many of them have been criticised in connection with the discussion of some educational problem. We are here concerned with them as involving deviations from that method which has proved most effective in achieving knowledge, for a consideration of the deviations may render clearer the true place of knowledge in experience. In brief, the function of knowledge is to make one experience freely available in other experiences. The word "freely" marks the difference between the principle of knowledge and that of habit.

Habit means that an individual undergoes a modification through an experience, which modification forms a predisposition to easier and more effective action in a like direction in the future. Thus it also has the function of making one experience available in subsequent experiences. Within certain limits, it performs this function successfully. But habit, apart from knowledge, does not make allowance for change of conditions, for novelty.

Prevision of change is not part of its scope, for habit assumes the essential likeness of the new situation with the old. Consequently it often leads astray, or comes between a person and the successful performance of his task, just as the skill, based on habit alone, of the mechanic will desert him when something unexpected occurs in the running of the machine. But a man who understands the machine is the man who knows what he is about. He knows the conditions under which a given habit works, and is in a position to introduce the changes which will readapt it to new conditions.

In other words, knowledge is a perception of those connections of an object which determine its applicability in a given situation. To take an extreme example; savages react to a flaming comet as they are accustomed to react to other events which threaten the security of their life. Since they try to frighten wild animals or their enemies by shrieks, beating of gongs, brandishing of weapons, etc., they use the same methods to scare away the comet. To us, the method is plainly absurd — so absurd that we fail to note that savages are simply falling back upon habit in a way which exhibits its limitations.

The only reason we do not act in some analogous fashion is because we do not take the comet as an isolated, disconnected event, but apprehend it in its connections with other events. We place it, as we say, in the astronomical system. We respond to its connections and not simply to the immediate occurrence. Thus our attitude to it is much freer. We may approach it, so to speak, from any one of the angles provided by its connections. We can bring into play, as we deem wise, any one of the habits appropriate to any one of the connected objects.

Thus we get at a new event indirectly instead of immediately — by invention, ingenuity, resourcefulness. An ideally perfect knowledge would represent such a network of interconnections that any past experience would offer a point of advantage from which to get at the problem presented in a new experience. In fine, while a habit apart from knowledge supplies us with a single fixed method of attack, knowledge means that selection may be made from a much wider range of habits.

Two aspects of this more general and freer availability of former experiences for subsequent ones may be distinguished. (i) One, the more tangible, is increased power of control. What cannot be managed directly may be handled indirectly; or we can interpose barriers between us and undesirable consequences; or we may evade them if we cannot overcome them. Genuine knowledge has all the practical value attaching to efficient habits in any case. (ii) But it also increases the meaning, the experienced significance, attaching to an experience. A situation to which we respond capriciously or by routine has only a minimum of conscious significance; we get nothing mentally from it. But wherever knowledge comes into play in determining a new experience there is mental reward; even if we fail practically in getting the needed control we have the satisfaction of experiencing a meaning instead of merely reacting physically.

While the content of knowledge is what has happened, what is taken as finished and hence settled and sure, the reference of knowledge is future or prospective. For knowledge furnishes the means of understanding or giving meaning to what is still going on and what is to be done. The knowledge of a physician is what he has found out by personal acquaintance and by study of what others have ascertained and recorded. But it is knowledge to him because it supplies the resources by which he interprets the unknown things which confront him, fills out the partial obvious facts with connected suggested phenomena, foresees their probable future, and makes plans accordingly. When knowledge is cut off from use in giving meaning to what is blind and baffling, it drops out of consciousness entirely or else becomes an object of aesthetic contemplation.

There is much emotional satisfaction to be had from a survey of the symmetry and order of possessed knowledge, and the satisfaction is a legitimate one. But this contemplative attitude is aesthetic, not intellectual. It is the same sort of joy that comes from viewing a finished picture or a well composed landscape. It would make no difference if the subject matter were totally different, provided it had the same harmonious organisation. Indeed, it would make no difference if it were wholly invented, a play of fancy.

Applicability to the world means not applicability to what is past and gone — that is out of the question by the nature of the case; it means applicability to what is still going on, what is still unsettled, in the moving scene in which we are implicated. The very fact that we so easily overlook this trait, and regard statements of what is past and out of reach as knowledge is because we assume the continuity of past and future. We cannot entertain the conception of a world in which knowledge of its past would not be helpful in forecasting and giving meaning to its future. We ignore the prospective reference just because it is so irretrievably implied.

Yet many of the philosophic schools of method which have been mentioned transform the ignoring into a virtual denial. They regard knowledge as something complete in itself irrespective of its availability in dealing with what is yet to be. And it is this omission which vitiates them and which makes them stand as sponsors for educational methods which an adequate conception of knowledge condemns. For one has only to call to mind what is sometimes treated in schools as acquisition of knowledge to realise how lacking it is in any fruitful connection with the ongoing experience of the students — how largely it seems to be believed that the mere appropriation of subject matter which happens to be stored in books constitutes knowledge. No matter how true what is learned to those who found it out and in whose experience it functioned, there is nothing which makes it knowledge to the pupils. It might as well be something about Mars or about some fanciful country unless it fructifies in the individual's own life.

At the time when scholastic method developed, it had relevancy to social conditions. It was a method for systematising and lending rational sanction to material accepted on authority. This subject matter meant so much that it vitalised the defining and systematising brought to bear upon it. Under present conditions the scholastic method, for most persons, means a form of knowing which has no especial connection with any particular subject matter. It includes making distinctions, definitions, divisions, and classifications for the mere sake of making them — with no objective in experience. The view of thought as a purely physical activity having its own forms, which are applied to any material as a seal may be stamped on any plastic stuff, the view which underlies what is termed formal logic is essentially the scholastic method generalised. The doctrine of formal discipline in education is the natural counterpart of the scholastic method.

The contrasting theories of the method of knowledge which go by the name of sensationalism and rationalism correspond to an exclusive emphasis upon the particular and the general respectively — or upon bare facts on one side and bare relations on the other. In real knowledge, there is a particularising and a generalising function working together. So far as a situation is confused, it has to be cleared up; it has to be resolved into details, as sharply defined as possible. Specified facts and qualities constitute the elements of the problem to be dealt with, and it is through our sense organs that they are specified.

As setting forth the problem, they may well be termed particulars, for they are fragmentary. Since our task is to discover their connections and to recombine them, for us at the time they are partial. They are to be given meaning; hence, just as they stand, they lack it. Anything which is to be known, whose meaning has still to be made out, offers itself as particular. But what is already known, if it has been worked over with a view to making it applicable to intellectually mastering new particulars, is general in function. Its function of introducing connection into what is otherwise unconnected constitutes its generality.

Any fact is general if we use it to give meaning to the elements of a new experience. "Reason" is just the ability to bring the subject matter of prior experience to bear to perceive the significance of the subject matter of a new experience. A person is reasonable in the degree in which he is habitually open to seeing an event which immediately strikes his senses not as an isolated thing but in its connection with the common experience of mankind.

Without the particulars as they are discriminated by the active responses of sense organs, there is no material for knowing and no intellectual growth. Without placing these particulars in the context of the meanings wrought out in the larger experience of the past — without the use of reason or thought — particulars are mere excitations or irritations. The mistake alike of the sensational and the rationalistic schools is that each fails to see that the function of sensory stimulation and thought is relative to reorganising experience in applying the old to the new, thereby maintaining the continuity or consistency of life.

2

Aims of Education

The nature of an aim so far as it falls within an activity, instead of being furnished from without. We approach the definition by a contrast of mere results with ends. Any exhibition of energy has results. The wind blows about the sands of the desert; the position of the grains is changed. Here is a result, an effect, but not an end. For there is nothing in the outcome which completes or fulfills what went before it. There is mere spatial redistribution. One state of affairs is just as good as any other. Consequently there is no basis upon which to select an earlier state of affairs as a beginning, a later as an end, and to consider what intervenes as a process of transformation and realisation.

Consider for example the activities of bees in contrast with the changes in the sands when the wind blows them about. The results of the bees' actions may be called ends not because they are designed or consciously intended, but because they are true terminations or completions of what has preceded. When the bees gather pollen and make wax and build cells, each step prepares the way for the next. When cells are built, the queen lays eggs in them; when eggs are laid, they are sealed and bees brood them and keep them at a temperature required to hatch them. When they are hatched, bees feed the young till they can take care of themselves. Now we are so familiar with such facts, that we are apt to dismis them on the ground that life and instinct are a kind o miraculous thing anyway. Thus we fail to note what th essential characteristic of the event is; namely, th significance of the temporal place and order of eacl element; the way each prior event leads into its successo while the successor takes up what is furnished an utilises it for some other stage, until we arrive at the end which, as it were, summarises and finishes off th process.

Since aims relate always to results, the first thing t look to when it is a question of aims, is whether the worl assigned possesses intrinsic continuity. Or is it a mer serial aggregate of acts, first doing one thing and the another? To talk about an educational aim whe approximately each act of a pupil is dictated by th teacher, when the only order in the sequence of his acts i that which comes from the assignment of lessons and th giving of directions by another, is to talk nonsense. It i equally fatal to an aim to permit capricious o discontinuous action in the name of spontaneous self expression.

An aim implies an orderly and ordered activity, on in which the order consists in the progressive completin of a process. Given an activity having a time span an cumulative growth within the time succession, an ai means foresight in advance of the end or possibl termination. If bees anticipated the consequences of thei activity, if they perceived their end in imaginativ foresight, they would have the primary element in a aim.

In the next place the aim as a foreseen end give direction to the activity; it is not an idle view of a mer spectator, but influences the steps taken to reach the end The foresight functions in three ways. In the first place, i involves careful observation of the given conditions to se what are the means available for reaching the end, and to discover the hindrances in the way. In the second place, it suggests the proper order or sequence in the use of means. It facilitates an economical selection and arrangement.

In the third place, it makes choice of alternatives possible. If we can predict the outcome of acting this way or that, we can then compare the value of the two courses of action; we can pass judgment upon their relative desirability. If we know that stagnant water breeds mosquitoes and that they are likely to carry disease, we can, disliking that anticipated result, take steps to avert it. Since we do not anticipate results as mere intellectual onlookers, but as persons concerned in the outcome, we are partakers in the process which produces the result. We intervene to bring about this result or that.

Of course these three points are closely connected with one another. We can definitely foresee results only as we make careful scrutiny of present conditions, and the importance of the outcome supplies the motive for observations. The more adequate our observations, the more varied is the scene of conditions and obstructions that presents itself, and the more numerous are the alternatives between which choice may be made.

In turn, the more numerous the recognised possibilities of the situation, or alternatives of action, the more meaning does the chosen activity possess, and the more flexibly controllable is it. Where only a single outcome has been thought of, the mind has nothing else to think of; the meaning attaching to the act is limited. One only steams ahead toward the mark. Sometimes such a narrow course may be effective. But if unexpected difficulties offer themselves, one has not as many resources at command as if he had chosen the same line of action after a broader survey of the possibilities of the field. He cannot make needed readjustments readily.

The net conclusion is that acting with an aim is all one with acting intelligently. To foresee a terminus of an act is to have a basis upon which to observe, to select, and to order objects and our own capacities. To do these things means to have a mind — for mind is precisely intentional purposeful activity controlled by perception of facts and their relationships to one another. To have a mind to do a thing is to foresee a future possibility; it is to have a plan for its accomplishment; it is to note the means which make the plan capable of execution and the obstructions in the way, — or, if it is really a mind to do the thing and not a vague aspiration — it is to have a plan which takes account of resources and difficulties.

Mind is capacity to refer present conditions to future results, and future consequences to present conditions. And these traits are just what is meant by having an aim or a purpose. A man is stupid or blind or unintelligent — lacking in mind — just in the degree in which in any activity he does not know what he is about, namely, the probable consequences of his acts. A man is imperfectly intelligent when he contents himself with looser guesses about the outcome than is needful, just taking a chance with his luck, or when he forms plans apart from study of the actual conditions, including his own capacities. Such relative absence of mind means to make our feelings the measure of what is to happen. To be intelligent we must "stop, look, listen" in making the plan of an activity.

To identify acting with an aim and intelligent activity is enough to show its value — its function in experience. We are only too given to making an entity out of the abstract noun "consciousness." We forget that it comes from the adjective "conscious." To be conscious is to be aware of what we are about; conscious signifies the deliberate, observant, planning traits of activity. Consciousness is nothing which we have which gazes idly on the scene around one or which has impressions made upon it by physical things; it is a name for the purposeful quality of an activity, for the fact that it is directed by an aim. Put the other way about, to have an aim is to act with meaning, not like an automatic machine; it is to mean to do something and to perceive the meaning of things in the light of that intent.

The Criteria of Good Aims.

We may apply the results of our discussion to a consideration of the criteria involved in a correct establishing of aims.

(1) The aim set up must be an outgrowth of existing conditions. It must be based upon a consideration of what is already going on; upon the resources and difficulties of the situation. Theories about the proper end of our activities — educational and moral theories — often violate this principle. They assume ends lying outside our activities; ends foreign to the concrete makeup of the situation; ends which issue from some outside source. Then the problem is to bring our activities to bear upon the realisation of these externally supplied ends. They are something for which we ought to act.

In any case such "aims" limit intelligence; they are not the expression of mind in foresight, observation, and choice of the better among alternative possibilities. They limit intelligence because, given ready-made, they must be imposed by some authority external to intelligence, leaving to the latter nothing but a mechanical choice of means.

(2) We have spoken as if aims could be completely formed prior to the attempt to realise them. This impression must now be qualified. The aim as it first emerges is a mere tentative sketch. The act of striving to realise it tests its worth. If it suffices to direct activity successfully, nothing more is required, since its whole

function is to set a mark in advance; and at times a mere hint may suffice. But usually — at least in complicated situations — acting upon it brings to light conditions which had been overlooked. This calls for revision of the original aim; it has to be added to and subtracted from.

An aim must, then, be flexible; it must be capable of alteration to meet circumstances. An end established externally to the process of action is always rigid. Being inserted or imposed from without, it is not supposed to have a working relationship to the concrete conditions of the situation. What happens in the course of action neither confirms, refutes, nor alters it. Such an end can only be insisted upon. The failure that results from its lack of adaptation is attributed simply to the perverseness of conditions, not to the fact that the end is not reasonable under the circumstances.

The value of a legitimate aim, on the contrary, lies in the fact that we can use it to change conditions. It is a method for dealing with conditions so as to effect desirable alterations in them. A farmer who should passively accept things just as he finds them would make as great a mistake as he who framed his plans in complete disregard of what soil, climate, etc., permit. One of the evils of an abstract or remote external aim in education is that its very inapplicability in practice is likely to react into a haphazard snatching at immediate conditions. A good aim surveys the present state of experience of pupils, and forming a tentative plan of treatment, keeps the plan constantly in view and yet modifies it as conditions develop. The aim, in short, is experimental, and hence constantly growing as it is tested in action.

(3) The aim must always represent a freeing of activities. The term end in view is suggestive, for it puts before the mind the termination or conclusion of some process. The only way in which we can define an activity

is by putting before ourselves the objects in which it terminates — as one's aim in shooting is the target. But we must remember that the object is only a mark or sign by which the mind specifies the activity one desires to carry out. Strictly speaking, not the target but hitting the target is the end in view; one takes aim by means of the target, but also by the sight on the gun.

The different objects which are thought of are means of directing the activity. Thus one aims at, say, a rabbit; what he wants is to shoot straight: a certain kind of activity. Or, if it is the rabbit he wants, it is not rabbit apart from his activity, but as a factor in activity; he wants to eat the rabbit, or to show it as evidence of his marksmanship — he wants to do something with it. The doing with the thing, not the thing in isolation, is his end. The object is but a phase of the active end, — continuing the activity successfully. This is what is meant by the phrase, used above, "freeing activity."

In contrast with fulfilling some process in order that activity may go on, stands the static character of an end which is imposed from without the activity. It is always conceived of as fixed; it is something to be attained and possessed. When one has such a notion, activity is a mere unavoidable means to something else; it is not significant or important on its own account. As compared with the end it is but a necessary evil; something which must be gone through before one can reach the object which is alone worth while.

In other words, the external idea of the aim leads to a separation of means from end, while an end which grows up within an activity as plan for its direction is always both ends and means, the distinction being only one of convenience. Every means is a temporary end until we have attained it. Every end becomes a means of carrying activity further as soon as it is achieved. We call it end when it marks off the future direction of the activity in which we are engaged; means when it marks off the present direction. Every divorce of end from means diminishes by that much the significance of the activity and tends to reduce it to a drudgery from which one would escape if he could.

A farmer has to use plants and animals to carry on his farming activities. It certainly makes a great difference to his life whether he is fond of them, or whether he regards them merely as means which he has to employ to get something else in which alone he is interested. In the former case, his entire course of activity is significant; each phase of it has its own value. He has the experience of realising his end at every stage; the postponed aim, or end in view, being merely a sight ahead by which to keep his activity going fully and freely. For if he does not look ahead, he is more likely to find himself blocked. The aim is as definitely a means of action as is any other portion of an activity.

Applications of Education

There is nothing peculiar about educational aims. They are just like aims in any directed occupation. The educator, like the farmer, has certain things to do, certain resources with which to do, and certain obstacles with which to contend. The conditions with which the farmer deals, whether as obstacles or resources, have their own structure and operation independently of any purpose of his. Seeds sprout, rain falls, the sun shines, insects devour, blight comes, the seasons change. His aim is simply to utilise these various conditions; to make his activities and their energies work together, instead of against one another. It would be absurd if the farmer set up a purpose of farming, without any reference to these conditions of soil, climate, characteristic of plant growth, etc. His purpose is simply a foresight of the consequences of his energies connected with those of the things about him, a foresight used to direct his movements from day to day. Foresight of possible consequences leads to more careful and extensive observation of the nature and performances of the things he had to do with, and to laying out a plan — that is, of a certain order in the acts to be performed.

It is the same with the educator, whether parent or teacher. It is as absurd for the latter to set up his "own" aims as the proper objects of the growth of the children as it would be for the farmer to set up an ideal of farming irrespective of conditions. Aims mean acceptance of responsibility for the observations, anticipations, and arrangements required in carrying on a function — whether farming or educating. Any aim is of value so far as it assists observation, choice, and planning in carrying on activity from moment to moment and hour to hour; if it gets in the way of the individual's own common sense it does harm.

And it is well to remind ourselves that education as such has no aims. Only persons, parents, and teachers, etc., have aims, not an abstract idea like education. And consequently their purposes are indefinitely varied, differing with different children, changing as children grow and with the growth of experience on the part of the one who teaches. Even the most valid aims which can be put in words will, as words, do more harm than good unless one recognises that they are not aims, but rather suggestions to educators as to how to observe, how to look ahead, and how to choose in liberating and directing the energies of the concrete situations in which they find themselves.

As a recent writer has said: "To lead this boy to read Scott's novels instead of old Sleuth's stories; to teach this girl to sew; to root out the habit of bullying from John's make-up; to prepare this class to study medicine, — these are samples of the millions of aims we have actually before us in the concrete work of education." Bearing these qualifications in mind, we shall proceed to state some of the characteristics found in all good educational aims.

(1) An educational aim must be founded upon the intrinsic activities and needs of the given individual to be educated. The tendency of such an aim as preparation is, as we have seen, to omit existing powers, and find the aim in some remote accomplishment or responsibility.

In general, there is a disposition to take considerations which are dear to the hearts of adults and set them up as ends irrespective of the capacities of those educated. There is also an inclination to propound aims which are so uniform as to neglect the specific powers and requirements of an individual, forgetting that all learning is something which happens to an individual at a given time and place.

The larger range of perception of the adult is of great value in observing the abilities and weaknesses of the young, in deciding what they may amount to. Thus the artistic capacities of the adult exhibit what certain tendencies of the child are capable of; if we did not have the adult achievements we should be without assurance as to the significance of the drawing, reproducing, modelling, colouring activities of childhood. So if it were not for adult language, we should not be able to see the import of the babbling impulses of infancy. But it is one thing to use adult accomplishments as a context in which to place and survey the doings of childhood and youth; it is quite another to set them up as a fixed aim without regard to the concrete activities of those educated.

(2) An aim must be capable of translation into a method of cooperating with the activities of those undergoing instruction. It must suggest the kind of environment needed to liberate and to organise their

capacities. Unless it lends itself to the construction of specific procedures, and unless these procedures test, correct, and amplify the aim, the latter is worthless. Instead of helping the specific task of teaching, it prevents the use of ordinary judgment in observing and sizing up the situation. It operates to exclude recognition of everything except what squares up with the fixed end in view. Every rigid aim just because it is rigidly given seems to render it unnecessary to give careful attention to concrete conditions. Since it must apply anyhow, what is the use of noting details which do not count?

The vice of externally imposed ends has deep roots. Teachers receive them from superior authorities; these authorities accept them from what is current in the community. The teachers impose them upon children. As a first consequence, the intelligence of the teacher is not free; it is confined to receiving the aims laid down from above. Too rarely is the individual teacher so free from the dictation of authoritative supervisor, textbook on methods, prescribed course of study, etc., that he can let his mind come to close quarters with the pupil's mind and the subject matter. This distrust of the teacher's experience is then reflected in lack of confidence in the responses of pupils.

The latter receive their aims through a double or treble external imposition, and are constantly confused by the conflict between the aims which are natural to their own experience at the time and those in which they are taught to acquiesce. Until the democratic criterion of the intrinsic significance of every growing experience is recognised, we shall be intellectually confused by the demand for adaptation to external aims.

(3) Educators have to be on their guard against ends that are alleged to be general and ultimate. Every activity, however specific, is, of course, general in its ramified connections, for it leads out indefinitely into other things.

So far as a general idea makes us more alive to these connections, it cannot be too general. But "general" also means "abstract," or detached from all specific context. And such abstractness means remoteness, and throws us back, once more, upon teaching and learning as mere means of getting ready for an end disconnected from the means. That education is literally and all the time its own reward means that no alleged study or discipline is educative unless it is worth while in its own immediate having.

A truly general aim broadens the outlook; it stimulates one to take more consequences (connections) into account. This means a wider and more flexible observation of means. The more interacting forces, for example, the farmer takes into account, the more varied will be his immediate resources. He will see a greater number of possible starting places, and a greater number of ways of getting at what he wants to do. The fuller one's conception of possible future achievements, the less his present activity is tied down to a small number of alternatives. If one knew enough, one could start almost anywhere and sustain his activities continuously and fruitfully.

Understanding then the term general or comprehensive aim simply in the sense of a broad survey of the field of present activities, we shall take up some of the larger ends which have currency in the educational theories of the day, and consider what light they throw upon the immediate concrete and diversified aims which are always the educator's real concern. We premise that there is no need of making a choice among them or regarding them as competitors. When we come to act in a tangible way we have to select or choose a particular act at a particular time, but any number of comprehensive ends may exist without competition, since they mean simply different ways of looking at the same scene.

One cannot climb a number of different mountains simultaneously, but the views had when different mountains are ascended supplement one another: they do not set up incompatible, competing worlds. Or, putting the matter in a slightly different way, one statement of an end may suggest certain questions and observations, and another statement another set of questions, calling for other observations. Then the more general ends we have, the better. One statement will emphasise what another slurs over. What a plurality of hypotheses does for the scientific investigator, a plurality of stated aims may do for the instructor.

Natural Development and Social Efficiency as Aims

Nature as Supplying the Aim

We have just pointed out the futility of trying to establish the aim of education — some one final aim which subordinates all others to itself. We have indicated that since general aims are but prospective points of view from which to survey the existing conditions and estimate their possibilities, we might have any number of them, all consistent with one another. As matter of fact, a large number have been stated at different times, all having great local value. For the statement of aim is a matter of emphasis at a given time. And we do not emphasise things which do not require emphasis — that is, such things as are taking care of themselves fairly well.

We tend rather to frame our statement on the basis of the defects and needs of the contemporary situation; we take for granted, without explicit statement which would be of no use, whatever is right or approximately so. We frame our explicit aims in terms of some alteration to be brought about. It is, then, DO paradox requiring explanation that a given epoch or generation tends to emphasise in its conscious projections just the things which it has least of in actual fact. A time of domination by authority will call out as response the desirability of great individual freedom; one of disorganised individual activities the need of social control as an educational aim.

The actual and implicit practice and the conscious or stated aim thus balance each other. At different times such aims as complete living, better methods of language study, substitution of things for words, social efficiency, personal culture, social service, complete development of personality, encyclopedic knowledge, discipline, a aesthetic contemplation, utility, etc., have served.

The following discussion takes up three statements of recent influence, and others will be considered later in a discussion of knowledge and of the values of studies. We begin with a consideration that education is a process of development in accordance with nature, taking Rousseau's statement, which opposed natural to social; and then pass over to the antithetical conception of social efficiency, which often opposes social to natural.

(1) Educational reformers disgusted with the conventionality and artificiality of the scholastic methods they find about them are prone to resort to nature as a standard. Nature is supposed to furnish the law and the end of development; ours it is to follow and conform to her ways.

The positive value of this conception lies in the forcible way in which it calls attention to the wrongness of aims which do not have regard to the natural endowment of those educated. Its weakness is the ease with which natural in the sense of normal is confused with the physical. The constructive use of intelligence in foresight, and contriving, is then discounted; we are just to get out of the way and allow nature to do the work. Since no one has stated in the doctrine both its truth and falsity better than Rousseau, we shall turn to him.

"Education," he says, "we receive from three sources — Nature, men, and things. The spontaneous development of our organs and capacities constitutes the education of Nature. The use to which we are taught to put this development constitutes that education given us by Men. The acquirement of personal experience from surrounding objects constitutes that of things. Only when these three kinds of education are consonant and make for the same end, does a man tend towards his true goal.... If we are asked what is this end, the answer is that of Nature.

For since the concurrence of the three kinds of education is necessary to their completeness, the kind which is entirely independent of our control must necessarily regulate us in determining the other two." Then he defines Nature to mean the capacities and dispositions which are inborn, "as they exist prior to the modification due to constraining habits and the influence of the opinion of others."

The wording of Rousseau will repay careful study. It contains as fundamental truths as have been uttered about education in conjunction with a curious twist. It would be impossible to say better what is said in the first sentences. The three factors of educative development are

(a) the native structure of our bodily organs and their functional activities;

(b) the uses to which the activities of these organs are put under the influence of other persons;

(c) their direct interaction with the environment.

This statement certainly covers the ground. His other two propositions are equally sound; namely, (a) that only when the three factors of education are consonant and cooperative does adequate development of the individual occur, and (b) that the native activities of the organs, being original, are basic in conceiving consonance.

But it requires but little reading between the lines, supplemented by other statements of Rousseau, to perceive that instead of regarding these three things as factors which must work together to some extent in order that any one of them may proceed educatively, he regards them as separate and independent operations. Especially does he believe that there is an independent and, as he says, "spontaneous" development of the native organs and faculties. He thinks that this development can go on irrespective of the use to which they are put.

And it is to this separate development that education coming from social contact is to be subordinated. Now there is an immense difference between a use of native activities in accord with those activities themselves — as distinct from forcing them and perverting them — and supposing that they have a normal development apart from any use, which development furnishes the standard and norm of all learning by use.

To recur to our previous illustration, the process of acquiring language is a practically perfect model of proper educative growth. The start is from native activities of the vocal apparatus, organs of hearing, etc. But it is absurd to suppose that these have an independent growth of their own, which left to itself would evolve a perfect speech. Taken literally, Rousseau's principle would mean that adults should accept and repeat the babblings and noises of children not merely as the beginnings of the development of articulate speech — which they are — but as furnishing language itself — the standard for all teaching of language.

The point may be summarised by saying that Rousseau was right, introducing a much-needed reform into education, in holding that the structure and activities of the organs furnish the conditions of all teaching of the use of the organs; but profoundly wrong in intimating that they supply not only the conditions but also the ends of their development.

As matter of fact, the native activities develop, in contrast with random and capricious exercise, through the uses to which they are put. And the office of the social medium is, as we have seen, to direct growth through putting powers to the best possible use. The instinctive activities may be called, metaphorically, spontaneous, in the sense that the organs give a strong bias for a certain sort of operation, — a bias so strong that we cannot go contrary to it, though by trying to go contrary we may pervert, stunt, and corrupt them. But the notion of a spontaneous normal development of these activities is pure mythology.

The natural, or native, powers furnish the initiating and limiting forces in all education; they do not furnish its ends or aims. There is no learning except from a beginning in unlearned powers, but learning is not a matter of the spontaneous overflow of the unlearned powers. Rousseau's contrary opinion is doubtless due to the fact that he identified God with Nature; to him the original powers are wholly good, coming directly from a wise and good creator. To paraphrase the old saying about the country and the town, God made the original human organs and faculties, man makes the uses to which they are put. Consequently the development of the former furnishes the standard to which the latter must be subordinated. When men attempt to determine the uses to which the original activities shall be put, they interfere with a divine plan.

The interference by social arrangements with Nature, God's work, is the primary source of corruption in individuals. Rousseau's passionate assertion of the intrinsic goodness of all natural tendencies was a reaction against the prevalent notion of the total depravity of innate human nature, and has had a powerful influence in modifying the attitude towards children's interests. But it is hardly necessary to say that primitive impulses are of themselves neither good nor evil, but become one or the other according to the objects for which they are employed. That neglect, suppression, and premature forcing of some instincts at the expense of others, are responsible for many avoidable ills, there can be no doubt. But the moral is not to leave them alone to follow their own "spontaneous development," but to provide an environment which shall organise them.

Returning to the elements of truth contained in Rousseau's statements, we find that natural development, as an aim, enables him to point the means of correcting many evils in current practices, and to indicate a number of desirable specific aims.

(1) Natural development as an aim fixes attention upon the bodily organs and the need of health and vigour. The aim of natural development says to parents and teachers: Make health an aim; normal development cannot be had without regard to the vigour of the body — an obvious enough fact and yet one whose due recognition in practice would almost automatically revolutionise many of our educational practices. "Nature" is indeed a vague and metaphorical term, but one thing that "Nature" may be said to utter is that there are conditions of educational efficiency, and that till we have learned what these conditions are and have learned to make our practices accord with them, the noblest and most ideal of our aims are doomed to suffer — are verbal and sentimental rather than efficacious.

(2) The aim of natural development translates into the aim of respect for physical mobility. In Rousseau's words: "Children are always in motion; a sedentary life is injurious." When he says that "Nature's intention is to strengthen the body before exercising the mind" he hardly states the fact fairly. But if he had said that

nature's "intention" (to adopt his poetical form of speech) is to develop the mind especially by exercise of the muscles of the body he would have stated a positive fact. In other words, the aim of following nature means, in the concrete, regard for the actual part played by use of the bodily organs in explorations, in handling of materials, in plays and games.

(3) The general aim translates into the aim of regard for individual differences among children. Nobody can take the principle of consideration of native powers into account without being struck by the fact that these powers differ in different individuals. The difference applies not merely to their intensity, but even more to their quality and arrangement. As Rouseau said: "Each individual is born with a distinctive temperament.... We indiscriminately employ children of different bents on the same exercises; their education destroys the special bent and leaves a dull uniformity. Therefore after we have wasted our efforts in stunting the true gifts of nature we see the short-lived and illusory brilliance we have substituted die away, while the natural abilities we have crushed do not revive."

Lastly, the aim of following nature means to note the origin, the waxing, and waning, of preferences and interests. Capacities bud and bloom irregularly; there is no even four-abreast development. We must strike while the iron is hot. Especially precious are the first dawnings of power. More than we imagine, the ways in which the tendencies of early childhood are treated fix fundamental dispositions and condition the turn taken by powers that show themselves later. Educational concern with the early years of life — as distinct from inculcation of useful arts — dates almost entirely from the time of the emphasis by Pestalozzi and Froebel, following Rousseau, of natural principles of growth.

The irregularity of growth and its significance is indicated in the following passage of a student of the growth of the nervous system. "While growth continues, things bodily and mental are lopsided, for growth is never general, but is accentuated now at one spot, now at another.... The methods which shall recognise in the presence of these enormous differences of endowment the dynamic values of natural inequalities of growth, and utilise them, preferring irregularity to the rounding out gained by pruning will most closely follow that which takes place in the body and thus prove most effective."

Observation of natural tendencies is difficult under conditions of restraint. They show themselves most readily in a child's spontaneous sayings and doings, — that is, in those he engages in when not put at set tasks and when not aware of being under observation. It does not follow that these tendencies are all desirable because they are natural; but it does follow that since they are there, they are operative and must be taken account of. We must see to it that the desirable ones have an environment which keeps them active, and that their activity shall control the direction the others take and thereby induce the disuse of the latter because they lead to nothing.

Many tendencies that trouble parents when they appear are likely to be transitory, and sometimes too much direct attention to them only fixes a child's attention upon them. At all events, adults too easily assume their own habits and wishes as standards, and regard all deviations of children's impulses as evils to be eliminated. That artificiality against which the conception of following nature is so largely a protest, is the outcome of attempts to force children directly into the mold of grown-up standards.

The early history of the idea of following nature combined two factors which had no inherent connection with one another. Before the time of Rousseau educational reformers had been inclined to urge the importance of education by ascribing practically unlimited power to it. All the differences between peoples and between classes and persons among the same people were said to be due to differences of training, of exercise, and practice. Originally, mind, reason, understanding is, for all practical purposes, the same in all. This essential identity of mind means the essential equality of all and the possibility of bringing them all to the same level.

As a protest against this view, the doctrine of accord with nature meant a much less formal and abstract view of mind and its powers. It substituted specific instincts and impulses and physiological capacities, differing from individual to individual, for abstract faculties of discernment, memory, and generalisation. Upon this side, the doctrine of educative accord with nature has been reinforced by the development of modern biology, physiology, and psychology. It means, in effect, that great as is the significance of nurture, of modification, and transformation through direct educational effort, nature, or unlearned capacities, affords the foundation and ultimate resources for such nurture.

On the other hand, the doctrine of following nature was a political dogma. It meant a rebellion against existing social institutions, customs, and ideals. Rousseau's statement that everything is good as it comes from the hands of the Creator has its signification only in its contrast with the concluding part of the same sentence: "Everything degenerates in the hands of man." And again he says: "Natural man has an absolute value; he is a numerical unit, a complete integer and has no relation save to himself and to his fellow man.

Civilized man is only a relative unit, the numerator of a fraction whose value depends upon its dominator, its relation to the integral body of society. Good political institutions are those which make a man unnatural." It is upon this conception of the artificial and harmful character of organised social life as it now exists that he rested the notion that nature not merely furnishes prime forces which initiate growth but also its plan and goal. That evil institutions and customs work almost automatically to give a wrong education which the most careful schooling cannot offset is true enough; but the conclusion is not to education apart from the environment, but to provide an environment in which native powers will be put to better uses.

Social Efficiency as Aim

A conception which made nature supply the end of a true education and society the end of an evil one, could hardly fail to call out a protest. The opposing emphasis took the form of a doctrine that the business of education is to supply precisely what nature fails to secure; namely, habituation of an individual to social control; subordination of natural powers to social rules. It is not surprising to find that the value in the idea of social efficiency resides largely in its protest against the points at which the doctrine of natural development went astray; while its misuse comes when it is employed to slur over the truth in that conception. It is a fact that we must look to the activities and achievements of associated life to find what the development of power — that is to say, efficiency — means.

The error is in implying that we must adopt measures of subordination rather than of utilisation to secure efficiency. The doctrine is rendered adequate when we recognise that social efficiency is attained not by negative constraint but by positive use of native individual capacities in occupations having a social meaning.

(1) Translated into specific aims, social efficiency indicates the importance of industrial competency. Persons cannot live without means of subsistence; the ways in which these means are employed and consumed have a profound influence upon all the relationships of persons to one another. If an individual is not able to earn his own living and that of the children dependent upon him, he is a drag or parasite upon the activities of others. He misses for himself one of the most educative experiences of life. If he is not trained in the right use of the products of industry, there is grave danger that he may deprave himself and injure others in his possession of wealth.

No scheme of education can afford to neglect such basic considerations. Yet in the name of higher and more spiritual ideals, the arrangements for higher education have often not only neglected them, but looked at them with scorn as beneath the level of educative concern. With the change from an oligarchical to a democratic society, it is natural that the significance of an education which should have as a result ability to make one's way economically in the world, and to manage economic resources usefully instead of for mere display and luxury, should receive emphasis.

There is, however, grave danger that in insisting upon this end, existing economic conditions and standards will be accepted as final. A democratic criterion requires us to develop capacity to the point of competency to choose and make its own career. This principle is violated when the attempt is made to fit individuals in advance for definite industrial callings, selected not on the basis of trained original capacities, but on that of the wealth or social status of parents.

As a matter of fact, industry at the present time undergoes rapid and abrupt changes through the evolution of new inventions. New industries spring up, and old ones are revolutionised. Consequently an attempt to train for too specific a mode of efficiency defeats its own purpose. When the occupation changes its methods, such individuals are left behind with even less ability to readjust themselves than if they had a less definite training. But, most of all, the present industrial constitution of society is, like every society which has ever existed, full of inequities. It is the aim of progressive education to take part in correcting unfair privilege and unfair deprivation, not to perpetuate them. Wherever social control means subordination of individual activities to class authority, there is danger that industrial education will be dominated by acceptance of the status quo. Differences of economic opportunity then dictate what the future callings of individuals are to be. We have an unconscious revival of the defects of the Platonic scheme without its enlightened method of selection.

(2) Civic efficiency, or good citizenship. It is, of course, arbitrary to separate industrial competency from capacity in good citizenship. But the latter term may be used to indicate a number of qualifications which are vaguer than vocational ability. These traits run from whatever make an individual a more agreeable companion to citizenship in the political sense: it denotes ability to judge men and measures wisely and to take a determining part in making as well as obeying laws.

The aim of civic efficiency has at least the merit of protecting us from the notion of a training of mental power at large. It calls attention to the fact that power must be relative to doing something, and to the fact that the things which most need to be done are things which involve one's relationships with others.

Here again we have to be on guard against understanding the aim too narrowly. An over-definite interpretation would at certain periods have excluded scientific discoveries, in spite of the fact that in the last analysis security of social progress depends upon them. For scientific men would have been thought to be mere theoretical dreamers, totally lacking in social efficiency. It must be borne in mind that ultimately social efficiency means neither more nor less than capacity to share in a give and take of experience. It covers all that makes one's own experience more worth while to others, and all that enables one to participate more richly in the worthwhile experiences of others. Ability to produce and to enjoy art, capacity for recreation, the significant utilisation of leisure, are more important elements in it than elements conventionally associated often times with citizenship.

In the broadest sense, social efficiency is nothing less than that socialisation of mind which is actively concerned in making experiences more communicable; in breaking down the barriers of social stratification which make individuals impervious to the interests of others. When social efficiency is confined to the service rendered by overt acts, its chief constituent (because its only guarantee) is omitted, — intelligent sympathy or good will.

For sympathy as a desirable quality is something more than mere feeling; it is a cultivated imagination for what men have in common and a rebellion at whatever unnecessarily divides them. What is sometimes called a benevolent interest in others may be but an unwitting mask for an attempt to dictate to them what their good shall be, instead of an endeavour to free them so that they may seek and find the good of their own choice. Social efficiency, even social service, are hard and metallic things when severed from an active acknowledgment of the diversity of goods which life may afford to different persons, and from faith in the social utility of encouraging every individual to make his own choice intelligent.

Culture as Aim

Whether or not social efficiency is an aim which is consistent with culture turns upon these considerations. Culture means at least something cultivated, something ripened; it is opposed to the raw and crude. When the "natural" is identified with this rawness, culture is opposed to what is called natural development. Culture is also something personal; it is cultivation with respect to appreciation of ideas and art and broad human interests.

When efficiency is identified with a narrow range of acts, instead of with the spirit and meaning of activity, culture is opposed to efficiency. Whether called culture or complete development of personality, the outcome is identical with the true meaning of social efficiency whenever attention is given to what is unique in an individual — and he would not be an individual if there were not something incommensurable about him. Its opposite is the mediocre, the average. Whenever distinctive quality is developed, distinction of personality results, and with it greater promise for a social service which goes beyond the supply in quantity of material commodities.

The fact is that the opposition of high worth of personality to social efficiency is a product of a feudally organised society with its rigid division of inferior and superior. The latter are supposed to have time and opportunity to develop themselves as human beings; the former are confined to providing external products. When social efficiency as measured by product or output is urged as an ideal in a would-be democratic society, it means that the depreciatory estimate of the masses characteristic of an aristocratic community is accepted and carried over. But if democracy has a moral and ideal meaning, it is that a social return be demanded from all and that opportunity for development of distinctive capacities be afforded all. The separation of the two aims in education is fatal to democracy; the adoption of the narrower meaning of efficiency deprives it of its essential justification.

The aim of efficiency must be included within the process of experience. When it is measured by tangible external products, and not by the achieving of a distinctively valuable experience, it becomes materialistic. Results in the way of commodities which may be the outgrowth of an efficient personality are, in the strictest sense, by-products of education: by-products which are inevitable and important, but nevertheless by-products. To set up an external aim strengthens by reaction the false conception of culture which identifies it with something purely "inner." And the idea of perfecting an "inner" personality is a sure sign of social divisions. What is called inner is simply that which does not connect with others — which is not capable of free and full communication. What is termed spiritual culture has usually been futile, with something rotten about it, just because it has been conceived as a thing which a man might have internally — and therefore exclusively. What one is as a person is what one is as associated with others, in a free give and take of intercourse. This transcends both the efficiency which consists in supplying products to others and the culture which is an exclusive refinement and polish.

Any individual has missed his calling, farmer, physician, teacher, student, who does not find that the accomplishments of results of value to others is an accompaniment of a process of experience inherently worth while. Why then should it be thought that one must take his choice between sacrificing himself to doing useful things for others, or sacrificing them to pursuit of his own exclusive ends, whether the saving of his own soul or the building of an inner spiritual life and personality? What happens is that since neither of these things is persistently possible, we get a compromise and an alternation.

One tries each course by turns. There is no greater tragedy than that so much of the professedly spiritual and religious thought of the world has emphasised the two ideals of self-sacrifice and spiritual self-perfecting instead of throwing its weight against this dualism of life. The dualism is too deeply established to be easily overthrown; for that reason, it is the particular task of education at the present time to struggle in behalf of an aim in which social efficiency and personal culture are synonyms instead of antagonists.

3

Educational Values

The specific values usually discussed in educational theories coincide with aims which are usually urged. They are such things as utility, culture, information, preparation for social efficiency, mental discipline or power, and so on.

The aspect of these aims in virtue of which they are valuable has been treated in our analysis of the nature of interest, and there is no difference between speaking of art as an interest or concern and referring to it as a value. It happens, however, that discussion of values has usually been centered about a consideration of the various ends subserved by specific subjects of the curriculum. It has been a part of the attempt to justify those subjects by pointing out the significant contributions to life accruing from their study. An explicit discussion of educational values thus affords an opportunity for reviewing the prior discussion of aims and interests on one hand and of the curriculum on the other, by bringing them into connection with one another.

Nature of Realization

Much of our experience is indirect; it is dependent upon signs which intervene between the things and ourselves, signs which stand for or represent the former. It is one thing to have been engaged in war, to have shared its dangers and hardships; it is another thing to hear or read about it. All language, all symbols, are implements of an indirect experience; in technical language the experience which is procured by their means is "mediated." It stands in contrast with an immediate, direct experience, something in which we take part vitally and at first hand, instead of through the intervention of representative media.

As we have seen, the scope of personal, vitally direct experience is very limited. If it were not for the intervention of agencies for representing absent and distant affairs, our experience would remain almost on the level of that of the brutes. Every step from savagery to civilization is dependent upon the invention of media which enlarge the range of purely immediate experience and give it deepened as well as wider meaning by connecting it with things which can only be signified or symbolized. It is doubtless this fact which is the cause of the disposition to identify an uncultivated person with an illiterate person — so dependent are we on letters for effective representative or indirect experience.

At the same time there is always a danger that symbols will not be truly representative; danger that instead of really calling up the absent and remote in a way to make it enter a present experience, the linguistic media of representation will become an end in themselves. Formal education is peculiarly exposed to this danger, with the result that when literacy supervenes, mere bookishness, what is popularly termed the academic, too often comes with it. In colloquial speech, the phrase a "realizing sense" is used to express the urgency, warmth, and intimacy of a direct experience in contrast with the remote, pallid, and coldly detached quality of a representative experience. The terms "mental realization" and "appreciation" (or genuine appreciation) are more elaborate names for the realizing sense of a thing. It is not possible to define these ideas except by synonyms, like "coming home to one" "really taking it in," etc., for the only way to appreciate what is meant by a direct experience of a thing is by having it. But it is the difference between reading a technical description of a picture, and seeing it; or between just seeing it and being moved by it; between learning mathematical equations about light and being carried away by some peculiarly glorious illumination of a misty landscape.

We are thus met by the danger of the tendency of technique and other purely representative forms to encroach upon the sphere of direct appreciations; in other words, the tendency to assume that pupils have a foundation of direct realization of situations sufficient for the superstructure of representative experience erected by formulated school studies. This is not simply a matter of quantity or bulk. Sufficient direct experience is even more a matter of quality; it must be of a sort to connect readily and fruitfully with the symbolic material of instruction.

Before teaching can safely enter upon conveying facts and ideas through the media of signs, schooling must provide genuine situations in which personal participation brings home the import of the material and the problems which it conveys. From the standpoint of the pupil, the resulting experiences are worth while on their own account; from the standpoint of the teacher they are also means of supplying subject matter required for understanding instruction involving signs, and of evoking attitudes of open-mindedness and concern as to the material symbolically conveyed.

In the outline given of the theory of educative subject matter, the demand for this background of realization or appreciation is met by the provision made for play and active occupations embodying typical situations. Nothing need be added to what has already been said except to point out that while the discussion dealt explicitly with the subject matter of primary education, where the demand for the available background of direct experience is most obvious, the principle applies to the primary or elementary phase of every subject. The first and basic function of laboratory work, for example, in a high school or college in a new field, is to familiarize the student at first hand with a certain range of facts and problems — to give him a "feeling" for them.

Getting command of technique and of methods of reaching and testing generalizations is at first secondary to getting appreciation. As regards the primary school activities, it is to be borne in mind that the fundamental intent is not to amuse nor to convey information with a minimum of vexation nor yet to acquire skill, — though these results may accrue as by-products, — but to enlarge and enrich the scope of experience, and to keep alert and effective the interest in intellectual progress.

The rubric of appreciation supplies an appropriate head for bringing out three further principles: the nature of effective or real (as distinct from nominal) standards of value; the place of the imagination in appreciative realizations; and the place of the fine arts in the course of study.

Nature of Standards of Valuation.

Every adult has acquired, in the course of his prior experience and education, certain measures of the worth of various sorts of experience. He has learned to look upon qualities like honesty, amiability, perseverance, loyalty, as moral goods; upon certain classics of literature, painting, music, as aesthetic values, and so on. Not only this, but he has learned certain rules for these values — the golden rule in morals; harmony, balance, etc., proportionate distribution in aesthetic goods; definition, clarity, system in intellectual accomplishments. These principles are so important as standards of judging the worth of new experiences that parents and instructors are always tending to teach them directly to the young. They overlook the danger that standards so taught will be merely symbolic; that is, largely conventional and verbal. In reality, working as distinct from professed standards depend upon what an individual has himself specifically appreciated to be deeply significant in concrete situations.

An individual may have learned that certain characteristics are conventionally esteemed in music; he may be able to converse with some correctness about classic music; he may even honestly believe that these traits constitute his own musical standards. But if in his own past experience, what he has been most accustomed to and has most enjoyed is ragtime, his active or working measures of valuation are fixed on the ragtime level. The appeal actually made to him in his own personal realization fixes his attitude much more deeply than what he has been taught as the proper thing to say; his habitual disposition thus fixed forms his real "norm" of valuation in subsequent musical experiences.

Probably few would deny this statement as to musical taste. But it applies equally well in judgments of moral and intellectual worth. A youth who has had repeated experience of the full meaning of the value of kindliness toward others built into his disposition has a measure of the worth of generous treatment of others. Without this vital appreciation, the duty and virtue of unselfishness impressed upon him by others as a standard remains purely a matter of symbols which he cannot adequately translate into realities. His "knowledge" is second-handed; it is only a knowledge that others prize unselfishness as an excellence, and esteem him in the degree in which he exhibits it. Thus there grows up a split between a person's professed standards and his actual ones. A person may be aware of the results of this struggle between his inclinations and his theoretical opinions; he suffers from the conflict between doing what is really dear to him and what he has learned will win the approval of others. But of the split itself he is unaware; the result is a kind of unconscious hypocrisy, an instability of disposition.

In similar fashion, a pupil who has worked through some confused intellectual situation and fought his way to clearing up obscurities in a definite outcome, appreciates the value of clarity and definition. He has a standard which can be depended upon. He may be trained externally to go through certain motions of analysis and division of subject matter and may acquire information about the value of these processes as standard logical functions, but unless it somehow comes home to him at some point as an appreciation of his own, the significance of the logical norms — so-called — remains as much an external piece of information as, say, the names of rivers in China. He may be able to recite, but the recital is a mechanical rehearsal.

It is, then, a serious mistake to regard appreciation as if it were confined to such things as literature and pictures and music. Its scope is as comprehensive as the work of education itself. The formation of habits is a purely mechanical thing unless habits are also tastes — habitual modes of preference and esteem, an effective sense of excellence. There are adequate grounds for asserting that the premium so often put in schools upon external "discipline," and upon marks and rewards, upon promotion and keeping back, are the obverse of the lack of attention given to life situations in which the meaning of facts, ideas, principles, and problems is vitally brought home.

Appreciative realizations are to be distinguished from symbolic or representative experiences. They are not to be distinguished from the work of the intellect or understanding. Only a personal response involving imagination can possibly procure realization even of pure "facts." The imagination is the medium of appreciation in every field.

The engagement of the imagination is the only thing that makes any activity more than mechanical. Unfortunately, it is too customary to identify the imaginative with the imaginary, rather than with a warm and intimate taking in of the full scope of a situation. This leads to an exaggerated estimate of fairy tales, myths, fanciful symbols, verse, and something labelled "Fine Art," as agencies for developing imagination and appreciation; and, by neglecting imaginative vision in other matters, leads to methods which reduce much instruction to an unimaginative acquiring of specialized skill and amassing of a load of information.

Theory, and — to some extent — practice, have advanced far enough to recognize that play-activity is an imaginative enterprise. But it is still usual to regard this activity as a specially marked-off stage of childish growth, and to overlook the fact that the difference between play and what is regarded as serious employment should be not a difference between the presence and absence of imagination, but a difference in the materials with which imagination is occupied.

The result is an unwholesome exaggeration of the fantastic and "unreal" phases of childish play and a deadly reduction of serious occupation to a routine efficiency prized simply for its external tangible results. Achievement comes to denote the sort of thing that a well-planned machine can do better than a human being can, and the main effect of education, the achieving of a life of rich significance, drops by the wayside. Meantime mind-wandering and wayward fancy are nothing but the unsuppressible imagination cut loose from concern with what is done.

An adequate recognition of the play of imagination as the medium of realization of every kind of thing which lies beyond the scope of direct physical response is the sole way of escape from mechanical methods in teaching. The emphasis put in this book, in accord with many tendencies in contemporary education, upon activity, will be misleading if it is not recognized that the imagination is as much a normal and integral part of human activity as is muscular movement.

The educative value of manual activities and of laboratory exercises, as well as of play, depends upon the extent in which they aid in bringing about a sensing of the meaning of what is going on. In effect, if not in name, they are dramatizations. Their utilitarian value in forming habits of skill to be used for tangible results is important, but not when isolated from the appreciative side. Were it not for the accompanying play of imagination, there would be no road from a direct activity to representative knowledge; for it is by imagination that symbols are translated over into a direct meaning and integrated with a narrower activity so as to expand and enrich it. When the representative creative imagination is made merely literary and mythological, symbols are rendered mere means of directing physical reactions of the organs of speech.

In the account previously given nothing was explicitly said about the place of literature and the fine arts in the course of study. The omission at that point was intentional. At the outset, there is no sharp demarcation of useful, or industrial, arts and fine arts. As engaging the emotions and the imagination, they have the qualities which give the fine arts their quality. As demanding method or skill, the adaptation of tools to materials with constantly increasing perfection, they involve the element of technique indispensable to artistic production.

From the standpoint of product, or the work of art, they are naturally defective, though even in this respect when they comprise genuine appreciation they often have a rudimentary charm. As experiences they have both an artistic and an aesthetic quality. When they emerge into activities which are tested by their product and when the socially serviceable value of the product is emphasized, they pass into useful or industrial arts. When they develop in the direction of an enhanced appreciation of the immediate qualities which appeal to taste, they grow into fine arts.

In one of its meanings, appreciation is opposed to depreciation. It denotes an enlarged, an intensified prizing, not merely a prizing, much less — like depreciation — a lowered and degraded prizing. This enhancement of the qualities which make any ordinary experience appealing, appropriable — capable of full assimilation — and enjoyable, constitutes the prime function of literature, music, drawing, painting, etc., in education. They are not the exclusive agencies of appreciation in the most general sense of that word; but they are the chief agencies of an intensified, enhanced appreciation.

As such, they are not only intrinsically and directly enjoyable, but they serve a purpose beyond themselves. They have the office, in increased degree, of all appreciation in fixing taste, in forming standards for the worth of later experiences. They arouse discontent with conditions which fall below their measure; they create a demand for surroundings coming up to their own level. They reveal a depth and range of meaning in experiences which otherwise might be mediocre and trivial. They supply, that is, organs of vision. Moreover, in their fullness they represent the concentration and consummation of elements of good which are otherwise scattered and incomplete. They select and focus the elements of enjoyable worth which make any experience directly enjoyable. They are not luxuries of education, but emphatic expressions of that which makes any education worth while.

Valuation of Studies

The theory of educational values involves not only an account of the nature of appreciation as fixing the measure of subsequent valuations, but an account of the specific directions in which these valuations occur. To value means primarily to prize, to esteem; but secondarily it means to apprise, to estimate. It means, that is, the act of cherishing something, holding it dear, and also the act of passing judgment upon the nature and amount of its value as compared with something else. To value in the latter sense is to valuate or evaluate.

The distinction coincides with that sometimes made between intrinsic and instrumental values. Intrinsic values are not objects of judgment, they cannot (as intrinsic) be compared, or regarded as greater and less, better or worse. They are invaluable; and if a thing is invaluable, it is neither more nor less so than any other invaluable. But occasions present themselves when it is necessary to choose, when we must let one thing go in order to take another. This establishes an order of preference, a greater and less, better and worse. Things judged or passed upon have to be estimated in relation to some third thing, some further end. With respect to that, they are means, or instrumental values.

We may imagine a man who at one time thoroughly enjoys converse with his friends, at another the hearing of a symphony; at another the eating of his meals; at another the reading of a book; at another the earning of money, and so on. As an appreciative realization, each of these is an intrinsic value. It occupies a particular place in life; it serves its own end, which cannot be supplied by a substitute. There is no question of comparative value, and hence none of valuation.

Each is the specific good which it is, and that is all that can be said. In its own place, none is a means to anything beyond itself. But there may arise a situation in which they compete or conflict, in which a choice has to be made. Now comparison comes in. Since a choice has to be made, we want to know the respective claims of each competitor.

Education is not a means to living, but is identical with the operation of living a life which is fruitful and inherently significant, the only ultimate value which can be set up is just the process of living itself. And this is not an end to which studies and activities are subordinate means; it is the whole of which they are ingredients. And what has been said about appreciation means that every study in one of its aspects ought to have just such ultimate significance. It is true of arithmetic as it is of poetry that in some place and at some time it ought to be a good to be appreciated on its own account — just as an enjoyable experience, in short. If it is not, then when the time and place come for it to be used as a means or instrumentality, it will be in just that much handicapped. Never having been realized or appreciated for itself, one will miss something of its capacity as a resource for other ends.

It equally follows that when we compare studies as to their values, that is, treat them as means to something beyond themselves, that which controls their proper valuation is found in the specific situation in which they are to be used. The way to enable a student to apprehend the instrumental value of arithmetic is not to lecture him upon the benefit it will be to him in some remote and uncertain future, but to let him discover that success in something he is interested in doing depends upon ability to use number.

It also follows that the attempt to distribute distinct sorts of value among different studies is a misguided one, in spite of the amount of time recently devoted to the undertaking. Science for example may have any kind of value, depending upon the situation into which it enters as a means. To some the value of science may be military; it may be an instrument in strengthening means of offense or defense; it may be technological, a tool for engineering; or it may be commercial — an aid in the successful conduct of business; under other conditions, its worth may be philanthropic — the service it renders in relieving human suffering; or again it may be quite conventional — of value in establishing one's social status as an "educated" person.

As matter of fact, science serves all these purposes, and it would be an arbitrary task to try to fix upon one of them as its "real" end. All that we can be sure of educationally is that science should be taught so as to be an end in itself in the lives of students — something worth while on account of its own unique intrinsic contribution to the experience of life. Primarily it must have "appreciation value." If we take something which seems to be at the opposite pole, like poetry, the same sort of statement applies. It may be that, at the present time, its chief value is the contribution it makes to the enjoyment of leisure. But that may represent a degenerate condition rather than anything necessary.

Poetry has historically been allied with religion and morals; it has served the purpose of penetrating the mysterious depths of things. It has had an enormous patriotic value. Homer to the Greeks was a Bible, a textbook of morals, a history, and a national inspiration. In any case, it may be said that an education which does not succeed in making poetry a resource in the business of life as well as in its leisure, has something the matter with it — or else the poetry is artificial poetry.

The same considerations apply to the value of a study or a topic of a study with reference to its motivating force. Those responsible for planning and teaching the course of study should have grounds for thinking that the studies and topics included furnish both direct increments to the enriching of lives of the pupils and also materials which they can put to use in other concerns of direct interest.

Since the curriculum is always getting loaded down with purely inherited traditional matter and with subjects which represent mainly the energy of some influential person or group of persons in behalf of something dear to them, it requires constant inspection, criticism, and revision to make sure it is accomplishing its purpose. Then there is always the probability that it represents the values of adults rather than those of children and youth, or those of pupils a generation ago rather than those of the present day. Hence a further need for a critical outlook and survey. But these considerations do not mean that for a subject to have motivating value to a pupil (whether intrinsic or instrumental) is the same thing as for him to be aware of the value, or to be able to tell what the study is good for.

In the first place, as long as any topic makes an immediate appeal, it is not necessary to ask what it is good for. This is a question which can be asked only about instrumental values. Some goods are not good for anything; they are just goods. Any other notion leads to an absurdity. For we cannot stop asking the question about an instrumental good, one whose value lies in its being good for something, unless there is at some point something intrinsically good, good for itself. To a hungry, healthy child, food is a good of the situation; we do not have to bring him to consciousness of the ends subserved by food in order to supply a motive to eat. The food in connection with his appetite is a motive. The same thing holds of mentally eager pupils with respect to many topics. Neither they nor the teacher could possibly foretell with any exactness the purposes learning is to accomplish in the future; nor as long as the eagerness continues is it advisable to try to specify particular goods which are to come of it.

The proof of a good is found in the fact that the pupil responds; his response is use. His response to the material shows that the subject functions in his life. It is unsound to urge that, say, Latin has a value per se in the abstract, just as a study, as a sufficient justification for teaching it. But it is equally absurd to argue that unless teacher or pupil can point out some definite assignable future use to which it is to be put, it lacks justifying value. When pupils are genuinely concerned in learning Latin, that is of itself proof that it possesses value. The most which one is entitled to ask in such cases is whether in view of the shortness of time, there are not other things of intrinsic value which in addition have greater instrumental value.

This brings us to the matter of instrumental values — topics studied because of some end beyond themselves. If a child is ill and his appetite does not lead him to eat when food is presented, or if his appetite is perverted so that he prefers candy to meat and vegetables, conscious reference to results is indicated. He needs to be made conscious of consequences as a justification of the positive or negative value of certain objects. Or the state of things may be normal enough, and yet an individual not be moved by some matter because he does not grasp how his attainment of some intrinsic good depends upon active concern with what is presented. In such cases, it is obviously the part of wisdom to establish consciousness of connection. In general what is desirable is that a topic be presented in such a way that it either have an immediate value, and require no justification, or else be perceived to be a means of achieving something of intrinsic value. An instrumental value then has the intrinsic value of being a means to an end.

It may be questioned whether some of the present pedagogical interest in the matter of values of studies is not either excessive or else too narrow. Sometimes it appears to be a laboured effort to furnish an apologetic for topics which no longer operate to any purpose, direct or indirect, in the lives of pupils. At other times, the reaction against useless lumber seems to have gone to the extent of supposing that no subject or topic should be taught unless some quite definite future utility can be pointed out by those making the course of study or by the pupil himself, unmindful of the fact that life is its own excuse for being; and that definite utilities which can be pointed out are themselves justified only because they increase the experienced content of life itself.

Segregation and Organization of Values.

It is of course possible to classify in a general way the various valuable phases of life. In order to get a survey of aims sufficiently wide to give breadth and flexibility to the enterprise of education, there is some advantage in such a classification. But it is a great mistake to regard these values as ultimate ends to which the concrete satisfactions of experience are subordinate. They are nothing but generalizations, more or less adequate, of concrete goods.

Health, wealth, efficiency, sociability, utility, culture, happiness itself are only abstract terms which sum up a multitude of particulars. To regard such things as standards for the valuation of concrete topics and process of education is to subordinate to an abstraction the concrete facts from which the abstraction is derived. They are not in any true sense standards of valuation; these are found, as we have previously seen, in the specific realizations which form tastes and habits of preference. They are, however, of significance as points of view elevated above the details of life whence to survey the field and see how its constituent details are distributed, and whether they are well proportioned.

No classification can have other than a provisional validity. The following may prove of some help. We may say that the kind of experience to which the work of the schools should contribute is one marked by executive competency in the management of resources and obstacles encountered (efficiency); by sociability, or interest in the direct companionship of others; by aesthetic taste or capacity to appreciate artistic excellence in at least some of its classic forms; by trained intellectual method, or interest in some mode of scientific achievement; and by sensitiveness to the rights and claims of others — conscientiousness. And while these considerations are not standards of value, they are useful criteria for survey, criticism, and better organization of existing methods and subject matter of instruction.

The need of such general points of view is the greater because of a tendency to segregate educational values due to the isolation from one another of the various pursuits of life. The idea is prevalent that different studies represent separate kinds of values, and that the curriculum should, therefore, be constituted by gathering together various studies till a sufficient variety of independent values have been cared for.

The following quotation does not use the word value, but it contains the notion of a curriculum constructed on the idea that there are a number of separate ends to be reached, and that various studies may be evaluated by referring each study to its respective end. "Memory is trained by most studies, but best by languages and history; taste is trained by the more advanced study of languages, and still better by English literature; imagination by all higher language teaching, but chiefly by Greek and Latin poetry; observation by science work in the laboratory, though some training is to be got from the earlier stages of Latin and Greek; for expression, Greek and Latin composition comes first and English composition next; for abstract reasoning, mathematics stands almost alone; for concrete reasoning, science comes first, then geometry; for social reasoning, the Greek and Roman historians and orators come first, and general history next. Hence the narrowest education which can claim to be at all complete includes Latin, one modern language, some history, some English literature, and one science."

There is much in the wording of this passage which is irrelevant to our point and which must be discounted to make it clear. The phraseology betrays the particular provincial tradition within which the author is writing. There is the unquestioned assumption of "faculties" to be trained, and a dominant interest in the ancient languages; there is comparative disregard of the earth on which men happen to live and the bodies they happen to carry around with them. But with allowances made for these matters (even with their complete abandonment) we find much in contemporary educational philosophy which parallels the fundamental notion of parcelling out special values to segregated studies.

Even when some one end is set up as a standard of value, like social efficiency or culture, it will often be found to be but a verbal heading under which a variety of disconnected factors are comprised. And although the general tendency is to allow a greater variety of values to a given study than does the passage quoted, yet the attempt to inventory a number of values attaching to each study and to state the amount of each value which the given study possesses emphasizes an implied educational disintegration.

As matter of fact, such schemes of values of studies are largely but unconscious justifications of the curriculum with which one is familiar. One accepts, for the most part, the studies of the existing course and then assigns values to them as a sufficient reason for their being taught. Mathematics is said to have, for example, disciplinary value in habituating the pupil to accuracy of statement and closeness of reasoning; it has utilitarian value in giving command of the arts of calculation involved in trade and the arts; culture value in its enlargement of the imagination in dealing with the most general relations of things; even religious value in its concept of the infinite and allied ideas. But clearly mathematics does not accomplish such results, because it is endowed with miraculous potencies called values; it has these values if and when it accomplishes these results, and not otherwise.

The statements may help a teacher to a larger vision of the possible results to be effected by instruction in mathematical topics. But unfortunately, the tendency is to treat the statement as indicating powers inherently residing in the subject, whether they operate or not, and thus to give it a rigid justification. If they do not operate, the blame is put not on the subject as taught, but on the indifference and recalcitrancy of pupils.

This attitude toward subjects is the obverse side of the conception of experience or life as a patchwork of independent interests which exist side by side and limit one another. Students of politics are familiar with a check and balance theory of the powers of government. There are supposed to be independent separate functions, like the legislative, executive, judicial, administrative, and all goes well if each of these checks all the others and thus creates an ideal balance. There is a philosophy which might well be called the check and balance theory of experience. Life presents a diversity of interests. Left to themselves, they tend to encroach on one another. The ideal is to prescribe a special territory for each till the whole ground of experience is covered, and then see to it each remains within its own boundaries.

Politics, business, recreation, art, science, the learned professions, polite intercourse, leisure, represent such interests. Each of these ramifies into many branches: business into manual occupations, executive positions, bookkeeping, railroading, banking, agriculture, trade and commerce, etc., and so with each of the others. An ideal education would then supply the means of meeting these separate and pigeon-holed interests. And when we look at the schools, it is easy to get the impression that they accept this view of the nature of adult life, and set for themselves the task of meeting its demands. Each interest is acknowledged as a kind of fixed institution to which something in the course of study must correspond.

The course of study must then have some civics and history politically and patriotically viewed: some utilitarian studies; some science; some art (mainly literature of course); some provision for recreation; some moral education; and so on. And it will be found that a large part of current agitation about schools is concerned with clamour and controversy about the due meed of recognition to be given to each of these interests, and with struggles to secure for each its due share in the course of study; or, if this does not seem feasible in the existing school system, then to secure a new and separate kind of schooling to meet the need. In the multitude of educations education is forgotten.

The obvious outcome is congestion of the course of study, overpressure and distraction of pupils, and a narrow specialization fatal to the very idea of education. But these bad results usually lead to more of the same sort of thing as a remedy. When it is perceived that after all the requirements of a full life experience are not met, the deficiency is not laid to the isolation and narrowness of the teaching of the existing subjects, and this recognition made the basis of reorganization of the system. No, the lack is something to be made up for by the introduction of still another study, or, if necessary, another kind of school. And as a rule those who object to the resulting overcrowding and consequent superficiality and distraction usually also have recourse to a merely quantitative criterion: the remedy is to cut off a great many studies as fads and frills, and return to the good old curriculum of the three R's in elementary education and the equally good and equally old-fashioned curriculum of the classics and mathematics in higher education.

The situation has, of course, its historic explanation. Various epochs of the past have had their own characteristic struggles and interests. Each of these great epochs has left behind itself a kind of cultural deposit, like a geologic stratum. These deposits have found their way into educational institutions in the form of studies, distinct courses of study, distinct types of schools.

With the rapid change of political, scientific, and economic interests in the last century, provision had to be made for new values. Though the older courses resisted, they have had at least in this country to retire their pretensions to a monopoly. They have not, however, been reorganized in content and aim; they have only been reduced in amount. The new studies, representing the new interests, have not been used to transform the method and aim of all instruction; they have been injected and added on. The result is a conglomerate, the cement of which consists in the mechanics of the school program or time table. Thence arises the scheme of values and standards of value which we have mentioned.

This situation in education represents the divisions and separations which obtain in social life. The variety of interests which should mark any rich and balanced experience have been torn asunder and deposited in separate institutions with diverse and independent purposes and methods. Business is business, science is science, art is art, politics is politics, social intercourse is social intercourse, morals is morals, recreation is recreation, and so on.

Each possesses a separate and independent province with its own peculiar aims and ways of proceeding. Each contributes to the others only externally and accidentally. All of them together make up the whole of life by just apposition and addition. What does one expect from business save that it should furnish money, to be used in turn for making more money and for support of self and family, for buying books and pictures, tickets to concerts which may afford culture, and for paying taxes, charitable gifts and other things of social and ethical value? How unreasonable to expect that the pursuit of business should be itself a culture of the imagination, in breadth and refinement; that it should directly, and not through the money which it supplies, have social service for its animating principle and be conducted as an enterprise in behalf of social organization! The same thing is to be said, mutatis mutandis, of the pursuit of art or science or politics or religion.

Each has become specialized not merely in its appliances and its demands upon time, but in its aim and animating spirit. Unconsciously, our course of studies and our theories of the educational values of studies reflect this division of interests. The point at issue in a theory of educational value is then the unity or integrity of experience.

Philosophic Theories of Morals

Inner and the Outer

Since morality is concerned with conduct, any dualisms which are set up between mind and activity must reflect themselves in the theory of morals. Since the formulations of the separation in the philosophic theory of morals are used to justify and idealize the practices employed in moral training, a brief critical discussion is in place. It is a commonplace of educational theory that the establishing of character is a comprehensive aim of school instruction and discipline. Hence it is important that we should be on our guard against a conception of the relations of intelligence to character which hampers the realization of the aim, and on the look-out for the conditions which have to be provided in order that the aim may be successfully acted upon.

The first obstruction which meets us is the currency of moral ideas which split the course of activity into two opposed factors, often named respectively the inner and outer, or the spiritual and the physical. This division is a culmination of the dualism of mind and the world, soul and body, end and means, which we have so frequently noted. In morals it takes the form of a sharp demarcation of the motive of action from its consequences, and of character from conduct.

Motive and character are regarded as something purely "inner," existing exclusively in consciousness, while consequences and conduct are regarded as outside of mind, conduct having to do simply with the movements which carry out motives; consequences with what happens as a result. Different schools identify morality with either the inner state of mind or the outer act and results, each in separation from the other.

Action with a purpose is deliberate; it involves a consciously foreseen end and a mental weighing of considerations pro and eon. It also involves a conscious state of longing or desire for the end. The deliberate choice of an aim and of a settled disposition of desire takes time. During this time complete overt action is suspended. A person who does not have his mind made up, does not know what to do. Consequently he postpones definite action so far as possible. His position may be compared to that of a man considering jumping across a ditch. If he were sure he could or could not make it, definite activity in some direction would occur. But if he considers, he is in doubt; he hesitates.

During the time in which a single overt line of action is in suspense, his activities are confined to such redistributions of energy within the organism as will prepare a determinate course of action. He measures the ditch with his eyes; he brings himself taut to get a feel of the energy at his disposal; he looks about for other ways across, he reflects upon the importance of getting across. All this means an accentuation of consciousness; it means a turning in upon the individual's own attitudes, powers, wishes, etc.

Obviously, however, this surging up of personal factors into conscious recognition is a part of the whole activity in its temporal development. There is not first a purely psychical process, followed abruptly by a radically different physical one. There is one continuous behaviour, proceeding from a more uncertain, divided, hesitating state to a more overt, determinate, or complete state.

The activity at first consists mainly of certain tensions and adjustments within the organism; as these are coordinated into a unified attitude, the organism as a whole acts — some definite act is undertaken. We may distinguish, of course, the more explicitly conscious phase of the continuous activity as mental or psychical. But that only identifies the mental or psychical to mean the indeterminate, formative state of an activity which in its fullness involves putting forth of overt energy to modify the environment.

Our conscious thoughts, observations, wishes, aversions are important, because they represent inchoate, nascent activities. They fulfill their destiny in issuing, later on, into specific and perceptible acts. And these inchoate, budding organic readjustments are important because they are our sole escape from the dominion of routine habits and blind impulse. They are activities having a new meaning in process of development. Hence, normally, there is an accentuation of personal consciousness whenever our instincts and ready formed habits find themselves blocked by novel conditions.

Then we are thrown back upon ourselves to reorganize our own attitude before proceeding to a definite and irretrievable course of action. Unless we try to drive our way through by sheer brute force, we must modify our organic resources to adapt them to the specific features of the situation in which we find ourselves. The conscious deliberating and desiring which precede overt action are, then, the methodic personal readjustment implied in activity in uncertain situations.

This role of mind in continuous activity is not always maintained, however. Desires for something different, aversion to the given state of things caused by the blocking of successful activity, stimulates the imagination. The picture of a different state of things does not always function to aid ingenious observation and recollection to find a way out and on. Except where there is a disciplined disposition, the tendency is for the imagination to run loose.

Instead of its objects being checked up by conditions with reference to their practicability in execution, they are allowed to develop because of the immediate emotional satisfaction which they yield. When we find the successful display of our energies checked by uncongenial surroundings, natural and social, the easiest way out is to build castles in the air and let them be a substitute for an actual achievement which involves the pains of thought. So in overt action we acquiesce, and build up an imaginary world in, mind. This break between thought and conduct is reflected in those theories which make a sharp separation between mind as inner and conduct and consequences as merely outer.

For the split may be more than an incident of a particular individual's experience. The social situation may be such as to throw the class given to articulate reflection back into their own thoughts and desires without providing the means by which these ideas and aspirations can be used to reorganize the environment. Under such conditions, men take revenge, as it were, upon the alien and hostile environment by cultivating contempt for it, by giving it a bad name. They seek refuge and consolation within their own states of mind, their own imaginings and wishes, which they compliment by calling both more real and more ideal than the despised outer world. Such periods have recurred in history. In the early centuries of the Christian era, the influential moral systems of Stoicism, of monastic and popular Christianity and other religious movements of the day, took shape under the influence of such conditions.

The more action which might express prevailing ideals was checked, the more the inner possession and cultivation of ideals was regarded as self-sufficient — as the essence of morality. The external world in which activity belongs was thought of as morally indifferent. Everything lay in having the right motive, even though that motive was not a moving force in the world. Much the same sort of situation recurred in Germany in the later eighteenth and early nineteenth centuries; it led to the Kantian insistence upon the good will as the sole moral good, the will being regarded as something complete in itself, apart from action and from the changes or consequences effected in the world. Later it led to any idealization of existing institutions as themselves the embodiment of reason.

The purely internal morality of "meaning well," of having a good disposition regardless of what comes of it, naturally led to a reaction. This is generally known as either hedonism or utilitarianism. It was said in effect that the important thing morally is not what a man is inside of his own consciousness, but what he does — the consequences which issue, the charges he actually effects. Inner morality was attacked as sentimental, arbitrary, dogmatic, subjective — as giving men leave to dignify and shield any dogma congenial to their self-interest or any caprice occurring to imagination by calling it an intuition or an ideal of conscience. Results, conduct, are what counts; they afford the sole measure of morality.

Ordinary morality, and hence that of the schoolroom, is likely to be an inconsistent compromise of both views. On one hand, certain states of feeling are made much of; the individual must "mean well," and if his intentions are good, if he had the right sort of emotional consciousness, he may be relieved of responsibility for full results in conduct. But since, on the other hand, certain things have to be done to meet the convenience and the requirements of others, and of social order in general, there is great insistence upon the doing of certain things, irrespective of whether the individual has any concern or intelligence in their doing. He must toe the mark; he must have his nose held to the grindstone; he must obey; he must form useful habits; he must learn self-control, — all of these precepts being understood in a way which emphasizes simply the immediate thing tangibly done, irrespective of the spirit of thought and desire in which it is done, and irrespective therefore of its effect upon other less obvious doings.

It is hoped that the prior discussion has sufficiently elaborated the method by which both of these evils are avoided. One or both of these evils must result wherever individuals, whether young or old, cannot engage in a progressively cumulative undertaking under conditions which engage their interest and require their reflection. For only in such cases is it possible that the disposition of desire and thinking should be an organic factor in overt and obvious conduct. Given a consecutive activity embodying the student's own interest, where a definite result is to be obtained, and where neither routine habit nor the following of dictated directions nor capricious improvising will suffice, and there the rise of conscious purpose, conscious desire, and deliberate reflection are inevitable. They are inevitable as the spirit and quality of an activity having specific consequences, not as forming an isolated realm of inner consciousness.

Duty and Interest.

Probably there is no antithesis more often set up in moral discussion than that between acting from "principle" and from "interest." To act on principle is to act disinterestedly, according to a general law, which is above all personal considerations. To act according to interest is, so the allegation runs, to act selfishly, with one's own personal profit in view. It substitutes the changing expediency of the moment for devotion to unswerving moral law. The false idea of interest underlying this opposition has already been criticized, but some moral aspects of the question will now be considered.

A clew to the matter may be found in the fact that the supporters of the "interest" side of the controversy habitually use the term "self-interest." Starting from the premises that unless there is interest in an object or idea, there is no motive force, they end with the conclusion that even when a person claims to be acting from principle or from a sense of duty, he really acts as he does because there "is something in it" for himself.

The premise is sound; the conclusion false. In reply the other school argues that since man is capable of generous self-forgetting and even self-sacrificing action, he is capable of acting without interest. Again the premise is sound, and the conclusion false. The error on both sides lies in a false notion of the relation of interest and the self.

Both sides assume that the self is a fixed and hence isolated quantity. As a consequence, there is a rigid dilemma between acting for an interest of the self and without interest. If the self is something fixed antecedent to action, then acting from interest means trying to get more in the way of possessions for the self — whether in the way of fame, approval of others, power over others, pecuniary profit, or pleasure. Then the reaction from this view as a cynical depreciation of human nature leads to the view that men who act nobly act with no interest at all. Yet to an unbiased judgment it would appear plain that a man must be interested in what he is doing or he would not do it.

A physician who continues to serve the sick in a plague at almost certain danger to his own life must be interested in the efficient performance of his profession — more interested in that than in the safety of his own bodily life. But it is distorting facts to say that this interest is merely a mask for an interest in something else which he gets by continuing his customary services — such as money or good repute or virtue; that it is only a means to an ulterior selfish end. The moment we recognize that the self is not something ready-made, but something in continuous formation through choice of action, the whole situation clears up.

A man's interest in keeping at his work in spite of danger to life means that his self is found in that work; if he finally gave up, and preferred his personal safety or comfort, it would mean that he preferred to be that kind of a self. The mistake lies in making a separation between interest and self, and supposing that the latter is the end to which interest in objects and acts and others is a mere means. In fact, self and interest are two names for the same fact; the kind and amount of interest actively taken in a thing reveals and measures the quality of selfhood which exists. Bear in mind that interest means the active or moving identity of the self with a certain object, and the whole alleged dilemma falls to the ground.

Unselfishness, for example, signifies neither lack of interest in what is done (that would mean only machine-like indifference) nor selflessness — which would mean absence of virility and character. As employed everywhere outside of this particular theoretical controversy, the term "unselfishness" refers to the kind of aims and objects which habitually interest a man.

And if we make a mental survey of the kind of interests which evoke the use of this epithet, we shall see that they have two intimately associated features. (i) The generous self consciously identifies itself with the full range of relationships implied in its activity, instead of drawing a sharp line between itself and considerations which are excluded as alien or indifferent; (ii) it readjusts and expands its past ideas of itself to take in new consequences as they become perceptible. When the physician began his career he may not have thought of a pestilence; he may not have consciously identified himself with service under such conditions. But, if he has a normally growing or active self, when he finds that his vocation involves such risks, he willingly adopts them as integral portions of his activity. The wider or larger self which means inclusion instead of denial of relationships is identical with a self which enlarges in order to assume previously unforeseen ties.

In such crises of readjustment — and the crisis may be slight as well as great — there may be a transitional conflict of "principle" with "interest." It is the nature of a habit to involve ease in the accustomed line of activity. It is the nature of a readjusting of habit to involve an effort which is disagreeable — something to which a man has deliberately to hold himself. In other words, there is a tendency to identify the self — or take interest — in what one has got used to, and to turn away the mind with aversion or irritation when an unexpected thing which involves an unpleasant modification of habit comes up.

Since in the past one has done one's duty without having to face such a disagreeable circumstance, why not go on as one has been? To yield to this temptation means to narrow and isolate the thought of the self — to treat it as complete. Any habit, no matter how efficient in the past, which has become set, may at any time bring this temptation with it. To act from principle in such an emergency is not to act on some abstract principle, or duty at large; it is to act upon the principle of a course of action, instead of upon the circumstances which have attended it.

The principle of a physician's conduct is its animating aim and spirit — the care for the diseased. The principle is not what justifies an activity, for the principle is but another name for the continuity of the activity. If the activity as manifested in its consequences is undesirable, to act upon principle is to accentuate its evil. And a man who prides himself upon acting upon principle is likely to be a man who insists upon having his own way without learning from experience what is the better way. He fancies that some abstract principle justifies his course of action without recognizing that his principle needs justification.

Assuming, however, that school conditions are such as to provide desirable occupations, it is interest in the occupation as a whole — that is, in its continuous development — which keeps a pupil at his work in spite of temporary diversions and unpleasant obstacles. Where there is no activity having a growing significance, appeal to principle is either purely verbal, or a form of obstinate pride or an appeal to extraneous considerations clothed with a dignified title. Undoubtedly there are junctures where momentary interest ceases and attention flags, and where reinforcement is needed. But what carries a person over these hard stretches is not loyalty to duty in the abstract, but interest in his occupation.

Duties are "offices" — they are the specific acts needed for the fulfilling of a function — or, in homely language — doing one's job. And the man who is genuinely interested in his job is the man who is able to stand temporary discouragement, to persist in the face of obstacles, to take the lean with the fat: he makes an interest out of meeting and overcoming difficulties and distraction.

Intelligence and Character

A noteworthy paradox often accompanies discussions of morals. On the one hand, there is an identification of the moral with the rational. Reason is set up as a faculty from which proceed ultimate moral intuitions, and sometimes, as in the Kantian theory, it is said to supply the only proper moral motive. On the other hand, the value of concrete, everyday intelligence is constantly underestimated, and even deliberately depreciated.

Morals is often thought to be an affair with which ordinary knowledge has nothing to do. Moral knowledge is thought to be a thing apart, and conscience is thought of as something radically different from consciousness. This separation, if valid, is of especial significance for education. Moral education in school is practically hopeless when we set up the development of character as a supreme end, and at the same time treat the acquiring of knowledge and the development of understanding, which of necessity occupy the chief part of school time, as having nothing to do with character. On such a basis, moral education is inevitably reduced to some kind of catechetical instruction, or lessons about morals.

Lessons "about morals" signify as matter of course lessons in what other people think about virtues and duties. It amounts to something only in the degree in which pupils happen to be already animated by a sympathetic and dignified regard for the sentiments of others. Without such a regard, it has no more influence on character than information about the mountains of Asia; with a servile regard, it increases dependence upon others, and throws upon those in authority the responsibility for conduct.

As a matter of fact, direct instruction in morals has been effective only in social groups where it was a part of the authoritative control of the many by the few. Not the teaching as such but the reinforcement of it by the whole regime of which it was an incident made it effective. To attempt to get similar results from lessons about morals in a democratic society is to rely upon sentimental magic.

At the other end of the scale stands the Socratic-Platonic teaching which identifies knowledge and virtue — which holds that no man does evil knowingly but only because of ignorance of the good. This doctrine is commonly attacked on the ground that nothing is more common than for a man to know the good and yet do the bad: not knowledge, but habituation or practice, and motive are what is required. Aristotle, in fact, at once attacked the Platonic teaching on the ground that moral virtue is like an art, such as medicine; the experienced practitioner is better than a man who has theoretical knowledge but no practical experience of disease and remedies.

The issue turns, however, upon what is meant by knowledge. Aristotle's objection ignored the gist of Plato's teaching to the effect that man could not attain a theoretical insight into the good except as he had passed through years of practical habituation and strenuous discipline. Knowledge of the good was not a thing to be got either from books or from others, but was achieved through a prolonged education. It was the final and culminating grace of a mature experience of life.

Irrespective of Plato's position, it is easy to perceive that the term knowledge is used to denote things as far apart as intimate and vital personal realization, — a conviction gained and tested in experience, — and a second-handed, largely symbolic, recognition that persons in general believe so and so — a devitalized remote information. That the latter does not guarantee conduct, that it does not profoundly affect character, goes without saying. But if knowledge means something of the same sort as our conviction gained by trying and testing that sugar is sweet and quinine bitter, the case stands otherwise.

Every time a man sits on a chair rather than on a stove, carries an umbrella when it rains, consults a doctor when ill — or in short performs any of the thousand acts which make up his daily life, he proves that knowledge of a certain kind finds direct issue in conduct. There is every reason to suppose that the same sort of knowledge of good has a like expression; in fact "good" is an empty term unless it includes the satisfactions experienced in such situations as those mentioned. Knowledge that other persons are supposed to know something might lead one to act so as to win the approbation others attach to certain actions, or at least so as to give others the impression that one agrees with them; there is no reason why it should lead to personal initiative and loyalty in behalf of the beliefs attributed to them.

It is not necessary, accordingly, to dispute about the proper meaning of the term knowledge. It is enough for educational purposes to note the different qualities covered by the one name, to realize that it is knowledge gained at first hand through the exigencies of experience which affects conduct in significant ways. If a pupil learns things from books simply in connection with school lessons and for the sake of reciting what he has learned when called upon, then knowledge will have effect upon some conduct — namely upon that of reproducing statements at the demand of others.

There is nothing surprising that such "knowledge" should not have much influence in the life out of school. But this is not a reason for making a divorce between knowledge and conduct, but for holding in low esteem this kind of knowledge. The same thing may be said of knowledge which relates merely to an isolated and technical speciality; it modifies action but only in its own narrow line.

In truth, the problem of moral education in the schools is one with the problem of securing knowledge — the knowledge connected with the system of impulses and habits. For the use to which any known fact is put depends upon its connections. The knowledge of dynamite of a safecracker may be identical in verbal form with that of a chemist; in fact, it is different, for it is knit into connection with different aims and habits, and thus has a different import.

Our prior discussion of subject-matter as proceeding from direct activity having an immediate aim, to the enlargement of meaning found in geography and history, and then to scientifically organized knowledge, was based upon the idea of maintaining a vital connection between knowledge and activity. What is learned and employed in an occupation having an aim and involving cooperation with others is moral knowledge, whether consciously so regarded or not. For it builds up a social interest and confers the intelligence needed to make that interest effective in practice. Just because the studies of the curriculum represent standard factors in social life, they are organs of initiation into social values. As mere school studies, their acquisition has only a technical worth.

Acquired under conditions where their social significance is realized, they feed moral interest and develop moral insight. Moreover, the qualities of mind discussed under the topic of method of learning are all of them intrinsically moral qualities. Open-mindedness, single-mindedness, sincerity, breadth of outlook, thoroughness, assumption of responsibility for developing the consequences of ideas which are accepted, are moral traits. The habit of identifying moral characteristics with external conformity to authoritative prescriptions may lead us to ignore the ethical value of these intellectual attitudes, but the same habit tends to reduce morals to a dead and machine like routine. Consequently while such an attitude has moral results, the results are morally undesirable — above all in a democratic society where so much depends upon personal disposition.

Social and Moral

Morals are as broad as acts which concern our relationships with others. And potentially this includes all our acts, even though their social bearing may not be thought of at the time of performance. For every act, by the principle of habit, modifies disposition — it sets up a certain kind of inclination and desire. And it is impossible to tell when the habit thus strengthened may have a direct and perceptible influence on our association with others.

Certain traits of character have such an obvious connection with our social relationships that we call them "moral" in an emphatic sense — truthfulness, honesty, chastity, amiability, etc. But this only means that they are, as compared with some other attitudes, central: — that they carry other attitudes with them. They are moral in an emphatic sense not because they are isolated and exclusive, but because they are so intimately connected with thousands of other attitudes which we do not explicitly recognize — which perhaps we have not even names for. To call them virtues in their isolation is like taking the skeleton for the living body.

The bones are certainly important, but their importance lies in the fact that they support other organs of the body in such a way as to make them capable of integrated effective activity. And the same is true of the qualities of character which we specifically designate virtues. Morals concern nothing less than the whole character, and the whole character is identical with the man in all his concrete make-up and manifestations. To possess virtue does not signify to have cultivated a few namable and exclusive traits; it means to be fully and adequately what one is capable of becoming through association with others in all the offices of life.

The moral and the social quality of conduct are, in the last analysis, identical with each other. The social function of education to say that the measure of the worth of the administration, curriculum, and methods of instruction of the school is the extent to which they are animated by a social spirit. And the great danger which threatens school work is the absence of conditions which make possible a permeating social spirit; this is the great enemy of effective moral training. For this spirit can be actively present only when certain conditions are met.

(i) In the first place, the school must itself be a community life in all which that implies. Social perceptions and interests can be developed only in a genuinely social medium — one where there is give and take in the building up of a common experience. Informational statements about things can be acquired in relative isolation by any one who previously has had enough intercourse with others to have learned language. But realization of the meaning of the linguistic signs is quite another matter. That involves a context of work and play in association with others.

The plea which has been made for education through continued constructive activities in this book rests upon the fact they afford an opportunity for a social atmosphere. In place of a school set apart from life as a place for learning lessons, we have a miniature social group in which study and growth are incidents of present shared experience. Playgrounds, shops, workrooms, laboratories not only direct the natural active tendencies of youth, but they involve intercourse, communication, and cooperation, — all extending the perception of connections.

(ii) The learning in school should be continuous with that out of school. There should be a free interplay between the two. This is possible only when there are numerous points of contact between the social interests of the one and of the other. A school is conceivable in which there should be a spirit of companionship and shared activity, but where its social life would no more represent or typify that of the world beyond the school walls than that of a monastery. Social concern and understanding

would be developed, but they would not be available outside; they would not carry over. The proverbial separation of town and gown, the cultivation of academic seclusion, operate in this direction. So does such adherence to the culture of the past as generates a reminiscent social spirit, for this makes an individual feel more at home in the life of other days than in his own.

A professedly cultural education is peculiarly exposed to this danger. An idealized past becomes the refuge and solace of the spirit; present-day concerns are found sordid, and unworthy of attention. But as a rule, the absence of a social environment in connection with which learning is a need and a reward is the chief reason for the isolation of the school; and this isolation renders school knowledge inapplicable to life and so infertile in character.

A narrow and moralistic view of morals is responsible for the failure to recognize that all the aims and values which are desirable in education are themselves moral. Discipline, natural development, culture, social efficiency, are moral traits — marks of a person who is a worthy member of that society which it is the business of education to further. There is an old saying to the effect that it is not enough for a man to be good; he must be good for something.

The something for which a man must be good is capacity to live as a social member so that what he gets from living with others balances with what he contributes. What he gets and gives as a human being, a being with desires, emotions, and ideas, is not external possessions, but a widening and deepening of conscious life — a more intense, disciplined, and expanding realization of meanings.

4

Education as Growth

The primary condition of growth is immaturity. This may seem to be a mere truism — saying that a being can develop only in some point in which he is undeveloped. But the prefix "im" of the word immaturity means something positive, not a mere void or lack. It is noteworthy that the terms "capacity" and "potentiality" have a double meaning, one sense being negative, the other positive.

Capacity may denote mere receptivity, like the capacity of a quart measure. We may mean by potentiality a merely dormant or quiescent state — a capacity to become something different under external influences. But we also mean by capacity an ability, a power; and by potentiality potency, force. Now when we say that immaturity means the possibility of growth, we are not referring to absence of powers which may exist at a later time; we express a force positively present — the ability to develop.

Our tendency to take immaturity as mere lack, and growth as something which fills up the gap between the immature and the mature is due to regarding childhood comparatively, instead of intrinsically. We treat it simply as a privation because we are measuring it by adulthood as a fixed standard. This fixes attention upon what the child has not, and will not have till he becomes a man.

This comparative standpoint is legitimate enough for some purposes, but if we make it final, the question arises whether we are not guilty of an overweening presumption. Children, if they could express themselves articulately and sincerely, would tell a different tale; and there is excellent adult authority for the conviction that for certain moral and intellectual purposes adults must become as little children.

The seriousness of the assumption of the negative quality of the possibilities of immaturity is apparent when we reflect that it sets up as an ideal and standard a static end. The fulfillment of growing is taken to mean an accomplished growth: that is to say, an Ungrowth, something which is no longer growing. The futility of the assumption is seen in the fact that every adult resents the imputation of having no further possibilities of growth; and so far as he finds that they are closed to him mourns the fact as evidence of loss, instead of falling back on the achieved as adequate manifestation of power. Why an unequal measure for child and man?

Taken absolutely, instead of comparatively, immaturity designates a positive force or ability, — the pouter to grow. We do not have to draw out or educe positive activities from a child, as some educational doctrines would have it. Where there is life, there are already eager and impassioned activities. Growth is not something done to them; it is something they do. The positive and constructive aspect of possibility gives the key to understanding the two chief traits of immaturity, dependence and plasticity.

(1) It sounds absurd to hear dependence spoken of as something positive, still more absurd as a power. Yet if helplessness were all there were in dependence, no development could ever take place. A merely impotent being has to be carried, forever, by others. The fact that

dependence is accompanied by growth in ability, not by an ever increasing lapse into parasitism, suggests that it is already something constructive. Being merely sheltered by others would not promote growth. For (2) it would only build a wall around impotence. With reference to the physical world, the child is helpless. He lacks at birth and for a long time thereafter power to make his way physically, to make his own living. If he had to do that by himself, he would hardly survive an hour. On this side his helplessness is almost complete. The young of the brutes are immeasurably his superiors. He is physically weak and not able to turn the strength which he possesses to coping with the physical environment.

1. The thoroughgoing character of this helplessness suggests, however, some compensating power. The relative ability of the young of brute animals to adapt themselves fairly well to physical conditions from an early period suggests the fact that their life is not intimately bound up with the life of those about them. They are compelled, so to speak, to have physical gifts because they are lacking in social gifts.

Human infants, on the other hand, can get along with physical incapacity just because of their social capacity. We sometimes talk and think as if they simply happened to be physically in a social environment; as if social forces exclusively existed in the adults who take care of them, they being passive recipients. If it were said that children are themselves marvelously endowed with power to enlist the cooperative attention of others, this would be thought to be a backhanded way of saying that others are marvelously attentive to the needs of children. But observation shows that children are gifted with an equipment of the first order for social intercourse.

Few grown-up persons retain all of the flexible and sensitive ability of children to vibrate sympathetically with the attitudes and doings of those about them.

Inattention to physical things is accompanied by a corresponding intensification of interest and attention as to the doings of people.

The native mechanism of the child and his impulses all tend to facile social responsiveness. The statement that children, before adolescence, are egotistically self-centered, even if it were true, would not contradict the truth of this statement. It would simply indicate that their social responsiveness is employed on their own behalf, not that it does not exist. But the statement is not true as matter of fact.

The facts which are cited in support of the alleged pure egoism of children really show the intensity and directness with which they go to their mark. If the ends which form the mark seem narrow and selfish to adults, it is only because adults have mastered these ends, which have consequently ceased to interest them. Most of the remainder of children's alleged native egoism is simply an egoism which runs counter to an adult's egoism. To a grown-up person who is too absorbed in his own affairs to take an interest in children's affairs, children doubtless seem unreasonably engrossed in their own affairs.

From a social standpoint, dependence denotes a power rather than a weakness; it involves interdependence. There is always a danger that increased personal independence will decrease the social capacity of an individual. In making him more self-reliant, it may make him more self-sufficient; it may lead to aloofness and indifference. It often makes an individual so insensitive in his relations to others as to develop an illusion of being really able to stand and act alone — an unnamed form of insanity which is responsible for a large part of the remediable suffering of the world.

2. The specific adaptability of an immature creature for growth constitutes his plasticity. This is something

quite different from the plasticity of putty or wax. It is not a capacity to take on change of form in accord with external pressure. It lies near the pliable elasticity by which some persons take on the colour of their surroundings while retaining their own bent. But it is something deeper than this. It is essentially the ability to learn from experience; the power to retain from one experience something which is of avail in coping with the difficulties of a later situation. This means power to modify actions on the basis of the results of prior experiences, the power to develop dispositions. Without it, the acquisition of habits is impossible.

It is a familiar fact that the young of the higher animals, and especially the human young, have to learn to utilise their instinctive reactions. The human being is born with a greater number of instinctive tendencies than other animals. But the instincts of the lower animals perfect themselves for appropriate action at an early period after birth, while most of those of the human infant are of little account just as they stand.

An original specialised power of adjustment secures immediate efficiency, but, like a railway ticket, it is good for one route only. A being who, in order to use his eyes, ears, hands, and legs, has to experiment in making varied combinations of their reactions, achieves a control that is flexible and varied. A chick, for example, pecks accurately at a bit of food in a few hours after hatching. This means that definite coordinations of activities of the eyes in seeing and of the body and head in striking are perfected in a few trials.

An infant requires about six months to be able to gauge with approximate accuracy the action in reaching which will coordinate with his visual activities; to be able, that is, to tell whether he can reach a seen object and just how to execute the reaching. As a result, the chick is limited by the relative perfection of its original endowment. The infant has the advantage of the multitude of instinctive tentative reactions and of the experiences that accompany them, even though he is at a temporary disadvantage because they cross one another.

In learning an action, instead of having it given ready-made, one of necessity learns to vary its factors, to make varied combinations of them, according to change of circumstances. A possibility of continuing progress is opened up by the fact that in learning one act, methods are developed good for use in other situations. Still more important is the fact that the human being acquires a habit of learning. He learns to learn.

The importance for human life of the two facts of dependence and variable control has been summed up in the doctrine of the significance of prolonged infancy. This prolongation is significant from the standpoint of the adult members of the group as well as from that of the young. The presence of dependent and learning beings is a stimulus to nurture and affection.

The need for constant continued care was probably a chief means in transforming temporary cohabitations into permanent unions. It certainly was a chief influence in forming habits of affectionate and sympathetic watchfulness; that constructive interest in the well-being of others which is essential to associated life. Intellectually, this moral development meant the introduction of many new objects of attention; it stimulated foresight and planning for the future. Thus there is a reciprocal influence.

Increasing complexity of social life requires a longer period of infancy in which to acquire the needed powers; this prolongation of dependence means prolongation of plasticity, or power of acquiring variable and novel modes of control. Hence it provides a further push to social progress.

Habits

We have already noted that plasticity is the capacity to retain and carry over from prior experience factors which modify subsequent activities. This signifies the capacity to acquire habits, or develop definite dispositions. We have now to consider the salient features of habits. In the first place, a habit is a form of executive skill, of efficiency in doing.

A habit means an ability to use natural conditions as means to ends. It is an active control of the environment through control of the organs of action. We are perhaps apt to emphasise the control of the body at the expense of control of the environment. We think of walking, talking, playing the piano, the specialised skills characteristic of the etcher, the surgeon, the bridge-builder, as if they were simply ease, deftness, and accuracy on the part of the organism. They are that, of course; but the measure of the value of these qualities lies in the economical and effective control of the environment which they secure. To be able to walk is to have certain properties of nature at our disposal — and so with all other habits.

Education is not infrequently defined as consisting in the acquisition of those habits that effect an adjustment of an individual and his environment. The definition expresses an essential phase of growth. But it is essential that adjustment be understood in its active sense of control of means for achieving ends. If we think of a habit simply as a change wrought in the organism, ignoring the fact that this change consists in ability to effect subsequent changes in the environment, we shall be led to think of "adjustment" as a conformity to environment as wax conforms to the seal which impresses it.

The environment is thought of as something fixed, providing in its fixity the end and standard of changes taking place in the organism; adjustment is just fitting ourselves to this fixity of external conditions. Habit as habituation is indeed something relatively passive; we get used to our surroundings — to our clothing, our shoes, and gloves; to the atmosphere as long as it is fairly equable; to our daily associates, etc.

Conformity to the environment, a change wrought in the organism without reference to ability to modify surroundings, is a marked trait of such habituations. Aside from the fact that we are not entitled to carry over the traits of such adjustments (which might well be called accommodations, to mark them off from active adjustments) into habits of active use of our surroundings, two features of habituations are worth notice. In the first place, we get used to things by first using them.

Consider getting used to a strange city. At first, there is excessive stimulation and excessive and ill-adapted response. Gradually certain stimuli are selected because of their relevancy, and others are degraded. We can say either that we do not respond to them any longer, or more truly that we have effected a persistent response to them — an equilibrium of adjustment. This means, in the second place, that this enduring adjustment supplies the background upon which are made specific adjustments, as occasion arises.

Adaptation, in fine, is quite as much adaptation of the environment to our own activities as of our activities to the environment. A savage tribe manages to live on a desert plain. It adapts itself. But its adaptation involves a maximum of accepting, tolerating, putting up with things as they are, a maximum of passive acquiescence, and a minimum of active control, of subjection to use. A civilised people enters upon the scene. It also adapts itself. It introduces irrigation; it searches the world for plants and animals that will flourish under such conditions; it improves, by careful selection, those which are growing there. As a consequence, the wilderness blossoms as a rose. The savage is merely habituated; the civilised man has habits which transform the environment.

The significance of habit is not exhausted, however, in its executive and motor phase. It means formation of intellectual and emotional disposition as well as an increase in ease, economy, and efficiency of action. Any habit marks an inclination — an active preference and choice for the conditions involved in its exercise. A habit does not wait, Micawber-like, for a stimulus to turn up so that it may get busy; it actively seeks for occasions to pass into full operation. If its expression is unduly blocked, inclination shows itself in uneasiness and intense craving.

A habit also marks an intellectual disposition. Where there is a habit, there is acquaintance with the materials and equipment to which action is applied. There is a definite way of understanding the situations in which the habit operates. Modes of thought, of observation and reflection, enter as forms of skill and of desire into the habits that make a man an engineer, an architect, a physician, or a merchant. In unskilled forms of labour, the intellectual factors are at minimum precisely because the habits involved are not of a high grade. But there are habits of judging and reasoning as truly as of handling a tool, painting a picture, or conducting an experiment.

Such statements are, however, understatements. The habits of mind involved in habits of the eye and hand supply the latter with their significance. Above all, the intellectual element in a habit fixes the relation of the habit to varied and elastic use, and hence to continued growth. We speak of fixed habits. Well, the phrase may mean powers so well established that their possessor always has them as resources when needed. But the phrase is also used to mean ruts, routine ways, with loss of freshness, open-mindedness, and originality.

Fixity of habit may mean that something has a fixed hold upon us, instead of our having a free hold upon things. This fact explains two points in a common notion about habits: their identification with mechanical and external modes of action to the neglect of mental and moral attitudes, and the tendency to give them a bad meaning, an identification with "bad habits." Many a person would feel surprised to have his aptitude in his chosen profession called a habit, and would naturally think of his use of tobacco, liquor, or profane language as typical of the meaning of habit. A habit is to him something which has a hold on him, something not easily thrown off even though judgment condemn it.

Habits reduce themselves to routine ways of acting, or degenerate into ways of action to which we are enslaved just in the degree in which intelligence is disconnected from them. Routine habits are unthinking habits: "bad" habits are habits so severed from reason that they are opposed to the conclusions of conscious deliberation and decision.

The acquiring of habits is due to an original plasticity of our natures: to our ability to vary responses till we find an appropriate and efficient way of acting. Routine habits, and habits that possess us instead of our possessing them, are habits which put an end to plasticity. They mark the close of power to vary. There can be no doubt of the tendency of organic plasticity, of the physiological basis, to lessen with growing years.

The instinctively mobile and eagerly varying action of childhood, the love of new stimuli and new developments, too easily passes into a "settling down," which means aversion to change and a resting on past achievements. Only an environment which secures the full use of intelligence in the process of forming habits can counteract this tendency.

Conception of Development

Life is development, and that developing, growing, is life. Translated into its educational equivalents, that means (i) that the educational process has no end beyond itself; it is its own end; and that (ii) the educational process is one of continual reorganising, reconstructing, transforming.

1. Development when it is interpreted in comparative terms, that is, with respect to the special traits of child and adult life, means the direction of power into special channels: the formation of habits involving executive skill, definiteness of interest, and specific objects of observation and thought. But the comparative view is not final. The child has specific powers; to ignore that fact is to stunt or distort the organs upon which his growth depends.

The adult uses his powers to transform his environment, thereby occasioning new stimuli which redirect his powers and keep them developing. Ignoring this fact means arrested development, a passive accommodation. Normal child and normal adult alike, in other words, are engaged in growing. The difference between them is not the difference between growth and no growth, but between the modes of growth appropriate to different conditions. With respect to the development of powers devoted to coping with specific scientific and economic problems we may say the child should be growing in manhood. With respect to sympathetic curiosity, unbiased responsiveness, and openness of mind, we may say that the adult should be growing in childlikeness. One statement is as true as the other.

Three ideas which have been criticised, namely, the merely privative nature of immaturity, static adjustment to a fixed environment, and rigidity of habit, are all connected with a false idea of growth or development, — that it is a movement toward a fixed goal. Growth is regarded as having an end, instead of being an end. The educational counterparts of the three fallacious ideas are first, failure to take account of the instinctive or native powers of the young; secondly, failure to develop initiative in coping with novel situations; thirdly, an undue emphasis upon drill and other devices which secure automatic skill at the expense of personal perception. In all cases, the adult environment is accepted as a standard for the child. He is to be brought up to it.

Natural instincts are either disregarded or treated as nuisances — as obnoxious traits to be suppressed, or at all events to be brought into conformity with external standards. Since conformity is the aim, what is distinctively individual in a young person is brushed aside, or regarded as a source of mischief or anarchy. Conformity is made equivalent to uniformity.

2. Since in reality there is nothing to which growth is relative save more growth, there is nothing to which education is subordinate save more education. It is a commonplace to say that education should not cease when one leaves school. The point of this commonplace is that the purpose of school education is to insure the continuance of education by organising the powers that insure growth. The inclination to learn from life itself and to make the conditions of life such that all will learn in the process of living is the finest product of schooling.

When we abandon the attempt to define immaturity by means of fixed comparison with adult accomplishments, we are compelled to give up thinking of it as denoting lack of desired traits. Abandoning this notion, we are also forced to surrender our habit of thinking of instruction as a method of supplying this lack by pouring knowledge into a mental and moral hole which awaits filling. Since life means growth, a living creature lives as truly and positively at one stage as at another, with the same intrinsic fullness and the same absolute claims.

Hence education means the enterprise of supplying the conditions which insure growth, or adequacy of life, irrespective of age. We first look with impatience upon immaturity, regarding it as something to be got over as rapidly as possible. Then the adult formed by such educative methods looks back with impatient regret upon childhood and youth as a scene of lost opportunities and wasted powers. This ironical situation will endure till it is recognised that living has its own intrinsic quality and that the business of education is with that quality.

Realisation that life is growth protects us from that so-called idealising of childhood which in effect is nothing but lazy indulgence. Life is not to be identified with every superficial act and interest. Even though it is not always easy to tell whether what appears to be mere surface fooling is a sign of some nascent as yet untrained power, we must remember that manifestations are not to be accepted as ends in themselves. They are signs of possible growth. They are to be turned into means of development, of carrying power forward, not indulged or cultivated for their own sake.

Excessive attention to surface phenomena may lead to their fixation and thus to arrested development. What impulses are moving toward, not what they have been, is the important thing for parent and teacher. The true principle of respect for immaturity cannot be better put than in the words of Emerson: "Respect the child. Be not too much his parent. Trespass not on his solitude. But I hear the outcry which replies to this suggestion: Would you verily throw up the reins of public and private discipline; would you leave the young child to the mad career of his own passions and whimsies, and call this anarchy a respect for the child's nature? I answer, — Respect the child, respect him to the end, but also respect yourself.... The two points in a boy's training are, to keep his naturel and train off all but that; to keep his naturel, but stop off his uproar, fooling, and horseplay; keep his nature and arm it with knowledge in the very direction in which it points." And as Emerson goes on to show this reverence for childhood and youth instead of opening up an easy and easy-going path to the instructors, "involves at once, immense claims on the time, the thought, on the life of the teacher. It requires time, use, insight, event, all the great lessons and assistances of God; and only to think of using it implies character and profoundness."

Preparation and Formal Discipline

Education as Preparation

We have laid it down that the educative process is a continuous process of growth, having as its aim at every stage an added capacity of growth. This conception contrasts sharply with other ideas which have influenced practice. By making the contrast explicit, the meaning of the conception will be brought more clearly to light. The first contrast is with the idea that education is a process of preparation or getting ready. What is to be prepared for is, of course, the responsibilities and privileges of adult life.

Children are not regarded as social members in full and regular standing. They are looked upon as candidates; they are placed on the waiting list. The conception is only carried a little farther when the life of adults is considered as not having meaning on its own account, but as a preparatory probation for "another life." The idea is but another form of the notion of the negative and privative character of growth already criticised; hence we shall not repeat the criticisms, but pass on to the evil consequences which flow from putting education on this basis.

In the first place, it involves loss of impetus. Motive power is not utilised. Children proverbially live in the present; that is not only a fact not to be evaded, but it is an excellence. The future just as future lacks urgency and body. To get ready for something, one knows not what nor why, is to throw away the leverage that exists, and to seek for motive power in a vague chance. Under such circumstances, there is, in the second place, a premium put on shilly-shallying and procrastination. The future prepared for is a long way off; plenty of time will intervene before it becomes a present.

The temptation to postpone is much increased because the present offers so many wonderful opportunities and proffers such invitations to adventure. Naturally attention and energy go to them; education accrues naturally as an outcome, but a lesser education than if the full stress of effort had been put upon making conditions as educative as possible.

A third undesirable result is the substitution of a conventional average standard of expectation and requirement for a standard which concerns the specific powers of the individual under instruction. For a severe and definite judgment based upon the strong and weak points of the individual is substituted a vague and wavering opinion concerning what youth may be expected, upon the average, to become in some more or less remote future; say, at the end of the year, when promotions are to take place, or by the time they are ready to go to college or to enter upon what, in contrast with the probationary stage, is regarded as the serious business of life. It is impossible to overestimate the loss which results from the deflection of attention from the strategic point to a comparatively unproductive point. It fails most just where it thinks it is succeeding — in getting a preparation for the future.

Finally, the principle of preparation makes necessary recourse on a large scale to the use of adventitious motives of pleasure and pain. The future having no stimulating and directing power when severed from the possibilities of the present, something must be hitched on to it to make it work. Promises of reward and threats of pain are employed. Healthy work, done for present reasons and as a factor in living, is largely unconscious.

The stimulus resides in the situation with which one is actually confronted. But when this situation is ignored, pupils have to be told that if they do not follow the prescribed course penalties will accrue; while if they do, they may expect, some time in the future, rewards for their present sacrifices. Everybody knows how largely systems of punishment have had to be resorted to by educational systems which neglect present possibilities in behalf of preparation for a future. Then, in disgust with the harshness and impotency of this method, the pendulum swings to the opposite extreme, and the dose of information required against some later day is sugar-coated, so that pupils may be fooled into taking something which they do not care for.

It is not of course a question whether education should prepare for the future. If education is growth, it must progressively realise present possibilities, and thus make individuals better fitted to cope with later requirements. Growing is not something which is completed in odd moments; it is a continuous leading into the future. If the environment, in school and out, supplies conditions which utilise adequately the present capacities of the immature, the future which grows out of the present is surely taken care of.

The mistake is not in attaching importance to preparation for future need, but in making it the mainspring of present effort. Because the need of preparation for a continually developing life is great, it is imperative that every energy should be bent to making the present experience as rich and significant as possible. Then as the present merges insensibly into the future, the future is taken care of.

Education as Unfolding

There is a conception of education which professes to be based upon the idea of development. But it takes back with one hand what it proffers with the other. Development is conceived not as continuous growing, but as the unfolding of latent powers toward a definite goal. The goal is conceived of as completion,-perfection. Life at any stage short of attainment of this goal is merely an unfolding toward it.

Logically the doctrine is only a variant of the preparation theory. Practically the two differ in that the adherents of the latter make much of the practical and professional duties for which one is preparing, while the developmental doctrine speaks of the ideal and spiritual qualities of the principle which is unfolding.

The conception that growth and progress are just approximations to a final unchanging goal is the last infirmity of the mind in its transition from a static to a dynamic understanding of life. It simulates the style of the latter. It pays the tribute of speaking much of development, process, progress. But all of these operations are conceived to be merely transitional; they lack meaning on their own account. They possess significance only as movements toward something away from what is now going on. Since growth is just a movement toward a completed being, the final ideal is immobile. An abstract and indefinite future is in control with all which that connotes in depreciation of present power and opportunity.

Since the goal of perfection, the standard of development, is very far away, it is so beyond us that, strictly speaking, it is unattainable. Consequently, in order to be available for present guidance it must be translated into something which stands for it. Otherwise we should be compelled to regard any and every manifestation of the child as an unfolding from within, and hence sacred. Unless we set up some definite criterion representing the ideal end by which to judge whether a given attitude or act is approximating or moving away, our sole alternative is to withdraw all influences of the environment lest they interfere with proper development. Since that is not practicable, a working substitute is set up. Usually, of course, this is some idea which an adult would like to have a child acquire.

Consequently, by "suggestive questioning" or some other pedagogical device, the teacher proceeds to "draw out" from the pupil what is desired. If what is desired is obtained, that is evidence that the child is unfolding properly. But as the pupil generally has no initiative of his own in this direction, the result is a random groping after what is wanted, and the formation of habits of dependence upon the cues furnished by others. Just because such methods simulate a true principle and claim to have its sanction they may do more harm than would outright "telling," where, at least, it remains with the child how much will stick.

Within the sphere of philosophic thought there have been two typical attempts to provide a working representative of the absolute goal. Both start from the conception of a whole — an absolute — which is "immanent" in human life. The perfect or complete ideal is not a mere ideal; it is operative here and now. But it is present only implicitly, "potentially," or in an enfolded condition. What is termed development is the gradual making explicit and outward of what is thus wrapped up.

Education as Training of Faculties.

A theory which has had great vogue and which came into existence before the notion of growth had much influence is known as the theory of "formal discipline." It has in view a correct ideal; one outcome of education should be the creation of specific powers of accomplishment.

A trained person is one who can do the chief things which it is important for him to do better than he could without training: "better" signifying greater ease, efficiency, economy, promptness, etc. That this is an outcome of education was indicated in what was said about habits as the product of educative development. But the theory in question takes, as it were, a short cut; it regards some powers as the direct and conscious aims of instruction, and not simply as the results of growth. There is a definite number of powers to be trained, as one might enumerate the kinds of strokes which a golfer has to master.

Consequently education should get directly at the business of training them. But this implies that they are already there in some untrained form; otherwise their creation would have to be an indirect product of other activities and agencies. Being there already in some crude form, all that remains is to exercise them in constant and graded repetitions, and they will inevitably be refined and perfected. In the phrase "formal discipline" as applied to this conception, "discipline" refers both to the outcome of trained power and to the method of training through repeated exercise.

The forms of powers in question are such things as the faculties of perceiving, retaining, recalling, associating, attending, willing, feeling, imagining, thinking, etc., which are then shaped by exercise upon material presented. In its classic form, this theory was expressed by Locke. The analogy constantly employed is that of a billiard player or gymnast, who by repeated use of certain muscles in a uniform way at last secures automatic skill. Even the faculty of thinking was to be formed into a trained habit by repeated exercises in making and combining simple distinctions, for which, Locke thought, mathematics affords unrivalled opportunity.

Locke's statements fitted well into the dualism of his day. It seemed to do justice to both mind and matter, the individual and the world. One of the two supplied the matter of knowledge and the object upon which mind should work. The other supplied definite mental powers, which were few in number and which might be trained by specific exercises.

The scheme appeared to give due weight to the subject matter of knowledge, and yet it insisted that the end of education is not the bare reception and storage of information, but the formation of personal powers of attention, memory, observation, abstraction, and generalisation. It was realistic in its emphatic assertion that all material whatever is received from without; it was idealistic in that final stress fell upon the formation of intellectual powers. It was objective and impersonal in its assertion that the individual cannot possess or generate any true ideas on his own account; it was individualistic in placing the end of education in the perfecting of certain faculties possessed at the outset by the individual. This kind of distribution of values expressed with nicety the state of opinion in the generations following upon Locke. It became, without explicit reference to Locke, a common-place of educational theory and of psychology. Practically, it seemed to provide the educator with definite, instead of vague, tasks. It made the elaboration of a technique of instruction relatively easy. All that was necessary was to provide for sufficient practice of each of the powers. This practice consists in repeated acts of attending, observing, memorising, etc. By grading the difficulty of the acts, making each set of repetitions somewhat more difficult than the set which preceded it, a complete scheme of instruction is evolved.

There are various ways, equally conclusive, of criticising this conception, in both its alleged foundations and in its educational application.

(1) Perhaps the most direct mode of attack consists in pointing out that the supposed original faculties of observation, recollection, willing, thinking, etc., are purely mythological. There are no such ready-made powers waiting to be exercised and thereby trained. There are, indeed, a great number of original native tendencies, instinctive modes of action, based on the original connections of neurones in the central nervous system.

There are impulsive tendencies of the eyes to follow and fixate light; of the neck muscles to turn toward light and sound; of the hands to reach and grasp; and turn and twist and thump; of the vocal apparatus to make sounds; of the mouth to spew out unpleasant substances; to gag and to curl the lip, and so on in almost indefinite number. But these tendencies (a) instead of being a small number sharply marked off from one another, are of an indefinite variety, interweaving with one another in all kinds of subtle ways. (b) Instead of being latent intellectual powers, requiring only exercise for their perfecting, they are tendencies to respond in certain ways to changes in the environment so as to bring about other changes. Something in the throat makes one cough; the tendency is to eject the obnoxious particle and thus modify the subsequent stimulus.

The hand touches a hot thing; it is impulsively, wholly unintellectually, snatched away. But the withdrawal alters the stimuli operating, and tends to make them more consonant with the needs of the organism. It is by such specific changes of organic activities in response to specific changes in the medium that control of the environment of which we have spoken is effected. Now all of our first seeings and hearings and touchings and smellings and tastings are of this kind. In any legitimate sense of the words mental or intellectual or cognitive, they are lacking in these qualities, and no amount of repetitious exercise could bestow any intellectual properties of observation, judgment, or intentional action (volition) upon them.

(2) Consequently the training of our original impulsive activities is not a refinement and perfecting achieved by "exercise" as one might strengthen a muscle by practice. It consists rather (a) in selecting from the diffused responses which are evoked at a given time those which are especially adapted to the utilisation of the stimulus. That is to say, among the reactions of the body in general and the hand in particular which instinctively occur upon stimulation of the eye by light, all except those which are specifically adapted to reaching, grasping, and manipulating the object effectively are gradually eliminated — or else no training occurs.

As we have already noted, the primary reactions, with a very few exceptions are too diffused and general to be practically of much use in the case of the human infant. Hence the identity of training with selective response. (b) Equally important is the specific coordination of different factors of response which takes place. There is not merely a selection of the hand reactions which effect grasping, but of the particular visual stimuli which call out just these reactions and no others, and an establishment of connection between the two. But the coordinating does not stop here.

Characteristic temperature reactions may take place when the object is grasped. These will also be brought in; later, the temperature reaction may be connected directly with the optical stimulus, the hand reaction being suppressed — as a bright flame, independent of close contact, may steer one away. Or the child in handling the object pounds with it, or crumples it, and a sound issues. The ear response is then brought into the system of response. If a certain sound is made by others and accompanies the activity, response of both ear and the vocal apparatus connected with auditory stimulation will also become an associated factor in the complex response.

(3) The more specialised the adjustment of response and stimulus to each other the more rigid and the less generally available is the training secured. In equivalent language, less intellectual or educative quality attaches to the training. The usual way of stating this fact is that the more specialised the reaction, the less is the skill acquired in practicing and perfecting it transferable to other modes of behaviour.

According to the orthodox theory of formal discipline, a pupil in studying his spelling lesson acquires, besides ability to spell those particular words, an increase of power of observation, attention, and recollection which may be employed whenever these powers are needed. As matter of fact, the more he confines himself to noticing and fixating the forms of words, irrespective of connection with other things the less likely is he to acquire an ability which can be used for anything except the mere noting of verbal visual forms. He may not even be increasing his ability to make accurate distinctions among geometrical forms, to say nothing of ability to observe in general. He is merely selecting the stimuli supplied by the forms of the letters and the motor reactions of oral or written reproduction. The scope of coordination is extremely limited.

The connections which are employed in other observations and recollections are deliberately eliminated when the pupil is exercised merely upon forms of letters and words. Having been excluded, they cannot be restored when needed. The ability secured to observe and to recall verbal forms is not available for perceiving and recalling other things. In the ordinary phraseology, it is not transferable. But the wider the context — that is to say, the more varied the stimuli and responses coordinated — the more the ability acquired is available for the effective performance of other acts; not, strictly speaking, because there is any "transfer," but because the wide range of factors employed in the specific act is equivalent to a broad range of activity, to a flexible, instead of to a narrow and rigid, coordination.

(4) Going to the root of the matter, the fundamental fallacy of the theory is its dualism; that is to say, its separation of activities and capacities from subject matter. There is no such thing as an ability to see or hear or remember in general; there is only the ability to see or hear or remember something. To talk about training a power, mental or physical, in general, apart from the subject matter involved in its exercise, is nonsense. Exercise may react upon circulation, breathing, and nutrition so as to develop vigour or strength, but this reservoir is available for specific ends only by use in connection with the material means which accomplish them.

Vigour will enable a man to play tennis or golf or to sail a boat better than he would if he were weak. But only by employing ball and racket, ball and club, sail and tiller, in definite ways does he become expert in any one of them; and expertness in one secures expertness in another only so far as it is either a sign of aptitude for fine muscular coordinations or as the same kind of coordination is involved in all of them. Moreover, the difference between the training of ability to spell which comes from taking visual forms in a narrow context and one which takes them in connection with the activities required to grasp meaning, such as context, affiliations of descent, etc., may be compared to the difference between exercises in the gymnasium with pulley weights to "develop" certain muscles, and a game or sport.

The former is uniform and mechanical; it is rigidly specialised. The latter is varied from moment to moment; no two acts are quite alike; novel emergencies have to be met; the coordinations forming have to be kept flexible and elastic. Consequently, the training is much more "general"; that is to say, it covers a wider territory and includes more factors. Exactly the same thing holds of special and general education of the mind.

A monotonously uniform exercise may by practice give great skill in one special act; but the skill is limited to that act, be it bookkeeping or calculations in logarithms or experiments in hydrocarbons. One may be an authority in a particular field and yet of more than usually poor judgment in matters not closely allied, unless the training in the special field has been of a kind to ramify into the subject matter of the other fields.

(5) Consequently, such powers as observation, recollection, judgment, aesthetic taste, represent organised results of the occupation of native active tendencies with certain subject matters. A man does not observe closely and fully by pressing a button for the observing faculty to get to work; but if he has something to do which can be accomplished successfully only through intensive and extensive use of eye and hand, he naturally observes. Observation is an outcome, a

consequence, of the interaction of sense organ and subject matter. It will vary, accordingly, with the subject matter employed.

It is consequently futile to set up even the ulterior development of faculties of observation, memory, etc. unless we have first determined what sort of subject matter we wish the pupil to become expert in observing and recalling and for what purpose. And it is only repeating in another form what has already been said, to declare that the criterion here must be social. We want the person to note and recall and judge those things which make him an effective competent member of the group in which he is associated with others. Otherwise we might as well set the pupil to observing carefully cracks on the wall and set him to memorising meaningless lists of words in an unknown tongue — which is about what we do in fact when we give way to the doctrine of formal discipline. If the observing habits of a botanist or chemist or engineer are better habits than those which are thus formed, it is because they deal with subject matter which is more significant in life.

In concluding this portion of the discussion, we note that the distinction between special and general education has nothing to do with the transferability of function or power. In the literal sense, any transfer is miraculous and impossible. But some activities are broad, they involve a coordination of many factors. Their development demands continuous alternation and readjustment.

As conditions change, certain factors are subordinated, and others which had been of minor importance come to the front. There is constant redistribution of the focus of the action, as is seen in the illustration of a game as over against pulling a fixed weight by a series of uniform motions. Thus there is practice in prompt making of new combinations with the focus of activity shifted to meet change in subject matter. Wherever an activity is broad in scope, and is constantly and unexpectedly obliged to change direction in its progressive development, general education is bound to result. For this is what "general" means; broad and flexible. In practice, education meets these conditions, and hence is general, in the degree in which it takes account of social relationships.

A person may become expert in technical philosophy, or philology, or mathematics or engineering or financiering, and be inept and ill-advised in his action and judgment outside of his speciality. If however his concern with these technical subject matters has been connected with human activities having social breadth, the range of active responses called into play and flexibly integrated is much wider. Isolation of subject matter from a social context is the chief obstruction in current practice to securing a general training of mind. Literature, art, religion, when thus dissociated, are just as narrowing as the technical things which the professional upholders of general education strenuously oppose.

Education as Conservative and Progressive

Education as Formation

We now come to a type of theory which denies the existence of faculties and emphasises the unique role of subject matter in the development of mental and moral disposition. according to it, education is neither a process of unfolding from within nor is it a training of faculties resident in mind itself. It is rather the formation of mind by setting up certain associations or connections of content by means of a subject matter presented from without.

Education proceeds by instruction taken in a strictly literal sense, a building into the mind from without. That education is formative of mind is not questioned; it is the conception already propounded. But formation here has a technical meaning dependent upon the idea of something operating from without.

Herbart is the best historical representative of this type of theory. He denies absolutely the existence of innate faculties. The mind is simply endowed with the power of producing various qualities in reaction to the various realities which act upon it. These qualitatively different reactions are called presentations.

Every presentation once called into being persists; it may be driven below the "threshold" of consciousness by new and stronger presentations, produced by the reaction of the soul to new material, but its activity continues by its own inherent momentum, below the surface of consciousness. What are termed faculties — attention, memory, thinking, perception, even the sentiments, are arrangements, associations, and complications, formed by the interaction of these submerged presentations with one another and with new presentations. Perception, for example, is the complication of presentations which result from the rise of old presentations to greet and combine with new ones; memory is the evoking of an old presentation above the threshold of consciousness by getting entangled with another presentation, etc. Pleasure is the result of reinforcement among the independent activities of presentations; pain of their pulling different ways, etc.

The concrete character of mind consists, then, wholly of the various arrangements formed by the various presentations in their different qualities. The "furniture" of the mind *is* the mind. Mind is wholly a matter of "contents." The educational implications of this doctrine are threefold.

(1) This or that kind of mind is formed by the use of objects which evoke this or that kind of reaction and which produce this or that arrangement among the reactions called out. The formation of mind is wholly a matter of the presentation of the proper educational materials.

(2) Since the earlier presentations constitute the "apperceiving organs" which control the assimilation of new presentations, their character is all important. The effect of new presentations is to reinforce groupings previously formed. The business of the educator is, first, to select the proper material in order to fix the nature of the original reactions, and, secondly, to arrange the sequence of subsequent presentations on the basis of the store of ideas secured by prior transactions. The control is from behind, from the past, instead of, as in the unfolding conception, in the ultimate goal.

(3) Certain formal steps of all method in teaching may be laid down. Presentation of new subject matter is obviously the central thing, but since knowing consists in the way in which this interacts with the contents already submerged below consciousness, the first thing is the step of "preparation," — that is, calling into special activity and getting above the floor of consciousness those older presentations which are to assimilate the new one. Then after the presentation, follow the processes of interaction of new and old; then comes the application of the newly formed content to the performance of some task. Everything must go through this course; consequently there is a perfectly uniform method in instruction in all subjects for all pupils of all ages.

Herbart's great service lay in taking the work of teaching out of the region of routine and accident. He brought it into the sphere of conscious method; it became a conscious business with a definite aim and procedure instead of being a compound of casual inspiration and subservience to tradition. Moreover, everything in teaching and discipline could be specified, instead of our having to be content with vague and more or less mystic generalities about ultimate ideals and speculative spiritual symbols. He abolished the notion of ready-made faculties, which might be trained by exercise upon any sort of material, and made attention to concrete subject matter, to the content, all-important.

Herbart undoubtedly has had a greater influence in bringing to the front questions connected with the material of study than any other educational philosopher. He stated problems of method from the standpoint of their connection with subject matter: method having to do with the manner and sequence of presenting new subject matter to insure its proper interaction with old.

The fundamental theoretical defect of this view lies in ignoring the existence in a living being of active and specific functions which are developed in the redirection and combination which occur as they are occupied with their environment. The theory represents the Schoolmaster come to his own. This fact expresses at once its strength and its weakness. The conception that the mind consists of what has been taught, and that the importance of what has been taught consists in its availability for further teaching, reflects the pedagogue's view of life.

The philosophy is eloquent about the duty of the teacher in instructing pupils; it is almost silent regarding his privilege of learning. It emphasises the influence of intellectual environment upon the mind; it slurs over the fact that the environment involves a personal sharing in common experiences. It exaggerates beyond reason the possibilities of consciously formulated and used methods and underestimates the role of vital, unconscious attitudes. It insists upon the old, the past, and passes lightly over the operation of the genuinely novel and unforeseeable. It takes, in brief, everything educational into account save its essence, — vital energy seeking opportunity for effective exercise.

All education forms character, mental and moral, but formation consists in the selection and coordination of native activities so that they may utilise the subject matter of the social environment. Moreover, the formation is not only a formation of native activities, but it takes place through them. It is a process of reconstruction, reorganisation.

Recapitulation and Retrospection

A peculiar combination of the ideas of development and formation from without has given rise to the recapitulation theory of education, biological and cultural. The individual develops, but his proper development consists in repeating in orderly stages the past evolution of animal life and human history. The former recapitulation occurs physiologically; the latter should be made to occur by means of education. The alleged biological truth that the individual in his growth from the simple embryo to maturity repeats the history of the evolution of animal life in the progress of forms from the simplest to the most complex does not concern us, save as it is supposed to afford scientific foundation for cultural recapitulation of the past.

Cultural recapitulation says, first, that children at a certain age are in the mental and moral condition of savagery; their instincts are vagrant and predatory because their ancestors at one time lived such a life. Consequently the proper subject matter of their education at this time is the material — especially the literary material of myths, folk-tale, and song — produced by humanity in the analogous stage. Then the child passes on to something corresponding, say, to the pastoral stage, and so on till at the time when he is ready to take part in contemporary life, he arrives at the present epoch of culture.

In this detailed and consistent form, the theory, outside of a small school in Germany, has had little currency. But the idea which underlies it is that education is essentially retrospective; that it looks primarily to the past and especially to the literary products of the past, and that mind is adequately formed in the degree in which it is patterned upon the spiritual heritage of the past. This idea has had such immense influence upon higher instruction especially, that it is worth examination in its extreme formulation.

In the first place, its biological basis is fallacious. Embyronic growth of the human infant preserves, without doubt, some of the traits of lower forms of life. But in no respect is it a strict traversing of past stages. If there were any strict "law" of repetition, evolutionary development would clearly not have taken place. Each new generation would simply have repeated its predecessors' existence. Development, in short, has taken place by the entrance of shortcuts and alterations in the prior scheme of growth. And this suggests that the aim of education is to facilitate such short-circuited growth. The great advantage of immaturity, educationally speaking, is that it enables us to emancipate the young from the need of dwelling in an outgrown past.

The business of education is rather to liberate the young from reviving and retraversing the past than to lead them to a recapitulation of it. The social environment of the young is constituted by the presence and action of the habits of thinking and feeling of civilised men. To ignore the directive influence of this present environment upon the young is simply to abdicate the educational function.

The two factors of truth in the conception may easily be disentangled from association with the false context which perverts them. On the biological side we have simply the fact that any infant starts with precisely the assortment of impulsive activities with which he does start, they being blind, and many of them conflicting with one another, casual, sporadic, and unadapted to their immediate environment.

Literatures produced in the past are, so far as men are now in possession and use of them, a part of the present environment of individuals; but there is an enormous difference between availing ourselves of them as present resources and taking them as standards and patterns in their retrospective character.

(1) The distortion of the first point usually comes about through misuse of the idea of heredity. It is assumed that heredity means that past life has somehow predetermined the main traits of an individual, and that they are so fixed that little serious change can be introduced into them. Thus taken, the influence of heredity is opposed to that of the environment, and the efficacy of the latter belittled. But for educational purposes heredity means neither more nor less than the original endowment of an individual. Education must take the being as he is; that a particular individual has just such and such an equipment of native activities is a basic fact. That they were produced in such and such a way, or that they are derived from one's ancestry, is not especially important for the educator, however it may be with the biologist, as compared with the fact that they now exist.

The relation of heredity and environment is well expressed in the case of language. If a being had no vocal organs from which issue articulate sounds, if he had no auditory or other sense-receptors and no connections between the two sets of apparatus, it would be a sheer waste of time to try to teach him to converse. He is born short in that respect, and education must accept the limitation. But if he has this native equipment, its possession in no way guarantees that he will ever talk any language or what language he will talk.

The environment in which his activities occur and by which they are carried into execution settles these things. If he lived in a dumb unsocial environment where men refused to talk to one another and used only that minimum of gestures without which they could not get along, vocal language would be as unachieved by him as if he had no vocal organs. If the sounds which he makes occur in a medium of persons speaking the Chinese language, the activities which make like sounds will be selected and coordinated. This illustration may be applied to the entire range of the educability of any individual. It places the heritage from the past in its right connection with the demands and opportunities of the present.

(2) The theory that the proper subject matter of instruction is found in the culture-products of past ages affords another instance of that divorce between the process and product of growth which has been criticised. To keep the process alive, to keep it alive in ways which make it easier to keep it alive in the future, is the function of educational subject matter. But an individual can live only in the present. The present is not just something which comes after the past; much less something produced by it. It is what life is in leaving the past behind it. The study of past products will not help us understand the present, because the present is not due to the products, but to the life of which they were the products.

A knowledge of the past and its heritage is of great significance when it enters into the present, hut not otherwise. And the mistake of making the records and remains of the past the main material of education is that it cuts the vital connection of present and past, and tends to make the past a rival of the present and the present a more or less futile imitation of the past. Under such circumstances, culture becomes an ornament and solace; a refuge and an asylum. Men escape from the crudities of the present to live in its imagined refinements, instead of using what the past offers as an agency for ripening these crudities.

The present, in short, generates the problems which lead us to search the past for suggestion, and which supplies meaning to what we find when we search. The past is the past precisely because it does not include what is characteristic in the present. The moving present includes the past on condition that it uses the past to direct its own movement. The past is a great resource for the imagination; it adds a new dimension to life, but OD condition that it be seen as the past of the present, and not as another and disconnected world.

The principle which makes little of the present act of living and operation of growing, the only thing always present, naturally looks to the past because the future goal which it sets up is remote and empty. But having turned its back upon the present, it has no way of returning to it laden with the spoils of the past. A mind that is adequately sensitive to the needs and occasions of the present actuality will have the liveliest of motives for interest in the background of the present, and will never have to hunt for a way back because it will never have lost connection.

Education as Reconstruction

In its contrast with the ideas both of unfolding of latent powers from within, and of the formation from without, whether by physical nature or by the cultural products of the past, the ideal of growth results in the conception that education is a constant reorganising or reconstructing of experience. It has all the time an immediate end, and so far as activity is educative, it reaches that end — the direct transformation of the quality of experience. Infancy, youth, adult life, — all stand on the same educative level in the sense that what is really learned at any and every stage of experience constitutes the value of that experience, and in the sense that it is the chief business of life at every point to make living thus contribute to an enrichment of its own perceptible meaning.

We thus reach a technical definition of education: It is that reconstruction or reorganisation of experience which adds to the meaning of experience, and which increases ability to direct the course of subsequent experience.

(1) The increment of meaning corresponds to the increased perception of the connections and continuities of the activities in which we are engaged. The activity begins in an impulsive form; that is, it is blind. It does not know what it is about; that is to say, what are its interactions with other activities. An activity which brings education or instruction with it makes one aware of some of the connections which had been imperceptible. To recur to our simple example, a child who reaches for a bright light gets burned. Henceforth he knows that a certain act of touching in connection with a certain act of vision (and vice-versa) means heat and pain; or, a certain light means a source of heat.

The acts by which a scientific man in his laboratory learns more about flame differ no whit in principle. By doing certain things, he makes perceptible certain connections of heat with other things, which had been previously ignored. Thus his acts in relation to these things get more meaning; he knows better what he is doing or "is about" when he has to do with them; he can intend consequences instead of just letting them happen — all synonymous ways of saying the same thing. At the same stroke, the flame has gained in meaning; all that is known about combustion, oxidation, about light and temperature, may become an intrinsic part of its intellectual content.

(2) The other side of an educative experience is an added power of subsequent direction or control. To say that one knows what he is about, or can intend certain consequences, is to say, of course, that he can better anticipate what is going to happen; that he can, therefore, get ready or prepare in advance so as to secure beneficial consequences and avert undesirable ones. A genuinely educative experience, then, one in which instruction is conveyed and ability increased, is contradistinguished from a routine activity on one hand, and a capricious activity on the other. (a) In the latter one "does not care what happens"; one just lets himself go and avoids connecting the consequences of one's act with the act. It is customary to frown upon such aimless random activity, treating it as willful mischief or carelessness or lawlessness. But there is a tendency to seek the cause of such aimless activities in the youth's own disposition, isolated from everything else. But in fact such activity is explosive, and due to maladjustment with surroundings.

Individuals act capriciously whenever they act under external dictation, or from being told, without having a purpose of their own or perceiving the bearing of the deed upon other acts. One may learn by doing something which he does not understand; even in the most intelligent action, we do much which we do not mean, because the largest portion of the connections of the act we consciously intend are not perceived or anticipated. (b) Routine action, action which is automatic, may increase skill to do a particular thing. In so far, it might be said to have an educative effect. But it does not lead to new perceptions of bearings and connections; it limits rather than widens the meaning-horizon. And since the environment changes and our way of acting has to be modified in order successfully to keep a balanced connection with things, an isolated uniform way of acting becomes disastrous at some critical moment. The vaunted "skill" turns out gross ineptitude.

like a silly truism. It ought to be one; but unfortunately it is not. On the contrary, thinking is often regarded both in philosophic theory and in educational practice as something cut off from experience, and capable of being cultivated in isolation. In fact, the inherent limitations of experience are often urged as the sufficient ground for attention to thinking.

Experience is then thought to be confined to the senses and appetites; to a mere material world, while thinking proceeds from a higher faculty (of reason), and is occupied with spiritual or at least literary things. So, oftentimes, a sharp distinction is made between pure mathematics as a peculiarly fit subject matter of thought and applied mathematics, which has utilitarian but not mental value.

Speaking generally, the fundamental fallacy in methods of instruction lies in supposing that experience on the part of pupils may be assumed. What is here insisted upon is the necessity of an actual empirical situation as the initiating phase of thought. Experience is here taken as previously defined: trying to do something and having the thing perceptibly do something to one in return. The fallacy consists in supposing that we can begin with ready-made subject matter of arithmetic, or geography, or whatever, irrespective of some direct personal experience of a situation.

Even the kindergarten and Montessori techniques are so anxious to get at intellectual distinctions, without "waste of time," that they tend to ignore — or reduce — the immediate crude handling of the familiar material of experience, and to introduce pupils at once to material which expresses the intellectual distinctions which adults have made. But the first stage of contact with any new material, at whatever age of maturity, must inevitably be of the trial and error sort. An individual must actually try, in play or work, to do something with material in

5

Modern Educational Thoughts

Thinking which is not connected with increase of efficiency in action, and with learning more about ourselves and the world in which we live, has something the matter with it just as thought. And skill obtained apart from thinking is not connected with any sense of the purposes for which it is to be used. It consequently leaves a man at the mercy of his routine habits and of the authoritative control of others, who know what they are about and who are not especially scrupulous as to their means of achievement. And information severed from thoughtful action is dead, a mind-crushing load. Since it simulates knowledge and thereby develops the poison of conceit, it is a most powerful obstacle to further growth in the grace of intelligence.

The sole direct path to enduring improvement in the methods of instruction and learning consists in centering upon the conditions which exact, promote, and test thinking. Thinking is the method of intelligent learning, of learning that employs and rewards mind. We speak, legitimately enough, about the method of thinking, but the important thing to bear in mind about method is that thinking is method, the method of intelligent experience in the course which it takes.

The initial stage of that developing experience which is called thinking is experience. This remark may sound carrying out his own impulsive activity, and then note the interaction of his energy and that of the material employed. This is what happens when a child at first begins to build with blocks, and it is equally what happens when a scientific man in his laboratory begins to experiment with unfamiliar objects.

Hence the first approach to any subject in school, if thought is to be aroused and not words acquired, should be as unscholastic as possible. To realize what an experience, or empirical situation, means, we have to call to mind the sort of situation that presents itself outside of school; the sort of occupations that interest and engage activity in ordinary life. And careful inspection of methods which are permanently successful in formal education, whether in arithmetic or learning to read, or studying geography, or learning physics or a foreign language, will reveal that they depend for their efficiency upon the fact that they go back to the type of the situation which causes reflection out of school in ordinary life. They give the pupils something to do, not something to learn; and the doing is of such a nature as to demand thinking, or the intentional noting of connections; learning naturally results.

That the situation should be of such a nature as to arouse thinking means of course that it should suggest something to do which is not either routine or capricious — something, in other words, presenting what is new and yet sufficiently connected with existing habits to call out an effective response. An effective response means one which accomplishes a perceptible result, in distinction from a purely haphazard activity, where the consequences cannot be mentally connected with what is done. The most significant question which can be asked, accordingly, about any situation or experience proposed to induce learning is what quality of problem it involves.

At first thought, it might seem as if usual school methods measured well up to the standard here set. The giving of problems, the putting of questions, the assigning of tasks, the magnifying of difficulties, is a large part of school work. But it is indispensable to discriminate between genuine and simulated or mock problems.

As a consequence of the absence of the materials and occupations which generate real problems, the pupil's problems are not his; or, rather, they are his only as a pupil, not as a human being. Hence the lamentable waste in carrying over such expertness as is achieved in dealing with them to the affairs of life beyond the schoolroom. A pupil has a problem, but it is the problem of meeting the peculiar requirements set by the teacher. His problem becomes that of finding out what the teacher wants, what will satisfy the teacher in recitation and examination and outward deportment. Relationship to subject matter is no longer direct.

The occasions and material of thought are not found in the arithmetic or the history or geography itself, but in skillfully adapting that material to the teacher's requirements. The pupil studies, but unconsciously to himself the objects of his study are the conventions and standards of the school system and school authority, not the nominal "studies."

The thinking thus evoked is artificially one-sided at the best. At its worst, the problem of the pupil is not how to meet the requirements of school life, but how to seem to meet them — or, how to come near enough to meeting them to slide along without an undue amount of friction. The type of judgment formed by these devices is not a desirable addition to character. If these statements give too highly colored a picture of usual school methods, the exaggeration may at least serve to illustrate the point: the need of active pursuits, involving the use of material to accomplish purposes, if there are to be situations which normally generate problems occasioning thoughtful inquiry.

There must be data at command to supply the considerations required in dealing with the specific difficulty which has presented itself. Teachers following a "developing" method sometimes tell children to think things out for themselves as if they could spin them out of their own heads. The material of thinking is not thoughts, but actions, facts, events, and the relations of things. In other words, to think effectively one must have had, or now have, experiences which will furnish him resources for coping with the difficulty at hand.

A difficulty is an indispensable stimulus to thinking, but not all difficulties call out thinking. Sometimes they overwhelm and submerge and discourage. The perplexing situation must be sufficiently like situations which have already been dealt with so that pupils will have some control of the meanings of handling it. A large part of the art of instruction lies in making the difficulty of new problems large enough to challenge thought, and small enough so that, in addition to the confusion naturally attending the novel elements, there shall be luminous familiar spots from which helpful suggestions may spring.

In one sense, it is a matter of indifference by what psychological means the subject matter for reflection is provided. Memory, observation, reading, communication, are all avenues for supplying data. The relative proportion to be obtained from each is a matter of the specific features of the particular problem in hand. It is foolish to insist upon observation of objects presented to the senses if the student is so familiar with the objects that he could just as well recall the facts independently. It is possible to induce undue and crippling dependence upon sense-presentations. No one can carry around with him a museum of all the things whose properties will assist the conduct of thought.

A well-trained mind is one that has a maximum of resources behind it, so to speak, and that is accustomed to go over its past experiences to see what they yield. On the other hand, a quality or relation of even a familiar object may previously have been passed over, and be just the fact that is helpful in dealing with the question. In this case direct observation is called for. The same principle applies to the use to be made of observation on one hand and of reading and "telling" on the other.

Direct observation is naturally more vivid and vital. But it has its limitations; and in any case it is a necessary part of education that one should acquire the ability to supplement the narrowness of his immediately personal experiences by utilizing the experiences of others. Excessive reliance upon others for data is to be depreciated. Most objectionable of all is the probability that others, the book or the teacher, will supply solutions ready-made, instead of giving material that the student has to adapt and apply to the question in hand for himself.

There is no inconsistency in saying that in schools there is usually both too much and too little information supplied by others. The accumulation and acquisition of information for purposes of reproduction in recitation and examination is made too much of. "Knowledge," in the sense of information, means the working capital, the indispensable resources, of further inquiry; of finding out, or learning, more things. Frequently it is treated as an end itself, and then the goal becomes to heap it up and display it when called for. This static, cold-storage ideal of knowledge is inimical to educative development. It not only lets occasions for thinking go unused, but it swamps thinking. No one could construct a house on ground cluttered with miscellaneous junk.

Pupils who have stored their "minds" with all kinds of material which they have never put to intellectual uses are sure to be hampered when they try to think. They have no practice in selecting what is appropriate, and no criterion to go by; everything is on the same dead static level. On the other hand, it is quite open to question whether, if information actually functioned in experience through use in application to the student's own purposes, there would not be need of more varied resources in books, pictures, and talks than are usually at command.

III. The correlate in thinking of facts, data, knowledge already acquired, is suggestions, inferences, conjectured meanings, suppositions, tentative explanations: — ideas, in short. Careful observation and recollection determine what is given, what is already there, and hence assured. They cannot furnish what is lacking. They define, clarify, and locate the question; they cannot supply its answer. Projection, invention, ingenuity, devising come in for that purpose. The data arouse suggestions, and only by reference to the specific data can we pass upon the appropriateness of the suggestions. But the suggestions run beyond what is, as yet, actually given in experience. They forecast possible results, things to do, not facts. Inference is always an invasion of the unknown, a leap from the known.

In this sense, a thought (what a thing suggests but is not as it is presented) is creative, — an incursion into the novel. It involves some inventiveness. What is suggested must, indeed, be familiar in some context; the novelty, the inventive devising, clings to the new light in which it is seen, the different use to which it is put. When Newton thought of his theory of gravitation, the creative aspect of his thought was not found in its materials. They were familiar; many of them commonplaces — sun, moon, planets, weight, distance, mass, square of numbers. These were not original ideas; they were established facts. His originality lay in the use to which these familiar acquaintances were put by introduction into an unfamiliar context. The same is true of every striking scientific discovery, every great invention, every admirable artistic production. Only silly folk identify creative originality with the extraordinary and fanciful; others recognize that its measure lies in putting everyday things to uses which had not occurred to others. The operation is novel, not the materials out of which it is constructed.

The educational conclusion which follows is that all thinking is original in a projection of considerations which have not been previously apprehended. The child of three who discovers what can be done with blocks, or of six who finds out what he can make by putting five cents and five cents together, is really a discoverer, even though everybody else in the world knows it. There is a genuine increment of experience; not another item mechanically added on, but enrichment by a new quality. The charm which the spontaneity of little children has for sympathetic observers is due to perception of this intellectual originality. The joy which children themselves experience is the joy of intellectual constructiveness — of creativeness, if the word may be used without misunderstanding.

The educational moral I am chiefly concerned to draw is not, however, that teachers would find their own work less of a grind and strain if school conditions favored learning in the sense of discovery and not in that of storing away what others pour into them; nor that it would be possible to give even children and youth the delights of personal intellectual productiveness — true and important as are these things. It is that no thought, no idea, can possibly be conveyed as an idea from one person to another. When it is told, it is, to the one to whom it is told, another given fact, not an idea. The communication may stimulate the other person to realize the question for himself and to think out a like idea, or it may smother his intellectual interest and suppress his dawning effort at thought. But what he directly gets cannot be an idea.

Only by wrestling with the conditions of the problem at first hand, seeking and finding his own way out, does he think. When the parent or teacher has provided the conditions which stimulate thinking and has taken a sympathetic attitude toward the activities of the learner by entering into a common or conjoint experience, all has been done which a second party can do to instigate learning.

The rest lies with the one directly concerned. If he cannot devise his own solution and find his own way out he will not learn, not even if he can recite some correct answer with one hundred per cent accuracy. We can and do supply ready-made "ideas" by the thousand; we do not usually take much pains to see that the one learning engages in significant situations where his own activities generate, support, and clinch ideas — that is, perceived meanings or connections. This does not mean that the teacher is to stand off and look on; the alternative to furnishing ready-made subject matter and listening to the accuracy with which it is reproduced is not quiescence, but participation, sharing, in an activity. In such shared activity, the teacher is a learner, and the learner is, without knowing it, a teacher — and upon the whole, the less consciousness there is, on either side, of either giving or receiving instruction, the better.

IV. Ideas, as we have seen, whether they be humble guesses or dignified theories, are anticipations of possible solutions. They are anticipations of some continuity or connection of an activity and a consequence which has not as yet shown itself. They are therefore tested by the operation of acting upon them. They are to guide and organize further observations, recollections, and experiments. They are intermediate in learning, not final. All educational reformers, as we have had occasion to remark, are given to attacking the passivity of traditional education. They have opposed pouring in from without, and absorbing like a sponge; they have attacked drilling in material as into hard and resisting rock. But it is not easy to secure conditions which will make the getting of an idea identical with having an experience which widens and makes more precise our contact with the environment. Activity, even self-activity, is too easily thought of as something merely mental, cooped up within the head, or finding expression only through the vocal organs.

While the need of application of ideas gained in study is acknowledged by all the more successful methods of instruction, the exercises in application are sometimes treated as devices for fixing what has already been learned and for getting greater practical skill in its manipulation. These results are genuine and not to be despised. But practice in applying what has been gained in study ought primarily to have an intellectual quality. As we have already seen, thoughts just as thoughts are incomplete. At best they are tentative; they are suggestions, indications. They are standpoints and methods for dealing with situations of experience. Till they are applied in these situations they lack full point and reality.

Only application tests them, and only testing confers full meaning and a sense of their reality. Short of use made of them, they tend to segregate into a peculiar world of their own. It may be seriously questioned whether the philosophies which isolate mind and set it over against the world did not have their origin in the fact that the reflective or theoretical class of men elaborated a large stock of ideas which social conditions did not allow them to act upon and test. Consequently men were thrown back into their own thoughts as ends in themselves.

However this may be, there can be no doubt that a peculiar artificiality attaches to much of what is learned in schools. It can hardly be said that many students consciously think of the subject matter as unreal; but it assuredly does not possess for them the kind of reality which the subject matter of their vital experiences possesses. They learn not to expect that sort of reality of it; they become habituated to treating it as having reality for the purposes of recitations, lessons, and examinations. That it should remain inert for the experiences of daily life is more or less a matter of course. The bad effects are twofold. Ordinary experience does not receive the enrichment which it should; it is not fertilized by school learning. And the attitudes which spring from getting used to and accepting half-understood and ill-digested material weaken vigor and efficiency of thought.

If we have dwelt especially on the negative side, it is for the sake of suggesting positive measures adapted to the effectual development of thought. Where schools are equipped with laboratories, shops, and gardens, where dramatizations, plays, and games are freely used, opportunities exist for reproducing situations of life, and for acquiring and applying information and ideas in the carrying forward of progressive experiences. Ideas are not segregated, they do not form an isolated island. They animate and enrich the ordinary course of life. Information is vitalized by its function; by the place it occupies in direction of action.

The phrase "opportunities exist" is used purposely. They may not be taken advantage of; it is possible to employ manual and constructive activities in a physical way, as means of getting just bodily skill; or they may be used almost exclusively for "utilitarian," i.e., pecuniary, ends. But the disposition on the part of upholders of 'cultural" education to assume that such activities are merely physical or professional in quality, is itself a product of the philosophies which isolate mind from direction of the course of experience and hence from action upon and with things. When the "mental" is regarded as a self-contained separate realm, a counterpart fate befalls bodily activity and movements. They are regarded as at the best mere external annexes to mind. They may be necessary for the satisfaction of bodily needs and the attainment of external decency and comfort, but they do not occupy a necessary place in mind nor enact an indispensable role in the completion of thought.

Hence they have no place in a liberal education — i.e., one which is concerned with the interests of intelligence. If they come in at all, it is as a concession to the material needs of the masses. That they should be allowed to invade the education of the elite is unspeakable. This conclusion follows irresistibly from the isolated conception of mind, but by the same logic it disappears when we perceive what mind really is — namely, the purposive and directive factor in the development of experience.

While it is desirable that all educational institutions should be equipped so as to give students an opportunity for acquiring and testing ideas and information in active pursuits typifying important social situations, it will, doubtless, be a long time before all of them are thus furnished. But this state of affairs does not afford instructors an excuse for folding their hands and persisting in methods which segregate school knowledge. Every recitation in every subject gives an opportunity for establishing cross connections between the subject matter of the lesson and the wider and more direct experiences of everyday life. Classroom instruction falls into three kinds.

The least desirable treats each lesson as an independent whole. It does not put upon the student the responsibility of finding points of contact between it and other lessons in the same subject, or other subjects of study. Wiser teachers see to it that the student is systematically led to utilize his earlier lessons to help understand the present one, and also to use the present to throw additional light upon what has already been acquired. Results are better, but school subject matter is still isolated. Save by accident, out-of-school experience is left in its crude and comparatively irreflective state. It is not subject to the refining and expanding influences of the more accurate and comprehensive material of direct instruction. The latter is not motivated and impregnated with a sense of reality by being intermingled with the realities of everyday life. The best type of teaching bears in mind the desirability of affecting this interconnection. It puts the student in the habitual attitude of finding points of contact and mutual bearings.

Experience and Thinking

The nature of experience can be understood only by noting that it includes an active and a passive element peculiarly combined. On the active hand, experience is trying — a meaning which is made explicit in the connected term experiment. On the passive, it is undergoing. When we experience something we act upon it, we do something with it; then we suffer or undergo the consequences. We do something to the thing and then it does something to us in return: such is the peculiar combination. The connection of these two phases of experience measures the fruitfulness or value of the experience. Mere activity does not constitute experience. It is dispersive, centrifugal, dissipating.

Experience as trying involves change, but change is meaningless transition unless it is consciously connected with the return wave of consequences which flow from it. When an activity is continued into the undergoing of consequences, when the change made by action is reflected back into a change made in us, the mere flux is loaded with significance. We learn something. It is not experience when a child merely sticks his finger into a flame; it is experience when the movement is connected with the pain which he undergoes in consequence. Henceforth the sticking of the finger into flame means a burn. Being burned is a mere physical change, like the burning of a stick of wood, if it is not perceived as a consequence of some other action.

Blind and capricious impulses hurry us on heedlessly from one thing to another. So far as this happens, everything is writ in water. There is none of that cumulative growth which makes an experience in any vital sense of that term. On the other hand, many things happen to us in the way of pleasure and pain which we do not connect with any prior activity of our own. They are mere accidents so far as we are concerned. There is no before or after to such experience; no retrospect nor outlook, and consequently no meaning. We get nothing which may be carried over to foresee what is likely to happen next, and no gain in ability to adjust ourselves to what is coming — no added control.

Only by courtesy can such an experience be called experience. To 'learn from experience" is to make a backward and forward connection between what we do to things and what we enjoy or suffer from things in consequence. Under such conditions, doing becomes a trying; an experiment with the world to find out what it is like; the undergoing becomes instruction — discovery of the connection of things.

Two conclusions important for education follow. (1) Experience is primarily an active-passive affair; it is not primarily cognitive. But (2) the measure of the value of an experience lies in the perception of relationships or continuities to which it leads up. It includes cognition in the degree in which it is cumulative or amounts to something, or has meaning. In schools, those under instruction are too customarily looked upon as acquiring knowledge as theoretical spectators, minds which appropriate knowledge by direct energy of intellect.

The very word pupil has almost come to mean one who is engaged not in having fruitful experiences but in absorbing knowledge directly. Something which is called mind or consciousness is severed from the physical organs of activity. The former is then thought to be purely intellectual and cognitive; the latter to be an irrelevant and intruding physical factor. The intimate union of activity and undergoing its consequences which leads to recognition of meaning is broken; instead we have two fragments: mere bodily action on one side, and meaning directly grasped by "spiritual" activity on the other. It would be impossible to state adequately the evil results which have flowed from this dualism of mind and body, much less to exaggerate them. Some of the more striking effects, may, however, be enumerated.

(a) In part bodily activity becomes an intruder. Having nothing, so it is thought, to do with mental activity, it becomes a distraction, an evil to be contended with. For the pupil has a body, and brings it to school along with his mind. And the body is, of necessity, a wellspring of energy; it has to do something. But its activities, not being utilized in occupation with things which yield significant results, have to be frowned upon. They lead the pupil away from the lesson with which his "mind" ought to be occupied; they are sources of mischief. The chief source of the "problem of discipline" in schools is that the teacher has often to spend the larger part of the time in suppressing the bodily activities which take the mind away from its material. A premium is put on physical quietude; on silence, on rigid uniformity of posture and movement; upon a machine-like simulation of the attitudes of intelligent interest. The teachers' business is to hold the pupils up to these requirements and to punish the inevitable deviations which occur.

The nervous strain and fatigue which result with both teacher and pupil are a necessary consequence of the abnormality of the situation in which bodily activity is divorced from the perception of meaning. Callous indifference and explosions from strain alternate. The neglected body, having no organized fruitful channels of activity, breaks forth, without knowing why or how, into meaningless boisterousness, or settles into equally meaningless fooling — both very different from the normal play of children.

Physically active children become restless and unruly; the more quiescent, socalled conscientious ones spend what energy they have in the negative task of keeping their instincts and active tendencies suppressed, instead of in a positive one of constructive planning and execution; they are thus educated not into responsibility for the significant and graceful use of bodily powers, but into an enforced duty not to give them free play. It may be seriously asserted that a chief cause for the remarkable achievements of Greek education was that it was never misled by false notions into an attempted separation of mind and body.

(b) Even, however, with respect to the lessons which have to be learned by the application of "mind," some bodily activities have to be used. The senses — especially the eye and ear — have to be employed to take in what the book, the map, the blackboard, and the teacher say.

The lips and vocal organs, and the hands, have to be used to reproduce in speech and writing what has been stowed away. The senses are then regarded as a kind of mysterious conduit through which information is conducted from the external world into the mind; they are spoken of as gateways and avenues of knowledge.

To keep the eyes on the book and the ears open to the teacher's words is a mysterious source of intellectual grace. Moreover, reading, writing, and figuring — important school arts — demand muscular or motor training. The muscles of eye, hand, and vocal organs accordingly have to be trained to act as pipes for carrying knowledge back out of the mind into external action. For it happens that using the muscles repeatedly in the same way fixes in them an automatic tendency to repeat.

(c) On the intellectual side, the separation of "mind" from direct occupation with things throws emphasis on things at the expense of relations or connections. It is altogether too common to separate perceptions and even ideas from judgments. The latter are thought to come after the former in order to compare them. It is alleged that the mind perceives things apart from relations; that it forms ideas of them in isolation from their connections — with what goes before and comes after. Then judgment or thought is called upon to combine the separated items of "knowledge" so that their resemblance or causal connection shall be brought out.

As matter of fact, every perception and every idea is a sense of the bearings, use, and cause, of a thing. We do not really know a chair or have an idea of it by inventorying and enumerating its various isolated qualities, but only by bringing these qualities into connection with something else — the purpose which makes it a chair and not a table; or its difference from the kind of chair we are accustomed to, or the "period" which it represents, and so on. A wagon is not perceived when all its parts are summed up; it is the characteristic connection of the parts which makes it a wagon. And these connections are not those of mere physical juxtaposition; they involve connection with the animals that draw it, the things that are carried on it, and so on. Judgment is employed in the perception; otherwise the perception is mere sensory excitation or else a recognition of the result of a prior judgment, as in the case of familiar objects.

Words, the counters for ideals, are, however, easily taken for ideas. And in just the degree in which mental activity is separated from active concern with the world, from doing something and connecting the doing with what is undergone, words, symbols, come to take the place of ideas. The substitution is the more subtle because some meaning is recognized. But we are very easily trained to be content with a minimum of meaning, and to fail to note how restricted is our perception of the relations which confer significance. We get so thoroughly used to a kind of pseudo-idea, a half perception, that we are not aware how half-dead our mental action is, and how much keener and more extensive our observations and ideas would be if we formed them under conditions of a vital experience which required us to use judgment: to hunt for the connections of the thing dealt with.

There is no difference of opinion as to the theory of the matter. All authorities agree that that discernment of relationships is the genuinely intellectual matter; hence, the educative matter. The failure arises in supposing that relationships can become perceptible without experience — without that conjoint trying and undergoing of which we have spoken. It is assumed that "mind" can grasp them if it will only give attention, and that this attention may be given at will irrespective of the situation.

Hence the deluge of half-observations, of verbal ideas, and unassimilated "knowledge" which afflicts the world. An ounce of experience is better than a ton of theory simply because it is only in experience that any theory has vital and verifiable significance. An experience, a very humble experience, is capable of generating and carrying any amount of theory, but a theory apart from an experience cannot be definitely grasped even as theory. It tends to become a mere verbal formula, a set of catchwords used to render thinking, or genuine theorizing, unnecessary and impossible. Because of our education we use words, thinking they are ideas, to dispose of questions, the disposal being in reality simply such an obscuring of perception as prevents us from seeing any longer the difficulty.

Reflection in Experience

Thought or reflection, as we have already seen virtually if not explicitly, is the discernment of the relation between what we try to do and what happens in consequence. No experience having a meaning is possible without some element of thought. But we may contrast two types of experience according to the proportion of reflection found in them.

All our experiences have a phase of "cut and try" in them — what psychologists call the method of trial and error. We simply do something, and when it fails, we do something else, and keep on trying till we hit upon something which works, and then we adopt that method as a rule of thumb measure in subsequent procedure. Some experiences have very little else in them than this hit and miss or succeed process. We see that a certain way of acting and a certain consequence are connected, but we do not see how they are. We do not see the details of the connection; the links are missing. Our discernment is very gross.

In other cases we push our observation farther. We analyze to see just what lies between so as to bind together cause and effect, activity and consequence. This extension of our insight makes foresight more accurate and comprehensive. The action which rests simply upon the trial and error method is at the mercy of circumstances; they may change so that the act performed does not operate in the way it was expected to. But if we know in detail upon what the result depends, we can look to see whether the required conditions are there. The method extends our practical control. For if some of the conditions are missing, we may, if we know what the needed antecedents for an effect are, set to work to supply them; or, if they are such as to produce undesirable effects as well, we may eliminate some of the superfluous causes and economize effort.

In discovery of the detailed connections of our activities and what happens in consequence, the thought implied in cut and try experience is made explicit. Its quantity increases so that its proportionate value is very different. Hence the quality of the experience changes; the change is so significant that we may call this type of experience reflective — that is, reflective par excellence. The deliberate cultivation of this phase of thought constitutes thinking as a distinctive experience. Thinking, in other words, is the intentional endeavor to discover specific connections between something which we do and the consequences which result, so that the two become continuous. Their isolation, and consequently their purely arbitrary going together, is canceled; a unified developing situation takes its place. The occurrence is now understood; it is explained; it is reasonable, as we say, that the thing should happen as it does.

Thinking is thus equivalent to an explicit rendering of the intelligent element in our experience. It makes it possible to act with an end in view. It is the condition of our having aims. As soon as an infant begins to expect he begins to use something which is now going on as a sign of something to follow; he is, in however simple a fashion, judging. For he takes one thing as evidence of something else, and so recognizes a relationship. Any future development, however elaborate it may be, is only an extending and a refining of this simple act of inference. All that the wisest man can do is to observe what is going on more widely and more minutely and then select more carefully from what is noted just those factors which point to something to happen.

The opposites, once more, to thoughtful action are routine and capricious behavior. The former accepts what has been customary as a full measure of possibility and omits to take into account the connections of the particular things done. The latter makes the momentary act a measure of value, and ignores the connections of our personal action with the energies of the environment. It says, virtually, "things are to be just as I happen to like them at this instant," as routine says in effect "let things continue just as I have found them in the past." Both refuse to acknowledge responsibility for the future consequences which flow from present action. Reflection is the acceptance of such responsibility.

The starting point of any process of thinking is something going on, something which just as it stands is incomplete or unfulfilled. Its point, its meaning lies literally in what it is going to be, in how it is going to turn out. As this is written, the world is filled with the clang of contending armies. For an active participant in the war, it is clear that the momentous thing is the issue, the future consequences, of this and that happening. He is identified, for the time at least, with the issue; his fate hangs upon the course things are taking. But even for an onlooker in a neutral country, the significance of every move made, of every advance here and retreat there, lies in what it portends. To think upon the news as it comes to us is to attempt to see what is indicated as probable or possible regarding an outcome.

To fill our heads, like a scrapbook, with this and that item as a finished and done-for thing, is not to think. It is to turn ourselves into a piece of registering apparatus. To consider the bearing of the occurrence upon what may be, but is not yet, is to think. Nor will the reflective experience be different in kind if we substitute distance in time for separation in space. Imagine the war done with, and a future historian giving an account of it. The episode is, by assumption, past. But he cannot give a thoughtful account of the war save as he preserves the time sequence; the meaning of each occurrence, as he deals with it, lies in what was future for it, though not for the historian. To take it by itself as a complete existence is to take it unreflectively.

Reflection also implies concern with the issue — a certain sympathetic identification of our own destiny, if only dramatic, with the outcome of the course of events. For the general in the war, or a common soldier, or a citizen of one of the contending nations, the stimulus to thinking is direct and urgent. For neutrals, it is indirect and dependent upon imagination. But the flagrant partisanship of human nature is evidence of the intensity of the tendency to identify ourselves with one possible course of events, and to reject the other as foreign. If we cannot take sides in overt action, and throw in our little weight to help determine the final balance, we take sides emotionally and imaginatively. We desire this or that outcome.

One wholly indifferent to the outcome does not follow or think about what is happening at all. From this dependence of the act of thinking upon a sense of sharing in the consequences of what goes on, flows one of the chief paradoxes of thought. Born in partiality, in order to accomplish its tasks it must achieve a certain detached impartiality. The general who allows his hopes and desires to affect his observations and interpretations of the existing situation will surely make a mistake in calculation. While hopes and fears may be the chief motive for a thoughtful following of the war on the part of an onlooker in a neutral country, he too will think ineffectively in the degree in which his preferences modify the stuff of his observations and reasonings. There is, however, no incompatibility between the fact that the occasion of reflection lies in a personal sharing in what is going on and the fact that the value of the reflection lies upon keeping one's self out of the data.

The almost insurmountable difficulty of achieving this detachment is evidence that thinking originates in situations where the course of thinking is an actual part of the course of events and is designed to influence the result. Only gradually and with a widening of the area of vision through a growth of social sympathies does thinking develop to include what lies beyond our direct interests: a fact of great significance for education.

To say that thinking occurs with reference to situations which are still going on, and incomplete, is to say that thinking occurs when things are uncertain or doubtful or problematic. Only what is finished, completed, is wholly assured. Where there is reflection there is suspense. The object of thinking is to help reach a conclusion, to project a possible termination on the basis of what is already given. Certain other facts about thinking accompany this feature. Since the situation in which thinking occurs is a doubtful one, thinking is a process of inquiry, of looking into things, of investigating. Acquiring is always secondary, and instrumental to the act of inquiring. It is seeking, a quest, for something that is not at hand. We sometimes talk as if "original research" were a peculiar prerogative of scientists or at least of advanced students. But all thinking is research, and all research is native, original, with him who carries it on, even if everybody else in the world already is sure of what he is still looking for.

A commanding general cannot base his actions upon either absolute certainty or absolute ignorance. He has a certain amount of information at hand which is, we will assume, reasonably trustworthy. He then infers certain prospective movements, thus assigning meaning to the bare facts of the given situation. His inference is more or less dubious and hypothetical. But he acts upon it. He develops a plan of procedure, a method of dealing with the situation. The consequences which directly follow from his acting this way rather than that test and reveal the worth of his reflections. What he already knows functions and has value in what he learns.

In form, yes, though not of course in content. It is self-evident that his guesses about the future indicated by present facts, guesses by which he attempts to supply meaning to a multitude of disconnected data, cannot be the basis of a method which shall take effect in the campaign. That is not his problem. But in the degree in which he is actively thinking, and not merely passively following the course of events, his tentative inferences will take effect in a method of procedure appropriate to his situation. He will anticipate certain future moves, and will be on the alert to see whether they happen or not.

In the degree in which he is intellectually concerned, or thoughtful, he will be actively on the lookout; he will take steps which although they do not affect the campaign, modify in some degree his subsequent actions. Otherwise his later "I told you so" has no intellectual quality at all; it does not mark any testing or verification of prior thinking, but only a coincidence that yields emotional satisfaction — and includes a large factor of self-deception.

The case is comparable to that of an astronomer who from given data has been led to foresee (infer) a future eclipse. No matter how great the mathematical probability, the inference is hypothetical — a matter of probability. The hypothesis as to the date and position of the anticipated eclipse becomes the material of forming a method of future conduct. Apparatus is arranged; possibly an expedition is made to some far part of the globe. In any case, some active steps are taken which actually change some physical conditions. And apart from such steps and the consequent modification of the situation, there is no completion of the act of thinking. It remains suspended. Knowledge, already attained knowledge, controls thinking and makes it fruitful.

So much for the general features of a reflective experience. They are

(i) perplexity, confusion, doubt, due to the fact that one is implicated in an incomplete situation whose full character is not yet determined;

(ii) a conjectural anticipation — a tentative interpretation of the given elements, attributing to them a tendency to effect certain consequences;

(iii) a careful survey of all attainable consideration which will define and clarify the problem in hand;

(iv) a consequent elaboration of the tentative hypothesis to make it more precise and more consistent, because squaring with a wider range of facts;

(v) taking one stand upon the projected hypothesis as a plan of action which is applied to the existing state of affairs: doing something overtly to bring about the anticipated result, and thereby testing the hypothesis.

It is the extent and accuracy of steps three and four which mark off a distinctive refiective experience from one on the trial and error plane. They make thinking itself into an experience. Nevertheless, we never get wholly beyond the trial and error situation. Our most elaborate and rationally consistent thought has to be tried in the world and thereby tried out. And since it can never take into account all the connections, it can never cover with perfect accuracy all the consequences. Yet a thoughtful survey of conditions is so careful, and the guessing at results so controlled, that we have a right to mark off the reflective experience from the grosser trial and error forms of action.

6

Education and Social Life

The most notable distinction between living and inanimate things is that the former maintain themselves by renewal. A stone when struck resists. If its resistance is greater than the force of the blow struck, it remains outwardly unchanged. Otherwise, it is shattered into smaller bits. Never does the stone attempt to react in such a way that it may maintain itself against the blow, much less so as to render the blow a contributing factor to its own continued action. While the living thing may easily be crushed by superior force, it none the less tries to turn the energies which act upon it into means of its own further existence. If it cannot do so, it does not just split into smaller pieces, but loses its identity as a living thing.

As long as it endures, it struggles to use surrounding energies in its own behalf. It uses light, air, moisture, and the material of soil. To say that it uses them is to say that it turns them into means of its own conservation. As long as it is growing, the energy it expends in thus turning the environment to account is more than compensated for by the return it gets: it grows. Understanding the word "control" in this sense, it may be said that a living being is one that subjugates and controls for its own continued activity the energies that would otherwise use it up. Life is a self-renewing process through action upon the environment.

In all the higher forms this process cannot be kept up indefinitely. After a while they succumb; they die. The creature is not equal to the task of indefinite self-renewal. But continuity of the life process is not dependent upon the prolongation of the existence of any one individual. Reproduction of other forms of life goes on in continuous sequence. And though, as the geological record shows, not merely individuals but also species die out, the life process continues in increasingly complex forms. As some species die out, forms better adapted to utilise the obstacles against which they struggled in vain come into being. Continuity of life means continual readaptation of the environment to the needs of living organisms.

We have been speaking of life in its lowest terms — as a physical thing. But we use the word Life" to denote the whole range of experience, individual and racial. When we see a book called the Life of Lincoln we do not expect to find within its covers a treatise on physiology. We look for an account of social antecedents; a description of early surroundings, of the conditions and occupation of the family; of the chief episodes in the development of character; of signal struggles and achievements; of the individual's hopes, tastes, joys and sufferings. In precisely similar fashion we speak of the life of a savage tribe, of the Athenian people, of the American nation. "Life" covers customs, institutions, beliefs, victories and defeats, recreations and occupations.

We employ the word "experience" in the same pregnant sense. And to it, as well as to life in the bare physiological sense, the principle of continuity through renewal applies. With the renewal of physical existence goes, in the case of human beings, the recreation of beliefs, ideals, hopes, happiness, misery, and practices. The continuity of any experience, through renewing of the social group, is a literal fact. Education, in its broadest sense, is the means of this social continuity of life. Every one of the constituent elements of a social group, in a modern city as in a savage tribe, is born immature, helpless, without language, beliefs, ideas, or social standards. Each individual, each unit who is the carrier of the life-experience of his group, in time passes away. Yet the life of the group goes on.

The primary ineluctable facts of the birth and death of each one of the constituent members in a social group determine the necessity of education. On one hand, there is the contrast between the immaturity of the new-born members of the group — its future sole representatives — and the maturity of the adult members who possess the knowledge and customs of the group. On the other hand, there is the necessity that these immature members be not merely physically preserved in adequate numbers, but that they be initiated into the interests, purposes, information, skill, and practices of the mature members: otherwise the group will cease its characteristic life.

Even in a savage tribe, the achievements of adults are far beyond what the immature members would be capable of if left to themselves. With the growth of civilization, the gap between the original capacities of the immature and the standards and customs of the elders increases. Mere physical growing up, mere mastery of the bare necessities of subsistence will not suffice to reproduce the life of the group. Deliberate effort and the taking of thoughtful pains are required. Beings who are born not only unaware of, but quite indifferent to, the aims and habits of the social group have to be rendered cognizant of them and actively interested. Education, and education alone, spans the gap.

Society exists through a process of transmission quite as much as biological life. This transmission occurs by means of communication of habits of doing, thinking, and feeling from the older to the younger. Without this communication of ideals, hopes, expectations, standards, opinions, from those members of society who are passing out of the group life to those who are coming into it, social life could not survive. If the members who compose a society lived on continuously, they might educate the new-born members, but it would be a task directed by personal interest rather than social need. Now it is a work of necessity.

If a plague carried off the members of a society all at once, it is obvious that the group would be permanently done for. Yet the death of each of its constituent members is as certain as if an epidemic took them all at once. But the graded difference in age, the fact that some are born as some die, makes possible through transmission of ideas and practices the constant reweaving of the social fabric. Yet this renewal is not automatic. Unless pains are taken to see that genuine and thorough transmission takes place, the most civilized group will relapse into barbarism and then into savagery. In fact, the human young are so immature that if they were left to themselves without the guidance and succor of others, they could not acquire the rudimentary abilities necessary for physical existence. The young of human beings compare so poorly in original efficiency with the young of many of the lower animals, that even the powers needed for physical sustentation have to be acquired under tuition. How much more, then, is this the case with respect to all the technological, artistic, scientific, and moral achievements of humanity!

Education and Communication

So obvious, indeed, is the necessity of teaching and learning for the continued existence of a society that we may seem to be dwelling unduly on a truism. But justification is found in the fact that such emphasis is a means of getting us away from an unduly scholastic and formal notion of education. Schools are, indeed, one important method of the transmission which forms the dispositions of the immature; but it is only one means, and, compared with other agencies, a relatively superficial means. Only as we have grasped the necessity of more fundamental and persistent modes of tuition can we make sure of placing the scholastic methods in their true context.

Society not only continues to exist by transmission, by communication, but it may fairly be said to exist in transmission, in communication. There is more than a verbal tie between the words common, community, and communication. Men live in a community in virtue of the things which they have in common; and communication is the way in which they come to possess things in common. What they must have in common in order to form a community or society are aims, beliefs, aspirations, knowledge — a common understanding — like-mindedness as the sociologists say. Such things cannot be passed physically from one to another, like bricks; they cannot be shared as persons would share a pie by dividing it into physical pieces. The communication which insures participation in a common understanding is one which secures similar emotional and intellectual dispositions — like ways of responding to expectations and requirements.

Persons do not become a society by living in physical proximity, any more than a man ceases to be socially influenced by being so many feet or miles removed from others. A book or a letter may institute a more intimate association between human beings separated thousands of miles from each other than exists between dwellers under the same roof. Individuals do not even compose a social group because they all work for a common end. The parts of a machine work with a maximum of cooperativeness for a common result, but they do not form a community. If, however, they were all cognizant of the common end and all interested in it so that they regulated their specific activity in view of it, then they would form a community. But this would involve communication. Each would have to know what the other was about and would have to have some way of keeping the other informed as to his own purpose and progress. Consensus demands communication.

We are thus compelled to recognize that within even the most social group there are many relations which are not as yet social. A large number of human relationships in any social group are still upon the machine-like plane. Individuals use one another so as to get desired results, without reference to the emotional and intellectual disposition and consent of those used. Such uses express physical superiority, or superiority of position, skill, technical ability, and command of tools, mechanical or fiscal. So far as the relations of parent and child, teacher and pupil, employer and employee, governor and governed, remain upon this level, they form no true social group, no matter how closely their respective activities touch one another. Giving and taking of orders modifies action and results, but does not of itself effect a sharing of purposes, a communication of interests.

Not only is social life identical with communication, but all communication is educative. To be a recipient of a communication is to have an enlarged and changed experience. One shares in what another has thought and felt and in so far, meagerly or amply, has his own attitude modified. Nor is the one who communicates left unaffected. Try the experiment of communicating, with fullness and accuracy, some experience to another, especially if it be somewhat complicated, and you will find your own attitude toward your experience changing; otherwise you resort to expletives and ejaculations. The experience has to be formulated in order to be communicated.

To formulate requires getting outside of it, seeing it as another would see it, considering what points of contact it has with the life of another so that it may be got into such form that he can appreciate its meaning. Except in dealing with commonplaces and catch phrases one has to assimilate, imaginatively, something of another's experience in order to tell him intelligently of one's own experience. All communication is like art. It may fairly be said, therefore, that any social arrangement that remains vitally social, or vitally shared, is educative to those who participate in it. Only when it becomes cast in a mold and runs in a routine way does it lose its educative power.

In final account, then, not only does social life demand teaching and learning for its own permanence, but the very process of living together educates. It enlarges and enlightens experience; it stimulates and enriches imagination; it creates responsibility for accuracy and vividness of statement and thought. A man really living alone (alone mentally as well as physically) would have little or no occasion to reflect upon his past experience to extract its net meaning. The inequality of achievement between the mature and the immature not only necessitates teaching the young, but the necessity of this teaching gives an immense stimulus to reducing experience to that order and form which will render it most easily communicable and hence most usable.

Place of Formal Education

There is, accordingly, a marked difference between the education which every one gets from living with others, as long as he really lives instead of just continuing to subsist, and the deliberate educating of the young. In the former case the education is incidental; it is natural and important, but it is not the express reason of the association. While it may be said, without exaggeration, that the measure of the worth of any social institution, economic, domestic, political, legal, religious, is its effect in enlarging and improving experience; yet this effect is not a part of its original motive, which is limited and more immediately practical.

Religious associations began, for example, in the desire to secure the favor of overruling powers and to ward off evil influences; family life in the desire to gratify appetites and secure family perpetuity; systematic labor, for the most part, because of enslavement to others, etc. Only gradually was the by-product of the institution, its effect upon the quality and extent of conscious life, noted, and only more gradually still was this effect considered as a directive factor in the conduct of the institution. Even today, in our industrial life, apart from certain values of industriousness and thrift, the intellectual and emotional reaction of the forms of human association under which the world's work is carried on receives little attention as compared with physical output.

But in dealing with the young, the fact of association itself as an immediate human fact, gains in importance. While it is easy to ignore in our contact with them the effect of our acts upon their disposition, or to subordinate that educative effect to some external and tangible result, it is not so easy as in dealing with adults.

The need of training is too evident; the pressure to accomplish a change in their attitude and habits is too urgent to leave these consequences wholly out of account. Since our chief business with them is to enable them to share in a common life we cannot help considering whether or no we are forming the powers which will secure this ability. If humanity has made some headway in realising that the ultimate value of every institution is its distinctively human effect — its effect upon conscious experience — we may well believe that this lesson has been learned largely through dealings with the young.

We are thus led to distinguish, within the broad educational process which we have been so far considering, a more formal kind of education — that of direct tuition or schooling. In undeveloped social groups, we find very little formal teaching and training. Savage groups mainly rely for instilling needed dispositions into the young upon the same sort of association which keeps adults loyal to their group. They have no special devices, material, or institutions for teaching save in connection with initiation ceremonies by which the youth are inducted into full social membership.

For the most part, they depend upon children learning the customs of the adults, acquiring their emotional set and stock of ideas, by sharing in what the elders are doing. In part, this sharing is direct, taking part in the occupations of adults and thus serving an apprenticeship; in part, it is indirect, through the dramatic plays in which children reproduce the actions of grown-ups and thus learn to know what they are like. To savages it would seem preposterous to seek out a place where nothing but learning was going on in order that one might learn.

But as civilisation advances, the gap between the capacities of the young and the concerns of adults widens. Learning by direct sharing in the pursuits of grown-ups becomes increasingly difficult except in the case of the less advanced occupations. Much of what adults do is so remote in space and in meaning that playful imitation is less and less adequate to reproduce its spirit. Ability to share effectively in adult activities thus depends upon a prior training given with this end in view. Intentional agencies — schools — and explicit material — studies — are devised. The task of teaching certain things is delegated to a special group of persons.

Without such formal education, it is not possible to transmit all the resources and achievements of a complex society. It also opens a way to a kind of experience which would not be accessible to the young, if they were left to pick up their training in informal association with others, since books and the symbols of knowledge are mastered.

But there are conspicuous dangers attendant upon the transition from indirect to formal education. Sharing in actual pursuit, whether directly or vicariously in play, is at least personal and vital. These qualities compensate, in some measure, for the narrowness of available opportunities. Formal instruction, on the contrary, easily becomes remote and dead — abstract and bookish, to use the ordinary words of depreciation. What accumulated knowledge exists in low grade societies is at least put into practice; it is transmuted into character; it exists with the depth of meaning that attaches to its coming within urgent daily interests.

But in an advanced culture much which has to be learned is stored in symbols. It is far from translation into familiar acts and objects. Such material is relatively technical and superficial. Taking the ordinary standard of reality as a measure, it is artificial. For this measure is connection with practical concerns. Such material exists in a world by itself, unassimilated to ordinary customs of thought and expression. There is the standing danger that the material of formal instruction will be merely the subject matter of the schools, isolated from the subject matter of life-experience.

The permanent social interests are likely to be lost from view. Those which have not been carried over into the structure of social life, but which remain largely matters of technical information expressed in symbols, are made conspicuous in schools. Thus we reach the ordinary notion of education: the notion which ignores its social necessity and its identity with all human association that affects conscious life, and which identifies it with imparting information about remote matters and the conveying of learning through verbal signs: the acquisition of literacy.

Hence one of the weightiest problems with which the philosophy of education has to cope is the method of keeping a proper balance between the informal and the formal, the incidental and the intentional, modes of education. When the acquiring of information and of technical intellectual skill do not influence the formation of a social disposition, ordinary vital experience fails to gain in meaning, while schooling, in so far, creates only "sharps" in learning — that is, egoistic specialists. To avoid a split between what men consciously know because they are aware of having learned it by a specific job of learning, and what they unconsciously know because they have absorbed it in the formation of their characters by intercourse with others, becomes an increasingly delicate task with every development of special schooling.

Education as a Social Function

We have seen that a community or social group sustains itself through continuous self-renewal, and that this renewal takes place by means of the educational growth of the immature members of the group. By various agencies, unintentional and designed, a society transforms uninitiated and seemingly alien beings into robust trustees of its own resources and ideals. Education is thus a fostering, a nurturing, a cultivating, process. All of these words mean that it implies attention to the conditions of growth. We also speak of rearing, raising, bringing up — words which express the difference of level which education aims to cover.

Etymologically, the word education means just a process of leading or bringing up. When we have the outcome of the process in mind, we speak of education as shaping, forming, molding activity — that is, a shaping into the standard form of social activity.

Since what is required is a transformation of the quality of experience till it partakes in the interests, purposes, and ideas current in the social group, the problem is evidently not one of mere physical forming. Things can be physically transported in space; they may be bodily conveyed. Beliefs and aspirations cannot be physically extracted and inserted. How then are they communicated? Given the impossibility of direct contagion or literal inculcation, our problem is to discover the method by which the young assimilate the point of view of the old, or the older bring the young into like-mindedness with themselves.

The answer, in general formulation, is: By means of the action of the environment in calling out certain responses. The required beliefs cannot be hammered in; the needed attitudes cannot be plastered on. But the particular medium in which an individual exists leads him to see and feel one thing rather than another; it leads him to have certain plans in order that he may act successfully with others; it strengthens some beliefs and weakens others as a condition of winning the approval of others. Thus it gradually produces in him a certain system of behavior, a certain disposition of action. The words "environment," "medium" denote something more than surroundings which encompass an individual. They denote the specific continuity of the surroundings with his own active tendencies.

An inanimate being is, of course, continuous with its surroundings; but the environing circumstances do not, save metaphorically, constitute an environment. For the inorganic being is not concerned in the influences which affect it. On the other hand, some things which are remote in space and time from a living creature, especially a human creature, may form his environment even more truly than some of the things close to him. The things with which a man varies are his genuine environment. Thus the activities of the astronomer vary with the stars at which he gazes or about which he calculates. Of his immediate surroundings, his telescope is most intimately his environment. The environment of an antiquarian, as an antiquarian, consists of the remote epoch of human life with which he is concerned, and the relics, inscriptions, etc., by which he establishes connections with that period.

In brief, the environment consists of those conditions that promote or hinder, stimulate or inhibit, the characteristic activities of a living being. Water is the environment of a fish because it is necessary to the fish's activities — to its life. The north pole is a significant element in the environment of an arctic explorer, whether he succeeds in reaching it or not, because it defines his activities, makes them what they distinctively are. Just because life signifies not bare passive existence (supposing there is such a thing), but a way of acting, environment or medium signifies what enters into this activity as a sustaining or frustrating condition.

Social Environment

A being whose activities are associated with others has a social environment. What he does and what he can do depend upon the expectations, demands, approvals, and condemnations of others. A being connected with other beings cannot perform his own activities without taking the activities of others into account. For they are the indispensable conditions of the realisation of his tendencies. When he moves he stirs them and reciprocally. We might as well try to imagine a business man doing business, buying and selling, all by himself, as to conceive it possible to define the activities of an individual in terms of his isolated actions. The manufacturer moreover is as truly socially guided in his activities when he is laying plans in the privacy of his own counting house as when he is buying his raw material or selling his finished goods. Thinking and feeling that have to do with action in association with others is as much a social mode of behavior as is the most overt cooperative or hostile act.

What we have more especially to indicate is how the social medium nurtures its immature members. There is no great difficulty in seeing how it shapes the external habits of action. Even dogs and horses have their actions modified by association with human beings; they form different habits because human beings are concerned with what they do.

Human beings control animals by controlling the natural stimuli which influence them; by creating a certain environment in other words. Food, bits and bridles, noises, vehicles, are used to direct the ways in which the natural or instinctive responses of horses occur. By operating steadily to call out certain acts, habits are formed which function with the same uniformity as the original stimuli. If a rat is put in a maze and finds food only by making a given number of turns in a given sequence, his activity is gradually modified till he habitually takes that course rather than another when he is hungry.

Human actions are modified in a like fashion. A burnt child dreads the fire; if a parent arranged conditions so that every time a child touched a certain toy he got burned, the child would learn to avoid that toy as automatically as he avoids touching fire. So far, however, we are dealing with what may be called training in distinction from educative teaching. The changes considered are in outer action rather than in mental and emotional dispositions of behavior. The distinction is not, however, a sharp one. The child might conceivably generate in time a violent antipathy, not only to that particular toy, but to the class of toys resembling it.

The aversion might even persist after he had forgotten about the original burns; later on he might even invent some reason to account for his seemingly irrational antipathy. In some cases, altering the external habit of action by changing the environment to affect the stimuli to action will also alter the mental disposition concerned in the action. Yet this does not always happen; a person trained to dodge a threatening blow, dodges automatically with no corresponding thought or emotion. We have to find, then, some differentia of training from education.

A clew may be found in the fact that the horse does not really share in the social use to which his action is put. Some one else uses the horse to secure a result which is advantageous by making it advantageous to the horse to perform the act — he gets food, etc. But the horse, presumably, does not get any new interest. He remains interested in food, not in the service he is rendering. He is not a partner in a shared activity. Were he to become a copartner, he would, in engaging in the conjoint activity, have the same interest in its accomplishment which others have. He would share their ideas and emotions.

Now in many cases — too many cases — the activity of the immature human being is simply played upon to secure habits which are useful. He is trained like an animal rather than educated like a human being. His instincts remain attached to their original objects of pain or pleasure. But to get happiness or to avoid the pain of failure he has to act in a way agreeable to others. In other cases, he really shares or participates in the common activity. In this case, his original impulse is modified. He not merely acts in a way agreeing with the actions of others, but, in so acting, the same ideas and emotions are aroused in him that animate the others. A tribe, let us say, is warlike.

The successes for which it strives, the achievements upon which it sets store, are connected with fighting and victory. The presence of this medium incites bellicose exhibitions in a boy, first in games, then in fact when he is strong enough. As he fights he wins approval and advancement; as he refrains, he is disliked, ridiculed, shut out from favorable recognition. It is not surprising that his original belligerent tendencies and emotions are strengthened at the expense of others, and that his ideas turn to things connected with war. Only in this way can he become fully a recognised member of his group. Thus his mental habitudes are gradually assimilated to those of his group.

If we formulate the principle involved in this illustration, we shall perceive that the social medium neither implants certain desires and ideas directly, nor yet merely establishes certain purely muscular habits of action, like "instinctively" winking or dodging a blow. Setting up conditions which stimulate certain visible and tangible ways of acting is the first step. Making the individual a sharer or partner in the associated activity so that he feels its success as his success, its failure as his failure, is the completing step. As soon as he is possessed by the emotional attitude of the group, he will be alert to recognise the special ends at which it aims and the means employed to secure success. His beliefs and ideas, in other words, will take a form similar to those of others in the group. He will also achieve pretty much the same stock of knowledge since that knowledge is an ingredient of his habitual pursuits.

The importance of language in gaining knowledge is doubtless the chief cause of the common notion that knowledge may be passed directly from one to another. It almost seems as if all we have to do to convey an idea into the mind of another is to convey a sound into his ear. Thus imparting knowledge gets assimilated to a purely physical process. But learning from language will be found, when analysed, to confirm the principle just laid down. It would probably be admitted with little hesitation that a child gets the idea of, say, a hat by using it as other persons do; by covering the head with it, giving it to others to wear, having it put on by others when going out, etc. But it may be asked how this principle of shared activity applies to getting through speech or reading the idea of, say, a Greek helmet, where no direct use of any kind enters in.

Since language tends to become the chief instrument of learning about many things, let us see how it works. The baby begins of course with mere sounds, noises, and tones having no meaning, expressing, that is, no idea. Sounds are just one kind of stimulus to direct response, some having a soothing effect, others tending to make one jump, and so on. The sound h-a-t would remain as meaningless as a sound in Choctaw, a seemingly inarticulate grunt, if it were not uttered in connection with an action which is participated in by a number of people.

When the mother is taking the infant out of doors, she says "hat" as she puts something on the baby's head. Being taken out becomes an interest to the child; mother and child not only go out with each other physically, but both are concerned in the going out; they enjoy it in common. By conjunction with the other factors in activity the sound "hat" soon gets the same meaning for the child that it has for the parent; it becomes a sign of the activity into which it enters. The bare fact that language consists of sounds which are mutually intelligible is enough of itself to show that its meaning depends upon connection with a shared experience.

In short, the sound h-a-t gains meaning in precisely the same way that the thing "hat" gains it, by being used in a given way. And they acquire the same meaning with the child which they have with the adult because they are used in a common experience by both. The guarantee for the same manner of use is found in the fact that the thing and the sound are first employed in a joint activity, as a means of setting up an active connection between the child and a grownup.

Similar ideas or meanings spring up because both persons are engaged as partners in an action where what each does depends upon and influences what the other does. If two savages were engaged in a joint hunt for game, and a certain signal meant "move to the right" to the one who uttered it, and "move to the left" to the one who heard it, they obviously could not successfully carry on their hunt together. Understanding one another means that objects, including sounds, have the same value for both with respect to carrying on a common pursuit.

After sounds have got meaning through connection with other things employed in a joint undertaking, they can be used in connection with other like sounds to develop new meanings, precisely as the things for which they stand are combined. Thus the words in which a child learns about, say, the Greek helmet originally got a meaning by use in an action having a common interest and end. They now arouse a new meaning by inciting the one who hears or reads to rehearse imaginatively the activities in which the helmet has its use.

Social Medium as Educative

Our net result thus far is that social environment forms the mental and emotional disposition of behavior in individuals by engaging them in activities that arouse and strengthen certain impulses, that have certain purposes and entail certain consequences. A child growing up in a family of musicians will inevitably have whatever capacities he has in music stimulated, and, relatively, stimulated more than other impulses which might have been awakened in another environment. Save as he takes an interest in music and gains a certain competency in it, he is "out of it"; he is unable to share in the life of the group to which he belongs. Some kinds of participation in the life of those with whom the individual is connected are inevitable; with respect to them, the social environment exercises an educative or formative influence unconsciously and apart from any set purpose.

In savage and barbarian communities, such direct participation furnishes almost the sole influence for rearing the young into the practices and beliefs of the group. Even in present-day societies, it furnishes the basic nurture of even the most insistently schooled youth. In accord with the interests and occupations of the group, certain things become objects of high esteem; others of aversion. Association does not create impulses or affection and dislike, but it furnishes the objects to which they attach themselves. The way our group or class does things tends to determine the proper objects of attention, and thus to prescribe the directions and limits of observation and memory. What is strange or foreign tends to be morally forbidden and intellectually suspect.

The main texture of disposition is formed, independently of schooling, by such influences. What conscious, deliberate teaching can do is at most to free the capacities thus formed for fuller exercise, to purge them of some of their grossness, and to furnish objects which make their activity more productive of meaning.

While this "unconscious influence of the environment" is so subtle and pervasive that it affects every fiber of character and mind, it may be worth while to specify a few directions in which its effect is most marked. First, the habits of language. Fundamental modes of speech, the bulk of the vocabulary, are formed in the ordinary intercourse of life, carried on not as a set means of instruction but as a social necessity. The babe acquires, as we well say, the mother tongue. While speech habits thus contracted may be corrected or even displaced by conscious teaching, yet, in times of excitement, intentionally acquired modes of speech often fall away, and individuals relapse into their really native tongue. Secondly, manners. Example is notoriously more potent than precept.

Good manners come, as we say, from good breeding or rather are good breeding; and breeding is acquired by habitual action, in response to habitual stimuli, not by conveying information. Despite the never ending play of conscious correction and instruction, the surrounding atmosphere and spirit is in the end the chief agent in forming manners. And manners are but minor morals. Moreover, in major morals, conscious instruction is likely to be efficacious only in the degree in which it falls in with the general "walk and conversation" of those who constitute the child's social environment. Thirdly, good taste and esthetic appreciation. If the eye is constantly greeted by harmonious objects, having elegance of form and color, a standard of taste naturally grows up. The effect of a tawdry, unarranged, and over-decorated environment works for the deterioration of taste, just as meager and barren surroundings starve out the desire for beauty.

Against such odds, conscious teaching can hardly do more than convey second-hand information as to what others think. Such taste never becomes spontaneous and personally engrained, but remains a labored reminder of what those think to whom one has been taught to look up. To say that the deeper standards of judgments of value are framed by the situations into which a person habitually enters is not so much to mention a fourth point, as it is to point out a fusion of those already mentioned.

We rarely recognise the extent in which our conscious estimates of what is worth while and what is not, are due to standards of which we are not conscious at all. But in general it may be said that the things which we take for granted without inquiry or reflection are just the things which determine our conscious thinking and decide our conclusions. And these habitudes which lie below the level of reflection are just those which have been formed in the constant give and take of relationship with others.

School as a Special Environment

The chief importance of this foregoing statement of the educative process which goes on willy-nilly is to lead us to note that the only way in which adults consciously control the kind of education which the immature get is by controlling the environment in which they act, and hence think and feel. We never educate directly, but indirectly by means of the environment. Whether we permit chance environments to do the work, or whether we design environments for the purpose makes a great difference. And any environment is a chance environment so far as its educative influence is concerned unless it has been deliberately regulated with reference to its educative effect.

An intelligent home differs from an unintelligent one chiefly in that the habits of life and intercourse which prevail are chosen, or at least colored, by the thought of their bearing upon the development of children. But schools remain, of course, the typical instance of environments framed with express reference to influencing the mental and moral disposition of their members.

Roughly speaking, they come into existence when social traditions are so complex that a considerable part of the social store is committed to writing and transmitted through written symbols. Written symbols are even more artificial or conventional than spoken; they cannot be picked up in accidental intercourse with others. In addition, the written form tends to select and record matters which are comparatively foreign to everyday life.

The achievements accumulated from generation to generation are deposited in it even though some of them have fallen temporarily out of use. Consequently as soon as a community depends to any considerable extent upon what lies beyond its own territory and its own immediate generation, it must rely upon the set agency of schools to insure adequate transmission of all its resources. To take an obvious illustration: The life of the ancient Greeks and Romans has profoundly influenced our own, and yet the ways in which they affect us do not present themselves on the surface of our ordinary experiences.

In similar fashion, peoples still existing, but remote in space, British, Germans, Italians, directly concern our own social affairs, but the nature of the interaction cannot be understood without explicit statement and attention. In precisely similar fashion, our daily associations cannot be trusted to make clear to the young the part played in our activities by remote physical energies, and by invisible structures. Hence a special mode of social intercourse is instituted, the school, to care for such matters.

This mode of association has three functions sufficiently specific, as compared with ordinary associations of life, to be noted. First, a complex civilization is too complex to be assimilated in toto. It has to be broken up into portions, as it were, and assimilated piecemeal, in a gradual and graded way. The relationships of our present social life are so numerous and so interwoven that a child placed in the most favorable position could not readily share in many of the most important of them. Not sharing in them, their meaning would not be communicated to him, would not become a part of his own mental disposition.

There would be no seeing the trees because of the forest. Business, politics, art, science, religion, would make all at once a clamor for attention; confusion would be the outcome. The first office of the social organ we call the school is to provide a simplified environment. It selects the features which are fairly fundamental and capable of being responded to by the young. Then it establishes a progressive order, using the factors first acquired as means of gaining insight into what is more complicated.

In the second place, it is the business of the school environment to eliminate, so far as possible, the unworthy features of the existing environment from influence upon mental habitudes. It establishes a purified medium of action. Selection aims not only at simplifying but at weeding out what is undesirable. Every society gets encumbered with what is trivial, with dead wood from the past, and with what is positively perverse.

The school has the duty of omitting such things from the environment which it supplies, and thereby doing what it can to counteract their influence in the ordinary social environment. By selecting the best for its exclusive use, it strives to reinforce the power of this best. As a society becomes more enlightened, it realises that it is responsible not to transmit and conserve the whole of its existing achievements, but only such as make for a better future society. The school is its chief agency for the accomplishment of this end.

In the third place, it is the office of the school environment to balance the various elements in the social environment, and to see to it that each individual gets an opportunity to escape from the limitations of the social group in which he was born, and to come into living contact with a broader environment. Such words as "society" and "community" are likely to be misleading, for they have a tendency to make us think there is a single thing corresponding to the single word.

As a matter of fact, a modern society is many societies more or less loosely connected. Each household with its immediate extension of friends makes a society; the village or street group of playmates is a community; each business group, each club, is another. Passing beyond these more intimate groups, there is in a country like our own a variety of races, religious affiliations, economic divisions. Inside the modern city, in spite of its nominal political unity, there are probably more communities, more differing customs, traditions, aspirations, and forms of government or control, than existed in an entire continent at an earlier epoch.

Each such group exercises a formative influence on the active dispositions of its members. A clique, a club, a gang, a Fagin's household of thieves, the prisoners in a jail, provide educative environments for those who enter into their collective or conjoint activities, as truly as a church, a labor union, a business partnership, or a political party. Each of them is a mode of associated or community life, quite as much as is a family, a town, or a state. There are also communities whose members have little or no direct contact with one another, like the guild of artists, the republic of letters, the members of the professional learned class scattered over the face of the earth. For they have aims in common, and the activity of each member is directly modified by knowledge of what others are doing.

In the olden times, the diversity of groups was largely a geographical matter. There were many societies, but each, within its own territory, was comparatively homogeneous. But with the development of commerce, transportation, intercommunication, and emigration, countries like the United States are composed of a combination of different groups with different traditional customs. It is this situation which has, perhaps more than any other one cause, forced the demand for an educational institution which shall provide something like a homogeneous and balanced environment for the young. Only in this way can the centrifugal forces set up by juxtaposition of different groups within one and the same political unit be counteracted.

The intermingling in the school of youth of different races, differing religions, and unlike customs creates for all a new and broader environment. Common subject matter accustoms all to a unity of outlook upon a broader horizon than is visible to the members of any group while it is isolated. The assimilative force of the American public school is eloquent testimony to the efficacy of the common and balanced appeal.

The school has the function also of coordinating within the disposition of each individual the diverse influences of the various social environments into which he enters. One code prevails in the family; another, on the street; a third, in the workshop or store; a fourth, in the religious association. As a person passes from one of the environments to another, he is subjected to antagonistic pulls, and is in danger of being split into a being having different standards of judgment and emotion for different occasions. This danger imposes upon the school a steadying and integrating office.

Democratic Conception in Education

For the most part, save incidentally, we have hitherto

been concerned with education as it may exist in any social group. We have now to make explicit the differences in the spirit, material, and method of education as it operates in different types of community life. To say that education is a social function, securing direction and development in the immature through their participation in the life of the group to which they belong, is to say in effect that education will vary with the quality of life which prevails in a group.

Particularly is it true that a society which not only changes but-which has the ideal of such change as will improve it, will have different standards and methods of education from one which aims simply at the perpetuation of its own customs. To make the general ideas set forth applicable to our own educational practice, it is, therefore, necessary to come to closer quarters with the nature of present social life.

Implications of Human Association

Society is one word, but many things. Men associate together in all kinds of ways and for all kinds of purposes. One man is concerned in a multitude of diverse groups, in which his associates may be quite different. It often seems as if they had nothing in common except that they are modes of associated life. Within every larger social organisation there are numerous minor groups: not only political subdivisions, but industrial, scientific, religious, associations.

There are political parties with differing aims, social sets, cliques, gangs, corporations, partnerships, groups bound closely together by ties of blood, and so on in endless variety. In many modern states and in some ancient, there is great diversity of populations, of varying languages, religions, moral codes, and traditions. From this standpoint, many a minor political unit, one of our large cities, for example, is a congeries of loosely associated societies, rather than an inclusive and permeating community of action and thought.

The terms society, community, are thus ambiguous. They have both a eulogistic or normative sense, and a descriptive sense; a meaning de jure and a meaning de facto. In social philosophy, the former connotation is almost always uppermost. Society is conceived as one by its very nature. The qualities which accompany this unity, praiseworthy community of purpose and welfare, loyalty to public ends, mutuality of sympathy, are emphasised. But when we look at the facts which the term denotes instead of confining our attention to its intrinsic connotation, we find not unity, but a plurality of societies, good and bad.

Men banded together in a criminal conspiracy, business aggregations that prey upon the public while serving it, political machines held together by the interest of plunder, are included. If it is said that such organisations are not societies because they do not meet the ideal requirements of the notion of society, the answer, in part, is that the conception of society is then made so "ideal" as to be of no use, having no reference to facts; and in part, that each of these organisations, no matter how opposed to the interests of other groups, has something of the praiseworthy qualities of "Society" which hold it together. There is honor among thieves, and a band of robbers has a common interest as respects its members.

Gangs are marked by fraternal feeling, and narrow cliques by intense loyalty to their own codes. Family life may be marked by exclusiveness, suspicion, and jealousy as to those without, and yet be a model of amity and mutual aid within. Any education given by a group tends to socialise its members, but the quality and value of the socialisation depends upon the habits and aims of the group.

Hence, once more, the need of a measure for the worth of any given mode of social life. In seeking this measure, we have to avoid two extremes. We cannot set up, out of our heads, something we regard as an ideal society. We must base our conception upon societies which actually exist, in order to have any assurance that our ideal is a practicable one. But, as we have just seen, the ideal cannot simply repeat the traits which are actually found. The problem is to extract the desirable traits of forms of community life which actually exist, and employ them to criticise undesirable features and suggest improvement. Now in any social group whatever, even in a gang of thieves, we find some interest held in common, and we find a certain amount of interaction and cooperative intercourse with other groups.

Let us apply the first element in this criterion to a despotically governed state. It is not true there is no common interest in such an organisation between governed and governors. The authorities in command must make some appeal to the native activities of the subjects, must call some of their powers into play. Talleyrand said that a government could do everything with bayonets except sit on them. This cynical declaration is at least a recognition that the bond of union is not merely one of coercive force. It may be said, however, that the activities appealed to are themselves unworthy and degrading — that such a government calls into functioning activity simply capacity for fear.

In a way, this statement is true. But it overlooks the fact that fear need not be an undesirable factor in experience. Caution, circumspection, prudence, desire to foresee future events so as to avert what is harmful, these desirable traits are as much a product of calling the impulse of fear into play as is cowardice and abject submission. The real difficulty is that the appeal to fear is isolated. In evoking dread and hope of specific tangible reward — say comfort and ease — many other capacities are left untouched. Or rather, they are affected, but in such a way as to pervert them. Instead of operating on their own account they are reduced to mere servants of attaining pleasure and avoiding pain.

This is equivalent to saying that there is no extensive number of common interests; there is no free play back and forth among the members of the social group. Stimulation and response are exceedingly one-sided. In order to have a large number of values in common, all the members of the group must have an equable opportunity to receive and to take from others. There must be a large variety of shared undertakings and experiences. Otherwise, the influences which educate some into masters, educate others into slaves. And the experience of each party loses in meaning, when the free interchange of varying modes of life-experience is arrested.

A separation into a privileged and a subject-class prevents social endosmosis. The evils thereby affecting the superior class are less material and less perceptible, but equally real. Their culture tends to be sterile, to be turned back to feed on itself; their art becomes a showy display and artificial; their wealth luxurious; their knowledge overspecialised; their manners fastidious rather than humane.

Lack of the free and equitable intercourse which springs from a variety of shared interests makes intellectual stimulation unbalanced. Diversity of stimulation means novelty, and novelty means challenge to thought. The more activity is restricted to a few definite lines — as it is when there are rigid class lines preventing adequate interplay of experiences — the more action tends to become routine on the part of the class at a disadvantage, and capricious, aimless, and explosive on the part of the class having the materially fortunate position.

Plato defined a slave as one who accepts from another the purposes which control his conduct. This condition obtains even where there is no slavery in the legal sense. It is found wherever men are engaged in activity which is socially serviceable, but whose service they do not understand and have no personal interest in. Much is said about scientific management of work. It is a narrow view which restricts the science which secures efficiency of operation to movements of the muscles.

The chief opportunity for science is the discovery of the relations of a man to his work — including his relations to others who take part — which will enlist his intelligent interest in what he is doing. Efficiency in production often demands division of labor. But it is reduced to a mechanical routine unless workers see the technical, intellectual, and social relationships involved in what they do, and engage in their work because of the motivation furnished by such perceptions.

The tendency to reduce such things as efficiency of activity and scientific management to purely technical externals is evidence of the one-sided stimulation of thought given to those in control of industry — those who supply its aims. Because of their lack of all-round and well-balanced social interest, there is not sufficient stimulus for attention to the human factors and relationships in industry. Intelligence is narrowed to the factors concerned with technical production and marketing of goods. No doubt, a very acute and intense intelligence in these narrow lines can be developed, but the failure to take into account the significant social factors means none the less an absence of mind, and a corresponding distortion of emotional life.

The isolation and exclusiveness of a gang or clique brings its antisocial spirit into relief. But this same spirit is found wherever one group has interests "of its own" which shut it out from full interaction with other groups, so that its prevailing purpose is the protection of what it has got, instead of reorganisation and progress through wider relationships. It marks nations in their isolation from one another; families which seclude their domestic concerns as if they had no connection with a larger life; schools when separated from the interest of home and community; the divisions of rich and poor; learned and unlearned.

The essential point is that isolation makes for rigidity and formal institutionalizing of life, for static and selfish ideals within the group. That savage tribes regard aliens and enemies as synonymous is not accidental. It springs from the fact that they have identified their experience with rigid adherence to their past customs. On such a basis it is wholly logical to fear intercourse with others, for such contact might dissolve custom. It would certainly occasion reconstruction. It is a commonplace that an alert and expanding mental life depends upon an enlarging range of contact with the physical environment. But the principle applies even more significantly to the field where we are apt to ignore it — the sphere of social contacts.

Every expansive era in the history of mankind has coincided with the operation of factors which have tended to eliminate distance between peoples and classes previously hemmed off from one another. Even the alleged benefits of war, so far as more than alleged, spring from the fact that conflict of peoples at least enforces intercourse between them and thus accidentally enables them to learn from one another, and thereby to expand their horizons. Travel, economic and commercial tendencies, have at present gone far to break down external barriers; to bring peoples and classes into closer and more perceptible connection with one another. It remains for the most part to secure the intellectual and emotional significance of this physical annihilation of space.

Democratic Ideal

The two elements in our criterion both point to democracy. The first signifies not only more numerous and more varied points of shared common interest, but greater reliance upon the recognition of mutual interests as a factor in social control. The second means not only freer interaction between social groups but change in social habit — its continuous readjustment through meeting the new situations produced by varied intercourse. And these two traits are precisely what characterise the democratically constituted society.

Upon the educational side, we note first that the realisation of a form of social life in which interests are mutually interpenetrating, and where progress, or readjustment, is an important consideration, makes a democratic community more interested than other communities have cause to be in deliberate and systematic education. The devotion of democracy to education is a familiar fact. The superficial explanation is that a government resting upon popular suffrage cannot be successful unless those who elect and who obey their governors are educated. Since a democratic society repudiates the principle of external authority, it must find a substitute in voluntary disposition and interest; these can be created only by education. But there is a deeper explanation.

A democracy is more than a form of government; it is primarily a mode of associated living, of conjoint communicated experience. The extension in space of the number of individuals who participate in an interest so that each has to refer his own action to that of others, and to consider the action of others to give point and direction to his own, is equivalent to the breaking down of those barriers of class, race, and national territory which kept men from perceiving the full import of their activity. These more numerous and more varied points of contact denote a greater diversity of stimuli to which an individual has to respond; they consequently put a premium on variation in his action. They secure a liberation of powers which remain suppressed as long as the incitations to action are partial, as they must be in a group which in its exclusiveness shuts out many interests.

The widening of the area of shared concerns, and the liberation of a greater diversity of personal capacities which characterize a democracy, are not of course the product of deliberation and conscious effort. On the contrary, they were caused by the development of modes of manufacture and commerce, travel, migration, and intercommunication which flowed from the command of science over natural energy. But after greater individualisation on one hand, and a broader community of interest on the other have come into existence, it is a matter of deliberate effort to sustain and extend them. Obviously a society to which stratification into separate classes would be fatal, must see to it that intellectual opportunities are accessible to all on equable and easy terms.

A society marked off into classes need he specially attentive only to the education of its ruling elements. A society which is mobile, which is full of channels for the distribution of a change occurring anywhere, must see to it that its members are educated to personal initiative and adaptability. Otherwise, they will be overwhelmed by the changes in which they are caught and whose significance or connections they do not perceive. The result will be a confusion in which a few will appropriate to themselves the results of the blind and externally directed activities of others.

Platonic Educational Philosophy

Consider the educational theories which have been evolved in three epochs when the social import of education was especially conspicuous. The first one to be considered is that of Plato. No one could better express than did he the fact that a society is stably organised when each individual is doing that for which he has aptitude by nature in such a way as to be useful to others; and that it is the business of education to discover these aptitudes and progressively to train them for social use.

Much which has been said so far is borrowed from what Plato first consciously taught the world. But conditions which he could not intellectually control led him to restrict these ideas in their application. He never got any conception of the indefinite plurality of activities which may characterise an individual and a social group, and consequently limited his view to a limited number of classes of capacities and of social arrangements.

Plato's starting point is that the organisation of society depends ultimately upon knowledge of the end of existence. If we do not know its end, we shall be at the mercy of accident and caprice. Unless we know the end, the good, we shall have no criterion for rationally deciding what the possibilities are which should be promoted, nor how social arrangements are to be ordered. We shall have no conception of the proper limits and distribution of activities — what he called justice — as a trait of both individual and social organisation. But how is the knowledge of the final and permanent good to be achieved? In dealing with this question we come upon the seemingly insuperable obstacle that such knowledge is not possible save in a just and harmonious social order. Everywhere else the mind is distracted and misled by false valuations and false perspectives.

A disorganised and factional society sets up a number of different models and standards. Under such conditions it is impossible for the individual to attain consistency of mind. Only a complete whole is fully self-consistent. A society which rests upon the supremacy of some factor over another irrespective of its rational or proportionate claims, inevitably leads thought astray. It puts a premium on certain things and slurs over others, and creates a mind whose seeming unity is forced and distorted. Education proceeds ultimately from the patterns furnished by institutions, customs, and laws.

Only in a just state will these be such as to give the right education; and only those who have rightly trained minds will be able to recognise the end, and ordering principle of things. We seem to be caught in a hopeless circle. However, Plato suggested a way out. A few men, philosophers or lovers of wisdom — or truth — may by study learn at least in outline the proper patterns of true existence. If a powerful ruler should form a state after these patterns, then its regulations could be preserved. An education could be given which would sift individuals, discovering what they were good for, and supplying a method of assigning each to the work in life for which his nature fits him. Each doing his own part, and never transgressing, the order and unity of the whole would be maintained.

It would be impossible to find in any scheme of philosophic thought a more adequate recognition on one hand of the educational significance of social arrangements and, on the other, of the dependence of those arrangements upon the means used to educate the young. It would be impossible to find a deeper sense of the function of education in discovering and developing personal capacities, and training them so that they would connect with the activities of others. Yet the society in which the theory was propounded was so undemocratic that Plato could not work out a solution for the problem whose terms he clearly saw.

While he affirmed with emphasis that the place of the individual in society should not be determined by birth or wealth or any conventional status, but by his own nature as discovered in the process of education, he had no perception of the uniqueness of individuals. For him they fall by nature into classes, and into a very small number of classes at that. Consequently the testing and sifting function of education only shows to which one of three classes an individual belongs. There being no recognition that each individual constitutes his own class, there could be no recognition of the infinite diversity of active tendencies and combinations of tendencies of which an individual is capable. There were only three types of faculties or powers in the individual's constitution. Hence education would soon reach a static limit in each class, for only diversity makes change and progress.

In some individuals, appetites naturally dominate; they are assigned to the laboring and trading class, which expresses and supplies human wants. Others reveal, upon education, that over and above appetites, they have a generous, outgoing, assertively courageous disposition. They become the citizen-subjects of the state; its defenders in war; its internal guardians in peace. But their limit is fixed by their lack of reason, which is a capacity to grasp the universal. Those who possess this are capable of the highest kind of education, and become in time the legislators of the state — for laws are the universals which control the particulars of experience. Thus it is not true that in intent, Plato subordinated the individual to the social whole. But it is true that lacking the perception of the uniqueness of every individual, his incommensurability with others, and consequently not recognising that a society might change and yet be stable, his doctrine of limited powers and classes came in net effect to the idea of the subordination of individuality.

"Individualistic" Ideal

In the eighteenth-century philosophy we find ourselves in a very different circle of ideas. "Nature" still means something antithetical to existing social organisation; Plato exercised a great influence upon Rousseau. But the voice of nature now speaks for the diversity of individual talent and for the need of free development of individuality in all its variety. Education in accord with nature furnishes the goal and the method of instruction and discipline. Moreover, the native or original endowment was conceived, in extreme cases, as nonsocial or even as antisocial. Social arrangements were thought of as mere external expedients by which these nonsocial individuals might secure a greater amount of private happiness for themselves.

Nevertheless, these statements convey only an inadequate idea of the true significance of the movement. In reality its chief interest was in progress and in social progress. The seeming antisocial philosophy was a somewhat transparent mask for an impetus toward a wider and freer society — toward cosmopolitanism. The positive ideal was humanity. In membership in humanity, as distinct from a state, man's capacities would be liberated; while in existing political organisations his powers were hampered and distorted to meet the requirements and selfish interests of the rulers of the state. The doctrine of extreme individualism was but the counterpart, the obverse, of ideals of the indefinite perfectibility of man and of a social organisation having a scope as wide as humanity. The emancipated individual was to become the organ and agent of a comprehensive and progressive society.

The heralds of this gospel were acutely conscious of the evils of the social estate in which they found themselves. They attributed these evils to the limitations imposed upon the free powers of man. Such limitation was both distorting and corrupting. Their impassioned devotion to emancipation of life from external restrictions which operated to the exclusive advantage of the class to whom a past feudal system consigned power, found intellectual formulation in a worship of nature. To give "nature" full swing was to replace an artificial, corrupt, and inequitable social order by a new and better kingdom of humanity.

Unrestrained faith in Nature as both a model and a working power was strengthened by the advances of natural science. Inquiry freed from prejudice and artificial restraints of church and state had revealed that the world is a scene of law. The Newtonian solar system, which expressed the reign of natural law, was a scene of wonderful harmony, where every force balanced with every other. Natural law would accomplish the same result in human relations, if men would only get rid of the artificial man-imposed coercive restrictions.

Education in accord with nature was thought to be the first step in insuring this more social society. It was plainly seen that economic and political limitations were ultimately dependent upon limitations of thought and feeling. The first step in freeing men from external chains was to emancipate them from the internal chains of false beliefs and ideals. What was called social life, existing institutions, were too false and corrupt to be intrusted with this work.

"Nature" must then be the power to which the enterprise was to be left. Even the extreme sensationalistic theory of knowledge which was current derived itself from this conception. To insist that mind is originally passive and empty was one way of glorifying the possibilities of education. If the mind was a wax tablet to be written upon by objects, there were no limits to the possibility of education by means of the natural environment. And since the natural world of objects is a scene of harmonious "truth," this education would infallibly produce minds filled with the truth.

Education as National

As soon as the first enthusiasm for freedom waned, the weakness of the theory upon the constructive side became obvious. Merely to leave everything to nature was, after all, but to negate the very idea of education; it was to trust to the accidents of circumstance. Not only was some method required but also some positive organ, some administrative agency for carrying on the process of instruction. The "complete and harmonious development of all powers," having as its social counterpart an enlightened and progressive humanity, required definite organisation for its realisation.

Private individuals here and there could proclaim the gospel; they could not execute the work. A Pestalozzi could try experiments and exhort philanthropically inclined persons having wealth and power to follow his example. But even Pestalozzi saw that any effective pursuit of the new educational ideal required the support of the state. The realization of the new education destined to produce a new society was, after all, dependent upon the activities of existing states. The movement for the democratic idea inevitably became a movement for publicly conducted and administered schools.

So far as Europe was concerned, the historic situation identified the movement for a state-supported education with the nationalistic movement in political life — a fact of incalculable significance for subsequent movements. Under the influence of German thought in particular, education became a civic function and the civic function was identified with the realisation of the ideal of the national state. The "state" was substituted for humanity; cosmopolitanism gave way to nationalism. To form the citizen, not the "man," became the aim of education.

The historic situation to which reference is made is the after-effects of the Napoleonic conquests, especially in Germany. The German states felt that systematic attention to education was the best means of recovering and maintaining their political integrity and power. Externally they were weak and divided. Under the leadership of Prussian statesmen they made this condition a stimulus to the development of an extensive and thoroughly grounded system of public education.

This change in practice necessarily brought about a change in theory. The individualistic theory receded into the background. The state furnished not only the instrumentalities of public education but also its goal. When the actual practice was such that the school system, from the elementary grades through the university faculties, supplied the patriotic citizen and soldier and the future state official and administrator and furnished the means for military, industrial, and political defense and expansion, it was impossible for theory not to emphasise the aim of social efficiency.

And with the immense importance attached to the nationalistic state, surrounded by other competing and more or less hostile states, it was equally impossible to interpret social efficiency in terms of a vague cosmopolitan humanitarianism. Since the maintenance of a particular national sovereignty required subordination of individuals to the superior interests of the state both in military defense and in struggles for international supremacy in commerce, social efficiency was understood to imply a like subordination.

The educational process was taken to be one of disciplinary training rather than of personal development. Since, however, the ideal of culture as complete development of personality persisted, educational philosophy attempted a reconciliation of the two ideas. The reconciliation took the form of the conception of the "organic" character of the state.

The individual in his isolation is nothing; only in and through an absorption of the aims and meaning of organised institutions does he attain true personality. What appears to be his subordination to political authority and the demand for sacrifice of himself to the commands of his superiors is in reality but making his own the objective reason manifested in the state — the only way in which he can become truly rational. The notion of development which we have seen to be characteristic of institutional idealism was just such a deliberate effort to combine the two ideas of complete realisation of personality and thoroughgoing "disciplinary" subordination to existing institutions.

The extent of the transformation of educational philosophy which occurred in Germany in the generation occupied by the struggle against Napoleon for national independence, may be gathered from Kant, who well expresses the earlier individual-cosmopolitan ideal. In his treatise on Pedagogics, consisting of lectures given in the later years of the eighteenth century, he defines education as the process by which man becomes man. Mankind begins its history submerged in nature — not as Man who is a creature of reason, while nature furnishes only instinct and appetite.

Nature offers simply the germs which education is to develop and perfect. The peculiarity of truly human life is that man has to create himself by his own voluntary efforts; he has to make himself a truly moral, rational, and free being. This creative effort is carried on by the educational activities of slow generations. Its acceleration depends upon men consciously striving to educate their successors not for the existing state of affairs but so as to make possible a future better humanity. But there is the great difficulty. Each generation is inclined to educate its young so as to get along in the present world instead of with a view to the proper end of education: the promotion of the best possible realisation of humanity as humanity. Parents educate their children so that they may get on; princes educate their subjects as instruments of their own purposes.

Who, then, shall conduct education so that humanity may improve? We must depend upon the efforts of enlightened men in their private capacity. "All culture begins with private men and spreads outward from them. Simply through the efforts of persons of enlarged inclinations, who are capable of grasping the ideal of a future better condition, is the gradual approximation of human nature to its end possible.... Rulers are simply interested in such training as will make their subjects better tools for their own intentions." Even the subsidy by rulers of privately conducted schools must be carefully safeguarded. For the rulers' interest in the welfare of their own nation instead of in what is best for humanity, will make them, if they give money for the schools, wish to draw their plans. We have in this view an express statement of the points characteristic of the eighteenth century individualistic cosmopolitanism.

The full development of private personality is identified with the aims of humanity as a whole and with the idea of progress. In addition we have an explicit fear of the hampering influence of a state-conducted and state-regulated education upon the attainment of these ideas. But in less than two decades after this time, Kant's philosophic successors, Fichte and Hegel, elaborated the idea that the chief function of the state is educational; that in particular the regeneration of Germany is to be accomplished by an education carried on in the interests of the state, and that the private individual is of necessity an egoistic, irrational being, enslaved to his appetites and to circumstances unless he submits voluntarily to the educative discipline of state institutions and laws. In this spirit, Germany was the first country to undertake a public, universal, and compulsory system of education extending from the primary school through the university, and to submit to jealous state regulation and supervision all private educational enterprises.

Two results should stand out from this brief historical survey. The first is that such terms as the individual and the social conceptions of education are quite meaningless taken at large, or apart from their context. Plato had the ideal of an education which should equate individual realisation and social coherency and stability. His situation forced his ideal into the notion of a society organised in stratified classes, losing the individual in the class. The eighteenth century educational philosophy was highly individualistic in form, but this form was inspired by a noble and generous social ideal: that of a society organised to include humanity, and providing for the indefinite perfectibility of mankind.

The idealistic philosophy of Germany in the early nineteenth century endeavored again to equate the ideals of a free and complete development of cultured personality with social discipline and political subordination. It made the national state an intermediary between the realisation of private personality on one side and of humanity on the other. Consequently, it is equally possible to state its animating principle with equal truth either in the classic terms of "harmonious development of all the powers of personality" or in the more recent terminology of "social efficiency." The conception of education as a social process and function has no definite meaning until we define the kind of society we have in mind.

These considerations pave the way for our second conclusion. One of the fundamental problems of education in and for a democratic society is set by the conflict of a nationalistic and a wider social aim. The earlier cosmopolitan and "humanitarian" conception suffered both from vagueness and from lack of definite organs of execution and agencies of administration. In Europe, in the Continental states particularly, the new idea of the importance of education for human welfare and progress was captured by national interests and harnessed to do a work whose social aim was definitely narrow and exclusive. The social aim of education and its national aim were identified, and the result was a marked obscuring of the meaning of a social aim.

This confusion corresponds to the existing situation of human intercourse. On the one hand, science, commerce, and art transcend national boundaries. They are largely international in quality and method. They involve interdependencies and cooperation among the peoples inhabiting different countries. At the same time, the idea of national sovereignty has never been as accentuated in politics as it is at the present time. Each nation lives in a state of suppressed hostility and incipient war with its neighbors.

Each is supposed to be the supreme judge of its own interests, and it is assumed as matter of course that each has interests which are exclusively its own. To question this is to question the very idea of national sovereignty which is assumed to be basic to political practice and political science. This contradiction between the wider sphere of associated and mutually helpful social life and the narrower sphere of exclusive and hence potentially hostile pursuits and purposes, exacts of educational theory a clearer conception of the meaning of "social" as a function and test of education than has yet been attained.

Is it possible for an educational system to be conducted by a national state and yet the full social ends of the educative process not be restricted, constrained, and corrupted? Internally, the question has to face the tendencies, due to present economic conditions, which split society into classes some of which are made merely tools for the higher culture of others.

Externally, the question is concerned with the reconciliation of national loyalty, of patriotism, with superior devotion to the things which unite men in common ends, irrespective of national political boundaries. Neither phase of the problem can be worked out by merely negative means. It is not enough to see to it that education is not actively used as an instrument to make easier the exploitation of one class by another.

School facilities must be secured of such amplitude and efficiency as will in fact and not simply in name discount the effects of economic inequalities, and secure to all the wards of the nation equality of equipment for their future careers.

Accomplishment of this end demands not only adequate administrative provision of school facilities, and such supplementation of family resources as will enable youth to take advantage of them, but also such modification of traditional ideals of culture, traditional subjects of study and traditional methods of teaching and discipline as will retain all the youth under educational influences until they are equipped to be masters of their own economic and social careers. The ideal may seem remote of execution, but the democratic ideal of education is a farcical yet tragic delusion except as the ideal more and more dominates our public system of education.

7

Education and Character Development

Temples have their sacred images, and we see what influence they have always had over a great part of mankind. But in truth the ideas and images in men's minds are the invisible powers that constantly govern them, and to these they all universally pay a ready submission. It is therefore of the highest concernment that great care should be taken of the understanding to conduct it right in the search of knowledge and in the judgments it makes.

The logic noes in use has so long possessed the chair, as the only art taught in the schools for the direction of the mind in the study of the arts and sciences, that it would perhaps be thought an affectation of novelty to suspect that rules that have served the learned world these two or three thousand years and which without any complaint of defects the learned have rested in are not sufficient to guide the understanding. This attempt would be censured as vanity or presumption did not the great Lord Verulam's authority justify it, who, not servilely thinking learning could not be advanced beyond what it was because for many ages it had not been, did not rest in the lazy approbation and applause of what was, because it was, but enlarged his mind to Chat might be. In his preface to his Norum Organum concerning logic he pronounces thus, Qui summas dialecticae partes tribuerunt atque inde fidissima scientiis praesidia comparari putarunt, verissime atque optime viderunt intellectum Slumanum sibi permissum merito suspectum esse debere.

Serum infirmior omnino est malo medicinal nec ipsa mali expers. Siquidem dialectica quae recepta est. licet ad ci-ailia et antes quae in sermone et opinione positae sunt rectissime adhibeatur, naturae tamen subtilitatem longo intervallo non attingit; et prensando quod non capit ad encores potius stabiliendos et quasi figendos qualn ad viam veritati aperiendam valuit.

"They," says he, "who attributed so much to logic perceived very well and truly that it seas not safe to trust the understanding to itself without the guard of any rules. But the remedy reached not the evil but became a part of it; for the logic which took place, though it might do well enough in civil affairs and the arts which consisted in talk and opinion, yet comes very far short of subtlety in the real performances of nature and, catching at what it cannot reach, has served to confirm and establish errors rather than to open a way to truth." And therefore a little after he says, "That it is absolutely necessary that a better and perfected use and employment of the mind and understanding should be introduced." Necessario requiritur ut melior et perfectior mentis et intellectus humani usus et adoperatio introducatur.

Parts. There is, it is visible, great variety in men's understandings, and their natural constitutions put so wide a difference between some men in this respect that art and industry would never be able to master, and their very natures seem to want a foundation to raise on it that which other men easily attain unto. Amongst men of equal education there is great inequality of parts. And the woods of America, as well as the schools of Athens, produce men of several abilities in the same kind. Though this be so, Whet I imagine most men come very short of what they might attain unto in their several degrees by a neglect of their understandings.

A few rules of logic are thought sufficient in this case for those who pretend to the highest improvement, whereas I think there are a great many natural defects in the understanding capable of amendment which are overlooked and wholly neglected. And it is easy to perceive that men are guilty of a great many faults in the exercise and improvement of this faculty of the mind which hinder them in their progress and keep them in ignorance and error all their lives. Some of them I shall take notice of and endeavor to point out proper remedies for in the following discourse.

Reasoning. Besides the want of determined ideas and of sagacity and exercise in finding out and laying in order intermediate ideas, there are three miscarriages that men are guilty of in reference to their reason, whereby this faculty is hindered in them from that service it might do and was designed for. And he that reflects upon the actions and discourses of mankind will find their defects in this kind very frequent and very observable.

(i) The first is of those who seldom reason at all, but do and think according to the example of others, whether parents, neighbors, ministers or who else they are pleased to make choice of to have an implicit faith in for the saving of themselves the pains and trouble of thinking and examining for themselves.

(ii) The second is of those w ho put passion in the place of reason and, being resolved that shall govern their actions and arguments, neither use their own nor hearken to other people's reason any further than it suits their humour, interest or party; and these, one may observe, commonly content themselves with words which have no distinct ideas to them, though in other matters that they come with an unbiased indifference to they want not abilities to talk and hear reason, where they have no secret inclination that hinders them from being tractable to it.

(iii) The third sort is of those who readily and sincerely follow reason but, for want of having that which one may call large, sound, roundabout sense, have not a full view of all that relates to the question and may be of moment to decide it. We are all shortsighted and very often see but one side of a matter; our views are not extended to all that has a connection with it. From this defect I think no man is free. We see but in part and we know but in part, and therefore it is no wonder we conclude not right from our partial views. This might instruct the proudest esteemer of his own parts how useful it is to talk and consult with others, even such as came short of him in capacity, quickness and penetration; for since no one sees all and we generally have different prospects of the same thing according to our different, as I may say, positions to it, it is not incongruous to think nor beneath any man to try whether another may not have notions of things which have escaped him and which his reason would make use of if they came into his mind. The faculty of reasoning seldom or never deceives those who trust to it; its consequences from what it builds on are evident and certain; but that which it oftenest, if not only, misleads us in is that the principles from which we conclude, the grounds upon which we bottom our reasoning are but a part; something is left out which should go into the reckoning to make it just and exact.

In this we may see the reason why some men of study and thought that reason right and are lovers of truth do make no great advances in their discoveries of it.

Error and truth are uncertainly blended in their minds; their decisions are lame and defective, and they are very often mistaken in their judgments; the reason whereof is, they converse but with one sort of men, they read but one sort of books, they will not come in the hearing but of one sort of notions; the truth is, they canton out to themselves a little Goshen in the intellectual world where light shines and, as they conclude, day blesses them; but the rest of that vast expansion they give up to night and darkness and so avoid coming near it.

Of practice and habits. We are born with faculties and powers capable almost of anything, such at least as would carry us further than can be easily imagined; but it is only the exercise of those powers which gives us ability and skill in anything and leads us towards perfection.

A middle-aged ploughman will scarce ever be brought to the carriage and language of a gentleman, though his body be as well proportioned and his joints as supple and his natural parts not any way inferior. The legs of a dancing-master and the fingers of a musician fall as it were naturally without thought or pains into regular and admirable motions. Bid them change their parts, and they will in vain endeavor to produce like motions in the members not used to them, and it will require length of time and long practice to attain but some degrees of a like ability.

What incredible and astonishing actions do we find rope-dancers and tumblers bring their bodies toÑnot but that sundry in almost all manual arts are as wonderful, but I name those which the world takes notice of for such, because on that very account they give money to see them. All these admired motions beyond the reach and almost the conception of unpracticed spectators are nothing but the mere effects of use and industry in men whose bodies have nothing peculiar in them from those of the amazed lookers on.

As it is in the body, so it is in the mind; practice makes it what it is, and most even of those excellences which are looked on as natural endowments will be found, when examined into more narrowly, to be the product of exercise and to be raised to that pitch only by repeated actions. Some men are remarked for pleasantness in raillery, others for apologues and apposite diverting stories. This is apt to be taken for the effect of pure nature, and that the rather, because it is not got by rules, and those who excel in either of them never purposely set themselves to the study of it as an art to be learnt. But yet it is true that at first some lucky hit, which took with somebody and gained him commendation, encouraged him to try again, inclined his thoughts and endeavours that way, till at last he insensibly got a facility in it without perceiving how, and that is attributed wholly to nature which was much more the effect of use and practice.

Many a good poetic vein is buried under a trade and never produces anything for want of improvement. We see the ways of discourse and reasoning are very different, even concerning the same matter, at Court and in the university. And he that will go but from Westminster Hall to the Exchange will find a different genius and turn in their ways of talking, and yet one cannot think that all whose lot fell in the City were born with different parts from those who were bred at the university or Inns of Court.

To what purpose all this but to show that the difference so observable in men's understandings and parts does not arise so much from their natural faculties as acquired habits. He would be laughed at that should go about to make a fine dancer out of a country hedger at past fifty; and he will not have much better success who shall endeavor at that age to make a man reason well or speak handsomely who has never been used to it, though you should lay before him a collection of all the best precepts of logic or orators.

Nobody is made anything by hearing of rules or laying them up in his memory; practice must settle the habit of doing without reflecting on the rule, and you may as well hope to make a good painter or musician extempore by a lecture and instruction in the arts of music and painting as a coherent thinker or strict reasoner be a set of rules showing him wherein right reasoning consists.

This being so, that defects and weaknesses in men's understandings, as well as other faculties, come from want of a right use of their own minds, I am apt to think the fault is generally mislaid upon nature and there is often a complaint of w ant of parts when the fault lies in want of a due improvement of them. We see men frequently dexterous and sharp enough in making a bargain Who, if you reason with them about matters of religion, appear perfectly stupid.

Ideas. I will not here, in what relates to the right conduct and improvement of the understanding, repeat again the getting clear and determined ideas and the employing our thoughts rather about them than about sounds put for them, nor of settling the signification of words which we use with ourselves in the search of truth or Pith others in discoursing about it. Those hindrances of our understandings in the pursuit of knowledge I have sufficiently enlarged upon in another place, so that nothing more needs here to be said of those matters.

Principles. There is another fault that stops or misleads men in their knowledge, Which I have also spoken something of but yet is necessary to mention here again, that we may examine it to the bottom and see the root it springs from, and that is a custom of taking up with principles that are not self-evident and very often not so much true. It is not unusual to see men rest their opinions upon foundations that have no more certainty nor solidity than the propositions built on them and embraced for their sake.

Such foundations are these and the like, viz.: the founders or leaders of my party are good men and therefore their tenets are true; it is the opinion of a sect that is erroneous, therefore it is false; it has been long received in the world, therefore it is true; or it is new, and therefore false.

These and mans the like, which are by no means the measures of truth and falsehood, the generality of men make the standards by which they accustom their understanding to judge. And thus they falling into a habit of determining of truth and falsehood by such wrong measures, it is no wonder they should embrace error for certainty and be very positive in things they have no ground for.

There is not any Who pretends to the least reason but, when any of these his false maxims are brought to the test, must acknowledge them to be fallible and such as he will not allow in those that differ from him; and yet after he is convinced of this you shall see him go on in the use of them and the very next occasion that offers argue again upon the same grounds. Would one not be ready to think that men are willing to impose upon themselves and mislead their own understanding who conduct them by such wrong measures even after they see they cannot be relied on? But yet they will not appear so blameable as may be thought at first sight; for I think there are a great many that argue thus in earnest and do it not to impose on themselves or others. They are persuaded of what they say and think there is weight in it, though in a like case they have been convinced there is none; but men would be intolerable to themselves and contemptible to others, if they should embrace opinions without any ground and hold what they could give no manner of reason for.

True or false, solid or sandy, the mind must have some foundation to rest itself upon, and, as I have remarked in another place, it no sooner entertains any proposition but it presently hastens to some hypothesis to bottom it on; till then it is unquiet and unsettled. So much do our own very tempers dispose us to a right use of our understandings, if we would follow as we should the inclinations of our nature.

In some matters of concernment, especially those of religion, men are not permitted to be always wavering and uncertain; they must embrace and profess some tenets or other; and it would be a shame, nay a contradiction, too heavy for anyone's mind to lie constantly under, for him to pretend seriously to be persuaded of the truth of any religion and yet not to be able to give any reason of one's belief or to say anything for his preference of this to any other opinion.

Nay, the most of men are so wholly strangers to this, that they do not so much as perceive their leant of it. They dispatch the ordinary business of their callings by rote, as we say, as they have learnt it, and if at any time they miss success, they impute it to anything rather than want of thought or skill; that they conclude (because they know no better) they have in perfection. Or if there be any subject that interest or fancy has recommended to their thoughts, their reasoning about it is still after their own fashion; be it better or worse, it serves their turns and is the best they are acquainted with; and therefore when they are led by it into mistakes and their business succeeds accordingly, they impute it to any cross accident or default of others rather than to their own want of understanding; that is what nobody discovers or complains of in himself.

Whatsoever made his business to miscarry, it leas not want of right thought and judgment in himself; he sees no such defect in himself, but is satisfied that he carries on his designs well enough by his own reasoning, or at least should have done, had it not been for unlucky traverses not in his power. Thus being content with this short and very imperfect use of his understanding, he never troubles himself to seek out methods of improving his mind, and lives all his life without any notion of close reasoning in a continued connection of a long train of consequences from sure foundations, such as is requisite for the making out and clearing most of the speculative truths most men own to believe and are most concerned in.

Not to mention here what I shall have occasion to insist on by and by more fully, viz., that in many cases it is not one series of consequences will serve the turn, but manor different and opposite deductions must be examined and laid together before a man can come to make a right judgment of the point in question. What then can be expected from men that neither see the want of any such kind of reasoning as this nor, if they do, know they how to set about it or could perform it? You may as well set a countryman who scarce knows the figures and never cast up a sum of three particulars to state a merchant's long account and find the true balance of it.

What then should be done in the case? I answer, we should always remember what I said above, that the faculties of our souls are improved and made useful to us just after the same manner as our bodies are. Would you have a man write or paint, dance or fence well, or perform any other manual operation dexterously and with ease, let him have never so much vigor and activity, suppleness and address naturally, yet nobody expects this from him unless he has been used to it and has employed time and pains in fashioning and forming his hand or outward parts to these motions.

Just so it is in the mind; would you have a man reason well, you must use him to it betimes, exercise his mind in observing the connection of ideas and following them in train. Nothing does this better than mathematics, which therefore I think should be taught all those who have the time and opportunity, not so much to make them mathematicians as to make them reasonable creatures; for though we all call ourselves so, because we are born to it if we please, yet we may truly say nature gives us but the seeds of it; we are born to be, if is e please, rational creatures, but it is use and exercise only that makes us so, and we are indeed so no further than industry and application has carried us. And therefore in ways of reasoning which men have not been used to, he that will observe the conclusions they take up must be satisfied they are not all rational.

This has been the less taken notice of, because everyone in his private affairs uses some sort of reasoning or other, enough to denominate him reasonable. But the mistake is that he that is found reasonable in one thing is concluded to be so in all, and to think or say otherwise is thought so unjust an affront and so senseless a censure that nobody ventures to do it. It looks like the degradation of a man below the dignity of his nature. It is true, that he that reasons well in any one thing has a mind naturally capable of reasoning well in others, and to the same degree of strength and clearness, and possibly much greater, had his understanding been so employed. But it is as true that he who can reason well today about one sort of matters cannot at all reason today about others, though perhaps a year hence he may. But wherever a man's rational faculty fails him and will not serve him to reason, there we cannot say he is rational, how capable however he may be by time and exercise to become so.

Try in men of holy and mean education, who have never elevated their thoughts above the spade and the plough nor looked beyond the ordinary drudgery of a day-laborer. Take the thoughts of such an one, used for many years to one tract, out of that narrow compass he has been all his life confined to, you will find him no more capable of reasoning than almost a perfect natural. Some one or two rules on which their conclusions immediately depend you will find in most men have governed all their thoughts; these, true or false, have been the maxims they have been guided by.

Take these from them, and they are perfectly at a loss, their compass and polestar then are gone and their understanding is perfectly at a nonplus; and therefore they either immediately return to their old maxims again as the foundations of all truth to them, notwithstanding all that can be said to show their weakness, or, if they give them up to their reasons, they with them give up all truth and further enquiry and think there is no such thing as certainty. For if you would enlarge their thoughts and settle them upon more remote and surer principles, they either cannot easily apprehend them, or, if they can, know not what use to make of them; for long deductions from remote principles is what they have not been used to and cannot manage.

What then, can grown men never be improved or enlarged in their understandings? I say not so, but this I think I may say, that it will not be done without industry and application, which will require more time and pains than grown men, settled in their course of life, will allow to it, and therefore very seldom is done. And this very capacity of attaining it by use and exercise only brings us back to that which I laid down before, that it is only practice that improves our minds as w ell as bodies, and we must expect nothing from our understandings any further than they are perfected by habits.

The Americans are not all born with worse understandings than the Europeans, though eve see none of them have such reaches in the arts and sciences. And among the children of a poor countryman the lucky chance of education and getting into the world gives one infinitely the superiority in parts over the rest, who, continuing at home, had continued also just of the same size with his brethren.

He that has to do with young scholars, especially in mathematics, may perceive how their minds open by degrees, and how it is exercise alone that opens them. Sometimes they would stick a long time at a part of a demonstration, not for want of will or application, but really for want of perceiving the connection of two ideas that, to one whose understanding is more exercised, is as visible as anything can be. The same would be with a grown man beginning to study mathematics; the understanding, for want of use, often sticks in very plain way, and he himself that is so puzzled, when he comes to see the connection, wonders what it was he stuck at in a case so plain.

Mathematics. I have mentioned mathematics as a way to settle in the mind a habit of reasoning closely and in train; not that I think it necessary that all men should be deep mathematicians, but that having got the way of reasoning, which that study necessarily brings the mind to, they might be able to transfer it to other parts of knowledge as they shall have occasion. For in all sorts of reasoning every single argument should be managed as a mathematical demonstration; the connection and dependence of ideas should be followed till the mind is brought to the source on which it bottoms and observes the coherence all along, though in proofs of probability one such train is not enough to settle the judgment as in demonstrative knowledge.

Where a truth is made out by one demonstration, there needs no further enquiry; but in probabilities, where there wants demonstration to establish the truth beyond doubt, there it is not enough to trace one argument to its source and observe its strength and weakness, but all the arguments, after having been so examined on both sides, must be laid in balance one against another, and upon the whole the understanding determine its assent.

This is a way of reasoning the understanding should be accustomed to, which is so different from what the illiterate are used to that even learned men oftentimes seem to have very little or no notion of it. Nor is it to be wondered, since the way of disputing in the schools leads them quite away from it by insisting on one topical argument, by the success of which the truth or falsehood of the question is to be determined and victory adjudged to the opponent or defendant; which is all one as if one should balance an account by one sum charged and discharged, when there are a hundred others to be taken into consideration.

This therefore it would be well if men's minds were accustomed to, and that early, that they might not erect their opinions upon one single view, when so many other are requisite to make up the account and must come into the reckoning before a man can form a right judgment. This would enlarge their minds and give a due freedom to their understandings, that they might not be led into error by presumption, laziness or precipitancy; for I think nobody can approve such a conduct of the understanding as should mislead it from truth, though it be never so much in fashion to make use of it.

Religion. Besides his particular calling for the support of his life, everyone has a concern in a future life which he is bound to look after. This engages his thoughts in religion; and here it mightily lies upon him to understand and reason right. Men therefore cannot be excused from understanding the words and framing the general notions relating to religion right.

The one day of seven, besides other days of rest, allows in the Christian world time enough for this if they would but make use of these vacancies from their daily labour and apply themselves to an improvement of knowledge with as much diligence as they often do to a great many other things that are useless, and had but those that would enter them according to their several capacities in a right way to this knowledge.

The original make of their minds is like that of other men, and they would be found not to want understanding fit to receive the knowledge of religion, if they were a little encouraged and helped in it as they should be. For there are instances of very mean people who have raised their minds to a great sense and understanding of religion. And though these have not been so frequent as could be wished, yet they are enough to clear that condition of life from a necessity of gross ignorance and to show that more might be brought to be rational creatures and Christians if due care were taken of them. For, if I mistake not, the peasantry lately in France of the reformed religion understood it much better and could say more for it than those of a higher condition among us.

But if it shall be concluded that the meaner sort of people must give themselves up to a brutish stupidity in the things of their nearest concernment, which I see no reason for, this excuses not those of a freer fortune and education, if they neglect their understandings and take no care to employ them as they ought and set them right in the knowledge of those things for which principally they were given them.

At least those whose plentiful fortunes allow them the opportunities and helps of improvements are not so few but that it might be hoped great advancements might be made in knowledge of all kinds, especially in that of the greatest concern and largest views, if men would make a right use of their faculties and study their own understandings.

Ideas. Outward corporeal objects that constantly importune our senses and captivate our appetites fail not to fill our heads with lively and lasting ideas of that kind. Here the mind needs not be set upon getting greater store; they offer themselves fast enough and are usually entertained in such plenty and lodged so carefully, that the mind wants room or attention for others that it has more use and need of.

To fit the understanding therefore for such reasoning as I have been above speaking of, care should be taken to fill it with moral and more abstract ideas; for these not offering themselves to the senses, but being to be framed to the understanding, people are generally so neglectful of a faculty they are apt to think wants nothing, that I fear most men's minds are more unfurnished with such ideas than is imagined. They often use the words, and how can they be suspected to want the ideas? What I have said in the third book of my essay will excuse me from any other answer to this question. But to convince people of what moment it is to their understandings to be furnished with such abstract ideas steady and settled in it, give me leave to ask how anyone shall be able to know whether he be obliged to be just, if he has not established ideas in his mind of obligation and of justice, since knowledge consists in nothing but the perceived agreement or disagreement of those ideas; and so of all others the like which concern our lives and manners.

And if men do find a difficulty to see the agreement or disagreement of two angles which lie before their eyes, unalterable in a diagram, how utterly impossible will it be to perceive it in ideas that have no other sensible objects to represent them to the mind but sounds, with which they have no manner of conformity and therefore had need to be clearly settled in the mind themselves if we would make any clear judgment about them. This, therefore, is one of the first things the mind should be employed about in the right conduct of the understanding, without which it is impossible it should be capable of reasoning right about those matters. But in these and all other ideas care must be taken that they harbor no inconsistencies, and that they have a real existence where real existence is supposed and are not mere chimeras with a supposed existence.

Prejudice. Everyone is forward to complain of the prejudices that mislead other men or parties, as if he were free and had none of his own. This being objected on all sides, it is agreed that it is a fault and a hindrance to knowledge. What now is the cure? No other but this, that every man should let alone others' prejudices and examine his own. Nobody is convinced of his by the accusation of another; he recriminates by the same rule and is clear.

The only way to remove this great cause of ignorance and error out of the world is for everyone impartially to examine himself. If others will not deal fairly faith their own minds, does that make my errors truths, or ought it to make me in love with them and willing to impose on myself? If others love cataracts on their eyes, should that hinder me from couching of mine as soon as I could? Everyone declares against blindness, and yet who almost is not fond of that which dims his sight and keeps the clear light out of his mind, which should lead him into truth and knowledge? False or doubtful positions, relied upon as unquestionable maxims, keep those in the dark from truth who build on them.

Such are usually the prejudices imbibed from education, party, reverence, fashion, interest, etc. This is the mote which everyone sees in his brother's eye, but never regards the beam in his own. For who is there almost that is ever brought fairly to examine his own principles and see whether they are such as will bear the trial? But yet this should be one of the first things everyone should set about and be scrupulous in, who would rightly conduct his understanding in the search of truth and knowledge.

Indifferency. First, he must not be in love with any opinion or wish it to be true till he knows it to be so, and then he will not need to wish it. For nothing that is false can deserve our good wishes nor a desire that it should have the place and force of truth; and yet nothing is more frequent than this. Often are fond of certain tenets upon no other evidence but respect and custom, and think they must maintain them or all is gone, though they have never examined the ground they stand on, nor have ever made them out to themselves or can make them out to others. We should contend earnestly for the truth, but we should first be sure that it is truth, or else we fight against God, who is the God of truth, and do the work of the devil, who is the father and propagator of lies; and our zeal, though never so warm, will not excuse us; for this is plainly prejudice.

Examine. Secondly, he must do that which he will find himself very averse to, as judging the thing unnecessary or himself incapable of doing it. He must try whether his principles be certainly true or not; and how far he may safely rely upon them. This, whether fewer have the heart or the skill to do, I shall not determine; but this I am sure, this is that which everyone ought to do who professes to love truth and would not impose upon himself which is a surer way to be made a fool of than by being exposed to the sophistry of others.

The disposition to put any cheat upon ourselves works constantly and we are pleased with it, but are impatient of being bantered or misled by others. The inability I here speak of is not any natural defect that makes men incapable of examining their own principles. To such, rules of conducting their understandings are useless, and that is the case of very few.

The great number is of those whom the ill habit of never exerting their thoughts has disabled; the powers of their minds are starved by disuse and have lost that reach and strength which nature fitted them to receive from exercise. Those who are in a condition to learn the first rules of plain arithmetic and could be brought to cast up an ordinary sum are capable of this, if they had but accustomed their minds to reasoning; but they that have wholly neglected the exercise of their understandings in this way will be very far at first from being able to do it and as unfit for it as one unpracticed in figures to cast up a shop-book, and perhaps think it as strange to be set about it.

And yet it must nevertheless be confessed to be a wrong use of our understandings to build our tenets upon principles that may lead us into error. We take our principles at haphazard upon trust and without ever having examined them, and then believe a whole system upon a presumption that they are true and solid. And what is all this but childish, shameful, senseless credulity?

In these two things, viz., an equal indifference for all truth and in the examination of our principles and not receiving any for such nor building on them till we are fully convinced, as rational creatures, of their solidity, truth and certainty, consists that freedom of the understanding which is necessary to a rational creature and without which it is not truly an understanding. It is conceit, fancy, extravagance, anything rather than understanding, if it must be under the constraint of receiving and holding opinions by the authority of anything but their own, not fancied but perceived, evidence. This was rightly called imposition, and is of all other the worst and most dangerous sort of it. For we impose upon ourselves, which is the strongest imposition of all others, and we impose upon ourselves in that part which ought with the greatest care to be kept free from all imposition.

The world is apt to cast great blame on those who have an indifferency for opinions, especially in religion. I fear this is the foundation of great error and worse consequences. To be indifferent which of two opinions is true is the right temper of the mind that preserves it from being imposed on and disposes it to examine with that indifference till it has done its best to find the truth;and this is the only direct and safe way to it. But to be indifferent whether we embrace falsehood for truth or no is the great road to error. Those who are not indifferent which opinion is true are guilty of this; they suppose, without examining, that what they hold is true and then think they ought to be zealous for it. Those, it is plain by their warmth and eagerness, are not indifferent for their own opinions, but methinks are very indifferent whether they be true or false, since they cannot endure to have any doubts raised or objections made against them; and it is visible they never have made any themselves, and so, never having examined them, know not nor are concerned, as they should be, to know whether they be true or false.

These are the common and most general miscarriages which I think men should avoid or rectify in a right conduct of their understandings, and should be particularly taken care of in education.

The business whereof in respect of knowledge is not, as I think, to perfect a learner in all or any one of the sciences, but to give his mínd that freedom, that disposition and those habits that may enable him to attain any part of knowledge he shall apply himself to or stand in need of in the future course of his life. This and this only is well principling, and not the instilling a reverence and veneration for certain dogmas under the specious title of principles, which are often so remote from that truth and evidence which belongs to principles, that they ought to be rejected as false and erroneous; and is often the cause to men so educated, when they come abroad into the world and find they cannot maintain the principles so taken up and rested in, to cast off all principles and turn perfect skeptics, regardless of knowledge and virtue.

There are several weaknesses and defects in the understanding, either from the natural temper of the mind or ill habits taken up, which hinder it in its progress to knowledge. Of these there are as many possibly to be found, if the mind were thoroughly studied, as there are diseases of the body, each whereof clogs and disables the understanding to some degree and therefore deserves to be looked after and cured. I shall set down some few to excite men, especially those who make knowledge their business, to look into themselves and observe whether they do not indulge some weakness, allow some miscarriages in the management of their intellectual faculty, which is prejudicial to them in the search for truth.

Observation. Particular matters of fact are the undoubted foundations on which our civil and natural knowledge is built; the benefit the understanding makes of them is to draw from them conclusions which may be as standing rules of knowledge and consequently of practice. The mind often makes not that benefit it should of the information it receives from the accounts of civil or natural historians, in being too forward or too slow in making observations on the particular facts recorded in them.

There are those who are very assiduous in reading and yet do not much advance their knowledge by it. They are delighted with the stories that are told and perhaps can tell them again, for they make all they read nothing but history to themselves; but not reflecting on it, not making to themselves observations from what they read, they are very little improved by all that crowd of particulars that either pass through or lodge themselves in their understandings. They dream on in a constant course of reading and cramming themselves; but, not digesting anything, it produces nothing but a heap of crudities.

If their memories retain well, one may say they have the materials of knowledge, but, like those for building, they are of no advantage if there be no other use made of them but to let them lie heaped up together. Opposite to these there are others who lose the improvement they should make of matters of fact by a quite contrary conduct. They are apt to draw general conclusions and raise axioms from every particular they meet with.

These make as little true benefit of history as the other, nay, being of forward and active spirits receive more harm by it; it being of worse consequence to steer one's thoughts by a wrong rule than to have none at all, error doing to busy men much more harm than ignorance to the slow and sluggish. Between these, those seem to do best who, taking material and useful hints, sometimes from single matters of fact, carry them in their minds to be judged of by what they shall find in history to confirm or reverse these imperfect observations; which may be established into rules fit to be relied on when they are justified by a sufficient and wary induction of particulars. He that makes no such reflections on what he reads only loads his mind with a rhapsody of tales fit in winter nights for the entertainment of others; and he that will improve every matter of fact into a maxim will abound in contrary observations that can be of no other use but to perplex and pudder him if he compares them; or else to misguide him, if he gives himself up to the authority of that which, for its novelty or for some other fancy, best pleases him.

Bias. Next to these we may place those who suffer their own natural tempers and passions they are possessed with to influence their judgments, especially of men and things that may any way relate to their present circumstances and interest. Truth is all simple, all pure, will bear no mixture of anything else with it. It is rigid and inflexible to any by-interests; and so should the understanding be, whose use and excellency lies in conforming itself to it.

To think of everything just as it is in itself is the proper business of the understanding, though it be not that which men always employ it to. This all men, at first hearing, allow is the right use everyone should make of his understanding. Nobody will be at such an open defiance with common sense as to profess that we should not endeavor to know and think of things as they are in themselves, and yet there is nothing more frequent than to do the contrary; and men are apt to excuse themselves, and think they have reason to do so, if they have but a pretense that it is for God or a good cause, that is, in effect, for themselves, their own persuasion or party; for those in their turns the several sects of men, especially in matters of religion, entitle God and a good cause.

But God requires not men to wrong or misuse their faculties for him, nor to lie to others or themselves for his sake; which they purposely do who will not suffer their understandings to have right conceptions of the things proposed to them and designedly restrain themselves from having just thoughts of everything, as far as they are concerned to enquire. And as for a good cause, that needs not such ill helps; if it be good, truth will support it and it has no need of fallacy or falsehood.

Arguments. Very much of kin to this is the hunting after arguments to make good one side of a question and wholly to neglect and refuse those which favor the other side. What is this but wailfully to misguide the understanding, espouse opinions that best comport with their porter, profit or credit and then seek arguments to support them? Truth lighted upon this way is of no more avail to us than error; for what is so taken up by us may be false as well as true, and he has not done his duty who has thus stumbled upon truth in his way to preferment.

There is another but more innocent way of collecting arguments, very familiar among bookish men, which is to furnish themselves with the arguments they meet with pro and con in the questions they study. This helps them not to judge right nor argue strongly, but only to talk copiously on either side, without being steady and settled in their own judgments; for such arguments gathered from other men's thoughts, floating only in the memory, are there ready indeed to supply copious talk with some appearance of reason, but are far from helping us to judge right. Such variety of arguments only distract the understanding that relies on them, unless it has gone further than such a superficial way of examining; this is to quit truth for appearance, only to serve our vanity.

The sure and only way to get true knowledge is to form in our minds clear settled notions of things, with names annexed to those determined ideas. These we are to consider, and with their several relations and habitudes, and not to amuse ourselves with floating names and words of indetermined signification, which we can use in several senses to serve a turn. It is in the perception of the habitudes and respects our ideas have one to another that real knowledge consists; and when a man once perceives how far they agree or disagree one with another, he will be able to judge of what other people say and will not need to be led by the arguments of others, which are many of them nothing but plausible sophistry. This will teach him to state the question right and see whereon it turns; and thus he will stand upon his own legs and know by his own understanding. Whereas by collecting and learning arguments by heart he will be but a retainer to others; and when anyone questions the foundations they are built upon, he will be at a nonplus and be fain to give up his implicit knowledge.

Haste. Labour for labour sake is against nature. The understanding, as well as all the other faculties, chooses always the shortest way to its end, would presently obtain the knowledge it is about and then set upon some new enquiry. But this whether laziness or haste often misleads it and makes it content itself with improper ways of search and such as will not serve the turn. Sometimes it rests upon testimony, when testimony of right has nothing to do, because it is easier to believe than to be scientifically instructed. Sometimes it contents itself with one argument and rests satisfied with that, as it were a demonstration; whereas the thing under proof is not capable of demonstration and therefore must be submitted to the trial of probabilities, and all the material arguments pro and con be examined and brought to a balance.

In some cases the mind is determined by probable topics in enquiries where demonstration may be had. All these and several others, which laziness, impatience, custom and want of use and attention lead men into, are misapplications of the understanding in the search of truth. In every question the nature and manner of the proof it is capable of should first be considered to make our enquiry such as it should be. This would save a great deal of frequently misemployed pains and lead us sooner to that discovery and possession of truth we are capable of.

The multiplying variety of arguments, especially frivolous ones, such as are all that are merely verbal, is not only lost labour, but Numbers the memory to no purpose and serves only to hinder it from seizing and holding of the truth in all those cases which are capable of demonstration. In such a way of proof the truth and certainty is seen and the mind fully possesses itself of it; when in the other way of assent it only hovers about it, is amused with uncertainties.

In this superficial way indeed the mind is capable of more variety of plausible talk, but is not enlarged as it should be in its knowledge. It is to this same haste and impatience of the mind also that a not due tracing of the arguments to their true foundation is owing; men see a little, presume a great deal, and so jump to the conclusion. This is a short way to fancy and conceit and to opiniatrety, but is certainly the furthest way about to knowledge. For he that will know must, by the connection of the proofs, see the truth and the ground it stands on; and therefore, if he has for haste skipped over what he should have examined, he must begin and go over all again, or else he will never come to knowledge.

Reading. This is that which I think great readers are apt to be mistaken in. Those who have read of everything are thought to understand everything too; but it is not always so. Reading furnishes the mind only with materials of knowledge; it is thinking makes what we read ours. We are of the ruminating kind, and it is not enough to cram ourselves with a great load of collections; unless we chew them over again, they will not give us strength and nourishment.

There are indeed in some writers risible instances of deep thought, close and acute reasoning and ideas well pursued. The light these would give would be of great use, if their readers would observe and imitate them; all the rest at best are but particulars fit to be turned into knowledge; but that can be done only by our own meditation and examining the reach, force and coherence of what is said; and then, as far as we apprehend and see the connection of ideas, so far it is ours; without that it is but so much loose matter floating in our brain.

The memory may be stored, but the judgment is little better and the stock of knowledge not increased by being able to repeat what others have said or produce the arguments we have found in them. Such a knowledge as this is but knowledge by hearsay, and the ostentation of it is at best but talking by rote, and very often upon weak and wrong principles. For all that is to be found in books is not built upon true foundations nor always rightly deduced from the principles it is pretended to be built on. Such an examen as is requisite to discover that, every reader's mind is not forward to make, especially in those who have given themselves up to a party and only hunt for what they can scrape together that may favor and support the tenets of it. Such men willfully exclude themselves from truth and from all true benefit to be received by reading. Others of more indifference often want attention and industry.

The mind is backward in itself to be at the pains to trace every argument to its original and to see upon what basis it stands and how firmly; but yet it is this that gives so much the advantage to one man more than another in reading. The mind should by severe rules be tied down to this at first uneasy task; use and exercise will give it facility, so that those who are accustomed to it, readily, as it were with one cast of the eye, take a view of the argument and presently in most cases see where it bottoms. Those who have got this faculty, one may say, have got the true key of books and the clue to lead them through the maze of variety of opinions and authors to truth and certainty. This young beginners should be entered in and showed the use of, that they might profit by their reading. Those who are strangers to it still be apt to think it too great a clog in the way of men's studies, and they will suspect they shall make but small progress if, in the books they read, they must stand to examine and unravel every argument and follow it step by step up to its original.

Practice. Though the faculties of the mind are improved by exercise, yet they must not be put to a stress beyond their strength. Quid valeant humeri, quid ferre recusent must be made the measure of everyone's understanding who has a desire not only to perform well but to keep up the vigor of his faculties and not to balk his understanding by what is too hard for it. The mind, by being engaged in a task beyond its strength, like the body strained by lifting at a weight too heavy, has often its force broken and thereby gets an ineptness or an aversion to any vigorous attempt ever after.

A sinew cracked seldom recovers its former strength, or at least the tenderness of the sprain remains a good while after and the memory of it longer, and leaves a lasting caution in the man not to put the part quickly again to any robust employment. So it fares in the mind once jaded by an attempt above its power; it either is disabled for the future or else checks at any vigorous undertaking ever after, at least is very hardly brought to exert its force again on any subject that requires thought and meditation.

The understanding should be brought to the difficult and knotty parts of knowledge, that try the strength of thought, and a full bent of the mind by insensible degrees; and in such a gradual proceeding nothing is too hard for it. Nor let it be objected that such a slow progress will never reach the extent of some sciences. It is not to be imagined how far constancy will carry a man; however, it is better walking slowly in a rugged way than to break a leg and be a cripple. He that begins with the calf may carry the ox; but he that will at first go to take up an ox may so disable himself as not be able to lift a calf after that.

When the mind by insensible degrees has brought itself to attention and close thinking, it will be able to cope with difficulties and master them without any prejudice to itself, and then it may go on roundly. Every abstruse problem, every intricate question will not baffle, discourage or break it. But though putting the mind unprepared upon an unusual stress that may discourage or damp it for the future ought to be avoided, yet this must not run it, by an over great shyness of difficulties, into a lazy sauntering about ordinary and obvious things that demand no thought or application.

This debases and enervates the understanding, makes it weak and unfit for labour. This is a sort of hovering about the surface of things without any insight into them or penetration; and when the mind has been once habituated to this lazy recumbency and satisfaction on the obvious surface of things, it is in danger to rest satisfied there and go no deeper, since it cannot do it without pains and digging. He that has for some time accustomed himself to take up with what easily offers itself at first view, has reason to fear he shall never reconcile himself to the fatigue of turning and tumbling things in his mind to discover their more retired and more valuable secrets.

It is not strange that methods of learning which scholars have been accustomed to in their beginning and entrance upon the sciences should influence them all their lives and be settled in their minds by an over-ruling reverence, especially if they be such as universal use has established. Learners must at first be believers, and, their master's rules having once been made axioms to them, it is no wonder they should keep that dignity and by the authority they have once got mislead those who think it sufficient to excuse them if they go out of their way in a well beaten tract.

Transferring of thoughts. There is scarce anything more for the improvement of knowledge, for the ease of life and the dispatch of business than for a man to be able to dispose of his own thoughts; and there is scarce anything harder in the whole conduct of the understanding than to get a full mastery over it. The mind in a waking man has always some object that it applies itself to, which, when we are lazier or unconcerned, we can easily change and at pleasure transfer our thoughts to another, and from thence to a third which has no relation to either of the former. Hence men forwardly conclude and frequently say, nothing is so free as thought; and it were well it were so; but the contrary will be found true in several instances; and there are many cases wherein there is nothing more resty and ungovernable than our thoughts; they will not be directed is hat objects to pursue nor be taken off from those they have once fixed on, but run away with a man in pursuit of those ideas they have in view, let him do what he can.

I will not here mention again what I have above taken notice of, how hard it is to get the mind, narrowed by a custom of thirty or forty years standing to a scant: collection of obvious and common ideas, to enlarge itself to a more copious stock and grow into an acquaintance with those that would afford more abundant matter of useful contemplation; it is not of this I am here speaking. The inconvenience I would here represent and find a remedy for is the difficulty there is sometimes to transfer our minds from one subject to another in cases where the ideas are equally familiar to us.

Matters that are recommended to our thoughts by any of our passions take possession of our minds with a kind of authority and will not be kept out or dislodged, but, as if the passion that rules were for the time the sheriff of the place and came with all the posse, the understanding is seized and taken with the object it introduces, as if it had a legal right to be alone considered there. There is scarce anybody, I think, of so calm a temper Who has not some time found this tyranny on his understanding and suffered under the inconvenience of it. who is there almost whose mind at some time or another love or anger, fear or grief has not so fastened to some clog, that it could not turn itself to any other object? I call it a clog, for it hangs upon the mind so as to hinder its vigor and activity in the pursuit of other contemplations, and advances itself little or not all in the knowledge of the thing which it so closely hugs and constantly pores on.

Men thus possessed are sometimes as if they care so in the worst sense and was under the power of an enchantment. They see not what passes before their eyes, hear not the audible discourse of the company; and is hen by any strong application to them they are roused a little, they are like men brought to themselves from some remote region; whereas in truth they come no further than their secret cabinet within, where they have been wholly taken up with the puppet which is for that time appointed for their entertainment.

The shame that such dumps cause to well bred people, when it carries them away from the company where they should bear a part in the conversation, is a sufficient argument that it is a fault in the conduct of our understanding not to have that power over it as to make use of it to those purposes and on those occasions wherein we have need of its assistance. The mind should be always free and ready to turn itself to the variety of objects that occur and allow them as much consideration as shall for that time be thought fit.

To be engrossed so by one object as not to be prevailed on to leave it for another that we judge fitter for our contemplation is to make it of no use to us. Did this state of mind remain always so, everyone would without scruple give it the name of perfect madness; and while it does last, at whatever intervals it returns, such a rotation of thoughts about the same object no more carries us for cards towards the attainment of knowledge than getting upon a mill horse whilst he jogs on in his circular tract would carry a man on a journey

I grant something must be allowed to legitimate passions and to natural inclinations Every man, besides occasional affections, has beloved studies, and those the mind will more closely stick to; but yet it is best that it should be always at liberty and under the free disposal of the man to act how and upon what he directs This we should endeavor to obtain, unless we would be content with such a flaw in our understandings that sometimes we should be as it were without it; for it is very little better than so in cases where we cannot make use of it to those purposes we would and which stand in present need of it

But before fit remedies can be thought on for this disease, we must know the several causes of it and thereby regulate the cure, if we will hope to labour with success

One we hare already instanced in, whereof all men that reflect have so general a knowledge and so often an experience in themselves, that nobody doubts of it A prevailing passion so pins down our thoughts to the object and concern of it, that a man passionately in love cannot bring himself to think of his ordinary affairs, nor a kind mother drooping under the loss of a child is not able to bear a part as she was wont in the discourse of the company or conversation of her friends.

But though passion be the most obvious and general, yet it is not the only cause that binds up the understanding and confines it for the time to one object, from which it w ill not be taken off.

Besides this, we may often find that the understanding, when it has a while employed itself upon a subject which either chance or some slight accident offered to it without the interest or recommendation of any passion, works itself into a warmth and by degrees gets into a career, wherein, like a bowl down a hill, it increases its motion by going and will not be stopped or diverted, though, when the heat is over, it sees all this earnest application was about a trifle not worth a thought and all the pains employed about it lost labour.

There is a third sort, if I mistake not, yet lower than this; it is a sort of childishness, if I may so say, of the understanding, wherein, during the fit, it plays with and dandies some insignificant puppet to no end nor with any design at all, and yet cannot easily be got off from it. Thus some trivial sentence or a scrap of poetry will sometimes get into men's heads and make such a chiming there, that there is no stilling of it, no peace to be obtained nor attention to anything else, but this impertinent guest will take up the mind and possess the thoughts in spite of all endeavors to get rid of it.

Whether everyone has experimented in themselves this troublesome intrusion of some striking ideas which thus importune the understanding and hinder it from being better employed, I know not. But persons of very good parts, and those more than one, I have heard speak and complain of it themselves. The reason I have to make this doubt is from what I have known in a case something of kin to this, though much odder, and that is of a sort of visions that some people have lying quiet but perfectly awake in the dark or with their eyes shut.

It is a great variety of faces, most commonly very odd ones, that appear to them in train one after another, so that, having had just the sight of one, it immediately passes away to give place to another that the same instant succeeds and has as quick an exit as its leader; and so they march on in a constant succession; nor can any one of them by any endeavor be stopped or retained beyond the instant of its appearance, but is thrust out by its follower, which will have its turn.

Concerning this fantastical phenomenon I have talked with several people, whereof some have been perfectly acquainted with it and others have been so wholly strangers to it, that they could hardly be brought to conceive or believe it. I knew a lady of excellent parts who had got past thirty without having ever had the least notice of any such thing. She was so great a stranger to it that, when she heard me and another talking of it, could scarce forbear thinking we bantered her; but some time after, drinking a large dose of dilute tea going to bed, she told us at next meeting that she had now experimented what our discourse had much ado to persuade her of.

She had seen a great variety of faces in a long train succeeding one another, as we had described; they were all strangers and intruders, such as she had no acquaintance with before nor sought after then, and as they came of themselves they went too; none of them stayed a moment nor could be detained by all the endeavors she could use, but went on in their solemn procession, just appeared and then vanished. This odd phenomenon seems to have a mechanical cause, and to depend upon the matter and motion of the blood or animal spirits.

When the fancy is bound by passion, I know no way to set the mind free and at liberty to prosecute what thoughts the man would make choice of, but to allay the present passion or counterbalance it with another, which is an art to be got by study and acquaintance with the passions.

Those as ho find themselves apt to be carried away with the spontaneous current of their own thoughts, not excited by any passion or interest, must be very wary and careful in all the instances of it to stop it and never humour their minds in being thus triflingly busy. Men know the value of their corporal liberty and therefore suffer not willingly fetters and chains to be put upon them.

To have the mind captivated is, for the time, certainly the greater evil of the two and deserves our utmost care and endeavors to preserve the freedom of our better part. And in this case our pains will not be lost; striving and struggling will prevail, if we constantly in all such occasions make use of it. We must never indulge these trivial attentions of thought; as soon as we find the mind makes itself a business of nothing, we should immediately disturb and check it, introduce new and more serious considerations, and not leave till we have beaten it off from the pursuit it was upon. This at first, if we have let the contrary practice grow to a habit, will perhaps be difficult; but constant endeavors will by degrees prevail and at last make it easy.

And when a man is pretty well advanced and can command his mind off at pleasure from incidental and undesigned pursuits, it may not be amiss for him to go on further and make attempts upon meditations of greater moment, that at the last he may have a full power over his own mind, and be so fully master of his own thoughts as to be able to transfer them from one subject to another with the same ease that he can lay by anything he has in his hand and take something else that he has a mind to in the room of it. This liberty of mind is of great use both in business and study, and he that has got it will have no small advantage of ease and dispatch in all that is the chosen and useful employment of his understanding.

The third and last way which I mentioned the mind to be sometimes taken up with seldom happens but w hen the mind is lazy or very loosely and negligently employed. It were better indeed be without such impertinent and useless repetitions; any obvious idea, when it is roving causelessly at a venture, being of more use and apter to suggest something worth consideration than the insignificant buzz of purely empty sounds.

8

Vocational Aspects of Education

At the present time the conflict of philosophic theories focuses in discussion of the proper place and function of vocational factors in education. The bald statement that significant differences in fundamental philosophical conceptions find their chief issue in connection with this point may arouse incredulity: there seems to be too great a gap between the remote and general terms in which philosophic ideas are formulated and the practical and concrete details of vocational education. But a mental review of the intellectual presuppositions underlying the oppositions in education of labor and leisure, theory and practice, body and mind, mental states and the world, will show that they culminate in the antithesis of vocational and cultural education.

Traditionally, liberal culture has been linked to the notions of leisure, purely contemplative knowledge and a spiritual activity not involving the active use of bodily organs. Culture has also tended, latterly, to be associated with a purely private refinement, a cultivation of certain states and attitudes of consciousness, separate from either social direction or service. It has been an escape from the former, and a solace for the necessity of the latter.

So deeply entangled are these philosophic dualisms with the whole subject of vocational education, that it is necessary to define the meaning of vocation with some fullness in order to avoid the impression that an education which centers about it is narrowly practical, if not merely pecuniary. A vocation means nothing but such a direction of life activities as renders them perceptibly significant to a person, because of the consequences they accomplish, and also useful to his associates.

The opposite of a career is neither leisure nor culture, but aimlessness, capriciousness, the absence of cumulative achievement in experience, on the personal side, and idle display, parasitic dependence upon the others, on the social side. Occupation is a concrete term for continuity. It includes the development of artistic capacity of any kind, of special scientific ability, of effective citizenship, as well as professional and business occupations, to say nothing of mechanical labor or engagement in gainful pursuits.

We must avoid not only limitation of conception of vocation to the occupations where immediately tangible commodities are produced, but also the notion that vocations are distributed in an exclusive way, one and only one to each person. Such restricted specialism is impossible; nothing could be more absurd than to try to educate individuals with an eye to only one line of activity. In the first place, each individual has of necessity a variety of callings, in each of which he should be intelligently effective; and in the second place any one occupation loses its meaning and becomes a routine keeping busy at something in the degree in which it is isolated from other interests.

(i) No one is just an artist and nothing else, and in so far as one approximates that condition, he is so much the less developed human being; he is a kind of monstrosity. He must, at some period of his life, be a member of a family; he must have friends and companions; he must either support himself or be supported by others, and thus he has a business career. He is a member of some organised political unit, and so on. We naturally name his vocation from that one of the callings which distinguishes him, rather than from those which he has in common with all others. But we should not allow ourselves to be so subject to words as to ignore and virtually deny his other callings when it comes to a consideration of the vocational phases of education.

(ii) As a man's vocation as artist is but the emphatically specialised phase of his diverse and variegated vocational activities, so his efficiency in it, in the humane sense of efficiency, is determined by its association with other callings. A person must have experience, he must live, if his artistry is to be more than a technical accomplishment. He cannot find the subject matter of his artistic activity within his art; this must be an expression of what he suffers and enjoys in other relationships — a thing which depends in turn upon the alertness and sympathy of his interests. What is true of an artist is true of any other special calling.

There is doubtless — in general accord with the principle of habit — a tendency for every distinctive vocation to become too dominant, too exclusive and absorbing in its specialised aspect. This means emphasis upon skill or technical method at the expense of meaning. Hence it is not the business of education to foster this tendency, but rather to safeguard against it, so that the scientific inquirer shall not be merely the scientist, the teacher merely the pedagogue, the clergyman merely one who wears the cloth, and so on.

Vocational Aims in Education

Bearing in mind the varied and connected content of the vocation, and the broad background upon which a particular calling is projected, we shall now consider education for the more distinctive activity of an individual.

1. An occupation is the only thing which balances the distinctive capacity of an individual with his social service. To find out what one is fitted to do and to secure an opportunity to do it is the key to happiness. Nothing is more tragic than failure to discover one's true business in life, or to find that one has drifted or been forced by circumstance into an uncongenial calling. A right occupation means simply that the aptitudes of a person are in adequate play, working with the minimum of friction and the maximum of satisfaction.

With reference to other members of a community, this adequacy of action signifies, of course, that they are getting the best service the person can render. It is generally believed, for example, that slave labor was ultimately wasteful even from the purely economic point of view — that there was not sufficient stimulus to direct the energies of slaves, and that there was consequent wastage. Moreover, since slaves were confined to certain prescribed callings, much talent must have remained unavailable to the community, and hence there was a dead loss.

Slavery only illustrates on an obvious scale what happens in some degree whenever an individual does not find himself in his work. And he cannot completely find himself when vocations are looked upon with contempt, and a conventional ideal of a culture which is essentially the same for all is maintained. Plato laid down the fundamental principle of a philosophy of education when he asserted that it was the business of education to discover what each person is good for, and to train him to mastery of that mode of excellence, because such development would also secure the fulfillment of social needs in the most harmonious way. His error was not in qualitative principle, but in his limited conception of the scope of vocations socially needed; a limitation of vision which reacted to obscure his perception of the infinite variety of capacities found in different individuals.

2. An occupation is a continuous activity having a purpose. Education through occupations consequently combines within itself more of the factors conducive to learning than any other method. It calls instincts and habits into play; it is a foe to passive receptivity. It has an end in view; results are to be accomplished. Hence it appeals to thought; it demands that an idea of an end be steadily maintained, so that activity cannot be either routine or capricious. Since the movement of activity must be progressive, leading from one stage to another, observation and ingenuity are required at each stage to overcome obstacles and to discover and readapt means of execution. In short, an occupation, pursued under conditions where the realisation of the activity rather than merely the external product is the aim, fulfills the requirements which were laid down earlier in connection with the discussion of aims, interest, and thinking.

A calling is also of necessity an organising principle for information and ideas; for knowledge and intellectual growth. It provides an axis which runs through an immense diversity of detail; it causes different experiences, facts, items of information to fall into order with one another. The lawyer, the physician, the laboratory investigator in some branch of chemistry, the parent, the citizen interested in his own locality, has a constant working stimulus to note and relate whatever has to do with his concern. He unconsciously, from the motivation of his occupation, reaches out for all relevant information, and holds to it.

The vocation acts as both magnet to attract and as glue to hold. Such organisation of knowledge is vital, because it has reference to needs; it is so expressed and readjusted in action that it never becomes stagnant. No classification, no selection and arrangement of facts, which is consciously worked out for purely abstract ends, can ever compare in solidity or effectiveness with that knit under the stress of an occupation; in comparison the former sort is formal, superficial, and cold.

3. The only adequate training for occupations is training through occupations. The principle stated early in this book that the educative process is its own end, and that the only sufficient preparation for later responsibilities comes by making the most of immediately present life, applies in full force to the vocational phases of education. The dominant vocation of all human beings at all times is living — intellectual and moral growth.

In childhood and youth, with their relative freedom from economic stress, this fact is naked and unconcealed. To predetermine some future occupation for which education is to be a strict preparation is to injure the possibilities of present development and thereby to reduce the adequacy of preparation for a future right employment. To repeat the principle we have had occasion to appeal to so often, such training may develop a machine-like skill in routine lines, but it will be at the expense of those qualities of alert observation and coherent and ingenious planning which make an occupation intellectually rewarding.

In an autocratically managed society, it is often a conscious object to prevent the development of freedom and responsibility, a few do the planning and ordering, the others follow directions and are deliberately confined to narrow and prescribed channels of endeavor. However much such a scheme may inure to the prestige and profit of a class, it is evident that it limits the development of the subject class; hardens and confines the opportunities for learning through experience of the master class, and in both ways hampers the life of the society as a whole.

The only alternative is that all the earlier preparation for vocations be indirect rather than direct; namely, through engaging in those active occupations which are indicated by the needs and interests of the pupil at the time. Only in this way can there be on the part of the educator and of the one educated a genuine discovery of personal aptitudes so that the proper choice of a specialised pursuit in later life may be indicated. Moreover, the discovery of capacity and aptitude will be a constant process as long as growth continues. It is a conventional and arbitrary view which assumes that discovery of the work to be chosen for adult life is made once for all at some particular date.

One has discovered in himself, say, an interest, intellectual and social, in the things which have to do with engineering and has decided to make that his calling. At most, this only blocks out in outline the field in which further growth is to be directed. It is a sort of rough sketch for use in direction of further activities. It is the discovery of a profession in the sense in which Columbus discovered America when he touched its shores.

Future explorations of an indefinitely more detailed and extensive sort remain to be made. When educators conceive vocational guidance as something which leads up to a definitive, irretrievable, and complete choice, both education and the chosen vocation are likely to be rigid, hampering further growth. In so far, the calling chosen will be such as to leave the person concerned in a permanently subordinate position, executing the intelligence of others who have a calling which permits more flexible play and readjustment.

And while ordinary usages of language may not justify terming a flexible attitude of readjustment a choice of a new and further calling, it is such in effect. If even adults have to be on the lookout to see that their calling does not shut down on them and fossilise them, educators must certainly be careful that the vocational preparation of youth is such as to engage them in a continuous reorganisation of aims and methods.

Opportunities and Dangers

In the past, education has been much more vocational in fact than in name. *(i)* The education of the masses was distinctly utilitarian. It was called apprenticeship rather than education, or else just learning from experience. The schools devoted themselves to the three R's in the degree in which ability to go through the forms of reading, writing, and figuring were common elements in all kinds of labor. Taking part in some special line of work, under the direction of others, was the out-of-school phase of this education. The two supplemented each other; the school work in its narrow and formal character was as much a part of apprenticeship to a calling as that explicitly so termed.

(ii) To a considerable extent, the education of the dominant classes was essentially vocational — it only happened that their pursuits of ruling and of enjoying were not called professions. For only those things were named vocations or employments which involved manual labor, laboring for a reward in keep, or its commuted money equivalent, or the rendering of personal services to specific persons. For a long time, for example, the profession of the surgeon and physician ranked almost with that of the valet or barber — partly because it had so much to do with the body, and partly because it involved rendering direct service for pay to some definite person.

But if we go behind words, the business of directing social concerns, whether politically or economically, whether in war or peace, is as much a calling as anything else; and where education has not been completely under the thumb of tradition, higher schools in the past have been upon the whole calculated to give preparation for this business. Moreover, display, the adornment of person, the kind of social companionship and entertainment which give prestige, and the spending of money, have been made into definite callings. Unconsciously to themselves the higher institutions of learning have been made to contribute to preparation for these employments. Even at present, what is called higher education is for a certain class mainly preparation for engaging effectively in these pursuits.

In other respects, it is largely, especially in the most advanced work, training for the calling of teaching and special research. By a peculiar superstition, education which has to do chiefly with preparation for the pursuit of conspicuous idleness, for teaching, and for literary callings, and for leadership, has been regarded as non-vocational and even as peculiarly cultural.

The literary training which indirectly fits for authorship, whether of books, newspaper editorials, or magazine articles, is especially subject to this superstition: many a teacher and author writes and argues in behalf of a cultural and humane education against the encroachments of a specialised practical education, without recognising that his own education, which he calls liberal, has been mainly training for his own particular calling. He has simply got into the habit of regarding his own business as essentially cultural and of overlooking the cultural possibilities of other employments. At the bottom of these distinctions is undoubtedly the tradition which recognises as employment only those pursuits where one is responsible for his work to a specific employer, rather than to the ultimate employer, the community.

There are, however, obvious causes for the present conscious emphasis upon vocational education — for the disposition to make explicit and deliberate vocational implications previously tacit.

(i) In the first place, there is an increased esteem, in democratic communities, of whatever has to do with manual labor, commercial occupations, and the rendering of tangible services to society. In theory, men and women are now expected to do something in return for their support — intellectual and economic — by society. Labor is extolled; service is a much-lauded moral ideal. While there is still much admiration and envy of those who can pursue lives of idle conspicuous display, better moral sentiment condemns such lives. Social responsibility for the use of time and personal capacity is more generally recognised than it used to be.

(ii) In the second place, those vocations which are specifically industrial have gained tremendously in importance in the last century and a half. Manufacturing and commerce are no longer domestic and local, and consequently more or less incidental, but are world-wide. They engage the best energies of an increasingly large number of persons. The manufacturer, banker, and captain of industry have practically displaced a hereditary landed gentry as the immediate directors of social affairs.

The problem of social readjustment is openly industrial, having to do with the relations of capital and labor. The great increase in the social importance of conspicuous industrial processes has inevitably brought to the front questions having to do with the relationship of schooling to industrial life. No such vast social readjustment could occur without offering a challenge to an education inherited from different social conditions, and without putting up to education new problems.

(iii) In the third place, there is the fact already repeatedly mentioned: Industry has ceased to be

essentially an empirical, rule-of-thumb procedure, handed down by custom. Its technique is now technological: that is to say, based upon machinery resulting from discoveries in mathematics, physics, chemistry, bacteriology, etc. The economic revolution has stimulated science by setting problems for solution, by producing greater intellectual respect for mechanical appliances. And industry received back payment from science with compound interest. As a consequence, industrial occupations have infinitely greater intellectual content and infinitely larger cultural possibilities than they used to possess.

The demand for such education as will acquaint workers with the scientific and social bases and bearings of their pursuits becomes imperative, since those who are without it inevitably sink to the role of appendages to the machines they operate. Under the old regime all workers in a craft were approximately equals in their knowledge and outlook.

Personal knowledge and ingenuity were developed within at least a narrow range, because work was done with tools under the direct command of the worker. Now the operator has to adjust himself to his machine, instead of his tool to his own purposes. While the intellectual possibilities of industry have multiplied, industrial conditions tend to make industry, for great masses, less of an educative resource than it was in the days of hand production for local markets. The burden of realising the intellectual possibilities inhering in work is thus thrown back on the school.

(iv) In the fourth place, the pursuit of knowledge has become, in science, more experimental, less dependent upon literary tradition, and less associated with dialectical methods of reasoning, and with symbols. As a result, the subject matter of industrial occupation presents not only more of the content of science than it used to,

but greater opportunity for familiarity with the method by which knowledge is made.

The ordinary worker in the factory is of course under too immediate economic pressure to have a chance to produce a knowledge like that of the worker in the laboratory. But in schools, association with machines and industrial processes may be had under conditions where the chief conscious concern of the students is insight. The separation of shop and laboratory, where these conditions are fulfilled, is largely conventional, the laboratory having the advantage of permitting the following up of any intellectual interest a problem may suggest; the shop the advantage of emphasising the social bearings of the scientific principle, as well as, with many pupils, of stimulating a livelier interest.

(v) Finally, the advances which have been made in the psychology of learning in general and of childhood in particular fall into line with the increased importance of industry in life. For modern psychology emphasises the radical importance of primitive unlearned instincts of exploring, experimentation, and "trying on." It reveals that learning is not the work of something ready-made called mind, but that mind itself is an organisation of original capacities into activities having significance. As we have already seen (ante, p. 204), in older pupils work is to educative development of raw native activities what play is for younger pupils. Moreover, the passage from play to work should be gradual, not involving a radical change of attitude but carrying into work the elements of play, plus continuous reorganisation in behalf of greater control.

The reader will remark that these five points practically resume the main contentions of the previous part of the work. Both practically and philosophically, the key to the present educational situation lies in a gradual reconstruction of school materials and methods so as to utilise various forms of occupation typifying social callings, and to bring out their intellectual and moral content. This reconstruction must relegate purely literary methods — including textbooks — and dialectical methods to the position of necessary auxiliary tools in the intelligent development of consecutive and cumulative activities.

Education would then become an instrument of perpetuating unchanged the existing industrial order of society, instead of operating as a means of its transformation. The desired transformation is not difficult to define in a formal way. It signifies a society in which every person shall be occupied in something which makes the lives of others better worth living, and which accordingly makes the ties which bind persons together more perceptible — which breaks down the barriers of distance between them. It denotes a state of affairs in which the interest of each in his work is uncoerced and intelligent: based upon its congeniality to his own aptitudes. It goes without saying that we are far from such a social state; in a literal and quantitative sense, we may never arrive at it. But in principle, the quality of social changes already accomplished lies in this direction. There are more ample resources for its achievement now than ever there have been before. No insuperable obstacles, given the intelligent will for its realisation, stand in the way.

Success or failure in its realisation depends more upon the adoption of educational methods calculated to effect the change than upon anything else. For the change is essentially a change in the quality of mental disposition — an educative change. This does not mean that we can change character and mind by direct instruction and exhortation, apart from a change in industrial and political conditions. Such a conception contradicts our basic idea that character and mind are attitudes of participative response in social affairs. But it does mean that we may produce in schools a projection in type of the society we should like to realise, and by forming minds in accord with it gradually modify the larger and more recalcitrant features of adult society.

Sentimentally, it may seem harsh to say that the greatest evil of the present regime is not found in poverty and in the suffering which it entails, but in the fact that so many persons have callings which make no appeal to them, which are pursued simply for the money reward that accrues. For such callings constantly provoke one to aversion, ill will, and a desire to slight and evade. Neither men's hearts nor their minds are in their work. On the other hand, those who are not only much better off in worldly goods, but who are in excessive, if not monopolistic, control of the activities of the many are shut off from equality and generality of social intercourse. They are stimulated to pursuits of indulgence and display; they try to make up for the distance which separates them from others by the impression of force and superior possession and enjoyment which they can make upon others.

It would be quite possible for a narrowly conceived scheme of vocational education to perpetuate this division in a hardened form. Taking its stand upon a dogma of social predestination, it would assume that some are to continue to be wage earners under economic conditions like the present, and would aim simply to give them what is termed a trade education — that is, greater technical efficiency.

Technical proficiency is often sadly lacking, and is surely desirable on all accounts — not merely for the sake of the production of better goods at less cost, but for the greater happiness found in work. For no one cares for what one cannot half do. But there is a great difference between a proficiency limited to immediate work, and a competency extended to insight into its social bearings; between efficiency in carrying out the plans of others and in one forming one's own. At present, intellectual and emotional limitation characterises both the employing and the employed class. While the latter often have no concern with their occupation beyond the money return it brings, the former's outlook may be confined to profit and power.

The latter interest generally involves much greater intellectual initiation and larger survey of conditions. For it involves the direction and combination of a large number of diverse factors, while the interest in wages is restricted to certain direct muscular movements. But none the less there is a limitation of intelligence to technical and non-humane, non-liberal channels, so far as the work does not take in its social bearings. And when the animating motive is desire for private profit or personal power, this limitation is inevitable. In fact, the advantage in immediate social sympathy and humane disposition often lies with the economically unfortunate, who have not experienced the hardening effects of a one-sided control of the affairs of others.

Any scheme for vocational education which takes its point of departure from the industrial regime that now exists, is likely to assume and to perpetuate its divisions and weaknesses, and thus to become an instrument in accomplishing the feudal dogma of social predestination. Those who are in a position to make their wishes good, will demand a liberal, a cultural occupation, and one which fits for directive power the youth in whom they are directly interested.

To split the system, and give to others, less fortunately situated, an education conceived mainly as specific trade preparation, is to treat the schools as an agency for transferring the older division of labor and leisure, culture and service, mind and body, directed and directive class, into a society nominally democratic. Such a vocational education inevitably discounts the scientific and historic human connections of the materials and processes dealt with. To include such things in narrow trade education would be to waste time; concern for them would not be "practical." They are reserved for those who have leisure at command — the leisure due to superior economic resources. Such things might even be dangerous to the interests of the controlling class, arousing discontent or ambitions "beyond the station" of those working under the direction of others.

But an education which acknowledges the full intellectual and social meaning of a vocation would include instruction in the historic background of present conditions; training in science to give intelligence and initiative in dealing with material and agencies of production; and study of economics, civics, and politics, to bring the future worker into touch with the problems of the day and the various methods proposed for its improvement.

Above all, it would train power of readaptation to changing conditions so that future workers would not become blindly subject to a fate imposed upon them. This ideal has to contend not only with the inertia of existing educational traditions, but also with the opposition of those who are entrenched in command of the industrial machinery, and who realise that such an educational system if made general would threaten their ability to use others for their own ends.

But this very fact is the presage of a more equitable and enlightened social order, for it gives evidence of the dependence of social reorganisation upon educational reconstruction. It is accordingly an encouragement to those believing in a better order to undertake the promotion of a vocational education which does not subject youth to the demands and standards of the present system, but which utilises its scientific and social factors to develop a courageous intelligence, and to make intelligence practical and executive.

Labor and Leisure

Origin of the Opposition

The isolation of aims and values which we have been considering leads to opposition between them. Probably the most deep-seated antithesis which has shown itself in educational history is that between education in preparation for useful labor and education for a life of leisure.

The bare terms "useful labor" and 'leisure" confirm the statement already made that the segregation and conflict of values are not self-inclosed, but reflect a division within social life. Were the two functions of gaining a livelihood by work and enjoying in a cultivated way the opportunities of leisure, distributed equally among the different members of a community, it would not occur to any one that there was any conflict of educational agencies and aims involved. It would be self-evident that the question was how education could contribute most effectively to both.

And while it might be found that some materials of instruction chiefly accomplished one result and other subject matter the other, it would be evident that care must be taken to secure as much overlapping as conditions permit; that is, the education which had leisure more directly in view should indirectly reinforce as much as possible the efficiency and the enjoyment of work, while that aiming at the latter should produce habits of emotion and intellect which would procure a worthy cultivation of leisure.

These general considerations are amply borne out by the historical development of educational philosophy. The separation of liberal education from professional and industrial education goes back to the time of the Greeks, and was formulated expressly on the basis of a division of classes into those who had to labor for a living and those who were relieved from this necessity.

The conception that liberal education, adapted to men in the latter class, is intrinsically higher than the servile training given to the latter class reflected the fact that one class was free and the other servile in its social status. The latter class labored not only for its own subsistence, but also for the means which enabled the superior class to live without personally engaging in occupations taking almost all the time and not of a nature to engage or reward intelligence.

That a certain amount of labor must be engaged in goes without saying. Human beings have to live and it requires work to supply the resources of life. Even if we insist that the interests connected with getting a living are only material and hence intrinsically lower than those connected with enjoyment of time released from labor, and even if it were admitted that there is something engrossing and insubordinate in material interests which leads them to strive to usurp the place belonging to the higher ideal interests, this would not — barring the fact of socially divided classes — lead to neglect of the kind of education which trains men for the useful pursuits. It would rather lead to scrupulous care for them, so that men were trained to be efficient in them and yet to keep them in their place; education would see to it that we avoided the evil results which flow from their being allowed to flourish in obscure purlieus of neglect.

Only when a division of these interests coincides with a division of an inferior and a superior social class will preparation for useful work be looked down upon with contempt as an unworthy thing: a fact which prepares one for the conclusion that the rigid identification of work with material interests, and leisure with ideal interests is itself a social product.

The educational formulations of the social situation made over two thousand years ago have been so influential and give such a clear and logical recognition of the implications of the division into laboring and leisure classes, that they deserve especial note. According to them, man occupies the highest place in the scheme of animate existence. In part, he shares the constitution and functions of plants and animals — nutritive, reproductive, motor or practical. The distinctively human function is reason existing for the sake of beholding the spectacle of the universe. Hence the truly human end is the fullest possible of this distinctive human prerogative.

The life of observation, meditation, cogitation, and speculation pursued as an end in itself is the proper life of man. From reason moreover proceeds the proper control of the lower elements of human nature — the appetites and the active, motor, impulses. In themselves greedy, insubordinate, lovers of excess, aiming only at their own satiety, they observe moderation — the law of the mean — and serve desirable ends as they are subjected to the rule of reason.

Such is the situation as an affair of theoretical psychology and as most adequately stated by Aristotle. But this state of things is reflected in the constitution of classes of men and hence in the organisation of society. Only in a comparatively small number is the function of reason capable of operating as a law of life. In the mass of people, vegetative and animal functions dominate. Their energy of intelligence is so feeble and inconstant that it is constantly overpowered by bodily appetite and passion. Such persons are not truly ends in themselves, for only reason constitutes a final end.

Like plants, animals and physical tools, they are means, appliances, for the attaining of ends beyond themselves, although unlike them they have enough intelligence to exercise a certain discretion in the execution of the tasks committed to them. Thus by nature, and not merely by social convention, there are those who are slaves — that is, means for the ends of others.

The great body of artisans are in one important respect worse off than even slaves. Like the latter they are given up to the service of ends external to themselves; but since they do not enjoy the intimate association with the free superior class experienced by domestic slaves they remain on a lower plane of excellence. Moreover, women are classed with slaves and craftsmen as factors among the animate instrumentalities of production and reproduction of the means for a free or rational life.

Individually and collectively there is a gulf between merely living and living worthily. In order that one may live worthily he must first live, and so with collective society. The time and energy spent upon mere life, upon the gaining of subsistence, detracts from that available for activities that have an inherent rational meaning; they also unfit for the latter. Means are menial, the serviceable is servile. The true life is possible only in the degree in which the physical necessities are had without effort and without attention. Hence slaves, artisans, and women are employed in furnishing the means of subsistence in order that others, those adequately equipped with intelligence, may live the life of leisurely concern with things intrinsically worth while.

To these two modes of occupation, with their distinction of servile and free activities (or "arts") correspond two types of education: the base or mechanical and the liberal or intellectual. Some persons are trained by suitable practical exercises for capacity in doing things, for ability to use the mechanical tools involved in turning out physical commodities and rendering personal service. This training is a mere matter of habituation and technical skill; it operates through repetition and assiduity in application, not through awakening and nurturing thought. Liberal education aims to train intelligence for its proper office: to know.

The less this knowledge has to do with practical affairs, with making or producing, the more adequately it engages intelligence. So consistently does Aristotle draw the line between menial and liberal education that he puts what are now called the "fine" arts, music, painting, sculpture, in the same class with menial arts so far as their practice is concerned. They involve physical agencies, assiduity of practice, and external results. In discussing, for example, education in music he raises the question how far the young should be practiced in the playing of instruments. His answer is that such practice and proficiency may be tolerated as conduce to appreciation; that is, to understanding and enjoyment of music when played by slaves or professionals. When professional power is aimed at, music sinks from the liberal to the professional level. One might then as well teach cooking, says Aristotle.

Even a liberal concern with the works of fine art depends upon the existence of a hireling class of practitioners who have subordinated the development of their own personality to attaining skill in mechanical execution. The higher the activity the more purely mental is it; the less does it have to do with physical things or with the body. The more purely mental it is, the more independent or self-sufficing is it.

These last words remind us that Aristotle again makes a distinction of superior and inferior even within those living the life of reason. For there is a distinction in ends and in free action, according as one's life is merely accompanied by reason or as it makes reason its own medium. That is to say, the free citizen who devotes himself to the public life of his community, sharing in the management of its affairs and winning personal honor and distinction, lives a life accompanied by reason.

Present Situation

If the Aristotelian conception represented just Aristotle's personal view, it would be a more or less interesting historical curiosity. It could be dismissed as an illustration of the lack of sympathy or the amount of academic pedantry which may coexist with extraordinary intellectual gifts. But Aristotle simply described without confusion and without that insincerity always attendant upon mental confusion, the life that was before him. That the actual social situation has greatly changed since his day there is no need to say.

Aristotle was certainly permanently right when he said that "any occupation or art or study deserves to be called mechanical if it renders the body or soul or intellect of free persons unfit for the exercise and practice of excellence." The force of the statement is almost infinitely increased when we hold, as we nominally do at present, that all persons, instead of a comparatively few, are free. For when the mass of men and all women were regarded as unfree by the very nature of their bodies and minds, there was neither intellectual confusion nor moral hypocrisy in giving them only the training which fitted them for mechanical skill, irrespective of its ulterior effect upon their capacity to share in a worthy life.

He was permanently right also when he went on to say that "all mercenary employments as well as those which degrade the condition of the body are mechanical, since they deprive the intellect of leisure and dignity," — permanently right, that is, if gainful pursuits as matter of fact deprive the intellect of the conditions of its exercise and so of its dignity. If his statements are false, it is because they identify a phase of social custom with a natural necessity. But a different view of the relations of mind and matter, mind and body, intelligence and social service, is better than Aristotle's conception only if it helps render the old idea obsolete in fact — in the actual conduct of life and education.

Aristotle was permanently right in assuming the inferiority and subordination of mere skill in performance and mere accumulation of external products to understanding, sympathy of appreciation, and the free play of ideas. If there was an error, it lay in assuming the necessary separation of the two: in supposing that there is a natural divorce between efficiency in producing commodities and rendering service, and self-directive thought; between significant knowledge and practical achievement. We hardly better matters if we just correct his theoretical misapprehension, and tolerate the social state of affairs which generated and sanctioned his conception. We lose rather than gain in change from serfdom to free citizenship if the most prized result of the change is simply an increase in the mechanical efficiency of the human tools of production. So we lose rather than gain in coming to think of intelligence as an organ of control of nature through action, if we are content that an unintelligent, unfree state persists in those who engage directly in turning nature to use, and leave the intelligence which controls to be the exclusive possession of remote scientists and captains of industry.

We are in a position honestly to criticize the division of life into separate functions and of society into separate classes only so far as we are free from responsibility for perpetuating the educational practices which train the many for pursuits involving mere skill in production, and the few for a knowledge that is an ornament and a cultural embellishment. In short, ability to transcend the Greek philosophy of life and education is not secured by a mere shifting about of the theoretical symbols meaning free, rational, and worthy. It is not secured by a change of sentiment regarding the dignity of labor, and the superiority of a life of service to that of an aloof self-sufficing independence.

Important as these theoretical and emotional changes are, their importance consists in their being turned to account in the development of a truly democratic society, a society in which all share in useful service and all enjoy a worthy leisure. It is not a mere change in the concepts of culture — or a liberal mind — and social service which requires an educational reorganisation; but the educational transformation is needed to give full and explicit effect to the changes implied in social life. The increased political and economic emancipation of the "masses" has shown itself in education; it has effected the development of a common school system of education, public and free. It has destroyed the idea that learning is properly a monopoly of the few who are predestined by nature to govern social affairs. But the revolution is still incomplete. The idea still prevails that a truly cultural or liberal education cannot have anything in common, directly at least, with industrial affairs, and that the education which is fit for the masses must be a useful or practical education in a sense which opposes useful and practical to nurture of appreciation and liberation of thought.

As a consequence, our actual system is an inconsistent mixture. Certain studies and methods are retained on the supposition that they have the sanction of peculiar liberality, the chief content of the term liberal being uselessness for practical ends. This aspect is chiefly visible in what is termed the higher education — that of the college and of preparation for it. But is has filtered through into elementary education and largely controls its processes and aims. But, on the other hand, certain concessions have been made to the masses who must engage in getting a livelihood and to the increased role of economic activities in modern life.

These concessions are exhibited in special schools and courses for the professions, for engineering, for manual training and commerce, in vocational and prevocational courses; and in the spirit in which certain elementary subjects, like the three R's, are taught. The result is a system in which both "cultural" and "utilitarian" subjects exist in an inorganic composite where the former are not by dominant purpose socially serviceable and the latter not liberative of imagination or thinking power.

In the inherited situation, there is a curious intermingling, in even the same study, of concession to usefulness and a survival of traits once exclusively attributed to preparation for leisure. The "utility" element is found in the motives assigned for the study, the "liberal" element in methods of teaching. The outcome of the mixture is perhaps less satisfactory than if either principle were adhered to in its purity.

The motive popularly assigned for making the studies of the first four or five years consist almost entirely of reading, spelling, writing, and arithmetic, is, for example, that ability to read, write, and figure accurately is indispensable to getting ahead. These studies are treated as mere instruments for entering upon a gainful employment or of later progress in the pursuit of learning, according as pupils do not or do remain in school. This attitude is reflected in the emphasis put upon drill and practice for the sake of gaining automatic skill. If we turn to Greek schooling, we find that from the earliest years the acquisition of skill was subordinated as much as possible to acquisition of literary content possessed of aesthetic and moral significance. Not getting a tool for subsequent use but present subject matter was the emphasised thing. Nevertheless the isolation of these studies from practical application, their reduction to purely symbolic devices, represents a survival of the idea of a liberal training divorced from utility.

A thorough adoption of the idea of utility would have led to instruction which tied up the studies to situations in which they were directly needed and where they were rendered immediately and not remotely helpful. It would be hard to find a subject in the curriculum within which there are not found evil results of a compromise between the two opposed ideals. Natural science is recommended on the ground of its practical utility, but is taught as a special accomplishment in removal from application. On the other hand, music and literature are theoretically justified on the ground of their culture value and are then taught with chief emphasis upon forming technical modes of skill.

If we had less compromise and resulting confusion, if we analysed more carefully the respective meanings of culture and utility, we might find it easier to construct a course of study which should be useful and liberal at the same time. Only superstition makes us believe that the two are necessarily hostile so that a subject is illiberal because it is useful and cultural because it is useless. It will generally be found that instruction which, in aiming at utilitarian results, sacrifices the development of imagination, the refining of taste and the deepening of intellectual insight — surely cultural values — also in the same degree renders what is learned limited in its use. Not that it makes it wholly unavailable but that its applicability is restricted to routine activities carried on under the supervision of others.

Narrow modes of skill cannot be made useful beyond themselves; any mode of skill which is achieved with deepening of knowledge and perfecting of judgment is readily put to use in new situations and is under personal control. It was not the bare fact of social and economic utility which made certain activities seem servile to the Greeks but the fact that the activities directly connected with getting a livelihood were not, in their days, the expression of a trained intelligence nor carried on because of a personal appreciation of their meaning.

So far as farming and the trades were rule-of-thumb occupations and so far as they were engaged in for results external to the minds of agricultural laborers and mechanics, they were illiberal — but only so far. The intellectual and social context has now changed. The elements in industry due to mere custom and routine have become subordinate in most economic callings to elements derived from scientific inquiry. The most important occupations of today represent and depend upon applied mathematics, physics, and chemistry.

The area of the human world influenced by economic production and influencing consumption has been so indefinitely widened that geographical and political considerations of an almost infinitely wide scope enter in. It was natural for Plato to deprecate the learning of geometry and arithmetic for practical ends, because as matter of fact the practical uses to which they were put were few, lacking in content and mostly mercenary in quality. But as their social uses have increased and enlarged, their liberalising or "intellectual" value and their practical value approach the same limit.

Doubtless the factor which chiefly prevents our full recognition and employment of this identification is the conditions under which so much work is still carried on. The invention of machines has extended the amount of leisure which is possible even while one is at work. It is a commonplace that the mastery of skill in the form of established habits frees the mind for a higher order of thinking. Something of the same kind is true of the introduction of mechanically automatic operations in industry. They may release the mind for thought upon other topics. But when we confine the education of those who work with their hands to a few years of schooling devoted for the most part to acquiring the use of rudimentary symbols at the expense of training in science, literature, and history, we fail to prepare the minds of workers to take advantage of this opportunity.

9

Transforming Education through Technology

Educators cannot resist new technologies, provided those technologies have characteristics suitable to educational purposes, foremost among those being a permanence in time. Stop for a moment to consider film, which encodes information in stable, material form yet has not come into robust use in education. Film is bulky, hard to store, costly to project, and easily damaged. It can be best disseminated in a quasi-broadcast fashion with prints distributed to numerous theaters more or less at the same time, with the production playing as long as it can command a full audience and then disappearing into an archive, from which films are not easy to retrieve. These distribution constraints have made movies, until very recently, far more effective as media of entertainment than of education.

Computers as a system will change that, and much more. Broadly speaking, the communication innovations since the mid- nineteenth century have created a family of technologies for encoding diverse forms of information in energy. The computer is the most recent in this series of innovations, and it is likely, historically, to incorporate all those leading up to it into itself. What seem to us to be separate industries with separate technologies will become branches of a single comprehensive industry and technology, the computer as a system.

One can now see large corporations jockeying to capitalise on this consolidation of technologies. For instance, the major Japanese electronics firms seem to be calculating that they can best shape this process by combining business communication with the entertainment industries, buying up major entertainment conglomerates while designing ever-more computing power into home entertainment devices. The emerging system, however, may in fact be far more robust if built on a combination of telecommunications and education. Digital technologies enhance the staying power of information in time, expanding its educative power relative to its currency as entertainment. We will be developing the thesis that the computer is rapidly incorporating the modern media in one comprehensive system, a system of knowledge and education.

Analog and the Digital Coding

We distinguished between technologies that locate information in matter, for instance sculpting and printing, and those that locate it in states of energy, for instance radio and computers. Among the latter, we need to make important further distinctions, which have to do with the techniques people use to encode information in energy. To grasp the cultural import of the computer as a system incorporating all the media of communication, to appreciate its potential power, we need to reflect on the way that it encodes information in energy, seeing how that differs from other techniques.

Analog coding serves effectively for some specialised computational purposes, but almost all computers, from tiny palm- tops to huge supercomputers, work with information stored in digital code. Such digital code differs profoundly from the analog codes used typically in radio and television. In the paragraphs that follow, we will reflect on how digital code differs from analog and then consider five matters that determine the value of information for human activity — production and reproduction, storage, transmission, selective retrieval, and intelligent processing. Through these considerations, we will form a sense of why the computer, as it matures, will be a very significant step in our history.

Note at the outset that we could apply this distinction between analog and digital coding to the media that use matter to carry information. For instance, painting and sculpture are highly analog media, whereas alphabetic writing is interestingly ambiguous. It is analog insofar as it is phonetic and digital insofar as it is a prescriptive set of legible conventions. But it would take us afield to pursue these distinctions with respect to media that locate information in matter, for our concerns here are primarily with the media that carry information in energy. How does the digital coding of information in energy differ from the analog?

Analog systems encode information in energy by using the properties of continuous waves so that each successive change in the amplitude of the wave will be analogous to a change in sound or appearance in the human world. Lets construct an example. Take a dishtowel.

Holding each corner of one end in each hand, flap it rhythmically in front of you, making it undulate up and down. It is not hard to control the beat of the flapping, making each flap identical in duration, perhaps slow and long or quick and short. That beat is like the frequency of an analog signal. Usually it does not carry the information, but when we are surrounded by many different signals, each with a different frequency, it allows us to find the one signal we want. Observe the flapping towel, however. From beat to beat, it will have all sorts of variations, curving this way then that, depending on subtle changes in the orientation of your hands to each other and the tension they put on the cloth.

Like the sound itself, the flapping is transient. Analog encoding depends on making significant changes in the energy state of the wave, a most unstable phenomena. Digital encoding is much more stable. Put down the towel and flip the light switch on the wall. The switch has gone from "on" to "off;" it was stable in its former state and is stable in its latter.

The light switch is a digital device, although one that does not accomplish much in the way of communication and control. To see simple signals controlling more complicated processes occurring around you, look at another digital switch, the stoplight at the corner. It has two basic states, red or green — amber is not really a state, but a cue that a change of state is about to happen. There are two unambiguous states, green-go, red-stop. These are easily standardised, stable, and remarkably effective in controlling complex flows of matter and energy. The stoplight is very much like the small charge in a transistor in that one state allows traffic to move and the other calls it to a halt.

Basic red-green stoplight is a binary digital system — binary because there are two alternatives and digital because those consist of discrete, unambiguously different states. The typical electric stove, with options on each burner running from warm to high, has a quinary digital control on its coils — quinary because there are five alternatives and digital because each of these is distinct from the others. Thus, digital systems can in principle have different numbers of basic alternatives, but computers almost always use a binary system, building many subtle variations from a multiplicity of either-ors.

A digital state is what it is, discrete, unambiguous, disjunctive. Digital code does not capture changes similar to other changes, it presents a set of values that are what they are. Digital coding follows a principle akin to encrypting — there is only one message, which, when encrypted, is put in a way that makes it look indecipherable. With the appropriate key, however, the cryptographer finds the message, not something like the original, but the original itself.

For instance, the apparatus for recording music digitally measures sound frequencies at successive instances and records the numeric value of the frequencies. These are samples of the actual sound, not likenesses to it. Digital coding samples a phenomenon, registers the sample, and then reproduces the phenomenon from the sample. If the sampling technique and the technique of reproducing from the sample are very good, it can be extremely hard to distinguish the original from the reproduction. What is coded is an exact value, precisely what it is and nothing else.

What is encoded digitally, therefore, is actually very different from what is encoded in an analog system. The digital system encodes a sample of the thing whereas the analog system encodes an analogy to it. Again, let us construct an example. Consider a full wheel of cheddar cheese. Describing the cheese by analogy can be difficult. I might say it is about the size and shape of an old-time hatbox and that it is heavy, as if the hatbox were filled with water. Its color is like custard and it tastes — this is the important, difficult part — somewhat like grapefruit, although its texture in the mouth is very different, a bit like a firm fudge that crumbles and then softens into a paste as one chews it. Describing the cheddar by a sample of it is much simpler. I cut you a little piece, perhaps several from different places in the wheel. The sample is the cheese and you can sniff it or taste it directly from the sample.

When we digitally code the sample, we register what the sample is on an appropriate scale and we code that value, not some approximate likeness to it. Consider recording a singer's voice digitally. At numerous intervals the recording samples the exact sound frequency of the voice, registering in a matrix of precise values what, at each sampling instant, the frequency was. The digital recording carries no information about the voice during the intervals between the sampling instants, but it carries the exact frequency of it at those instants. If the sampling frequency is sufficiently rapid, the sound of the reproduced voice will be essentially identical to the original. Digital code allows the playback to reconstruct the voice. Thus, digital coding registers sampled values, not approximate similarities. That is its first point of difference with analog coding.

Secondly digital code differs from analog because it resists degradation far more effectively. Electrical systems, like everything else, are subject to entropy. Every circuit has in it random fluctuations. Computers are not wondrously free of such static. Minor fluxes are a big problem in analog coding because the locus of information is in tiny incremental differences in the amplitude of waves, which the random fluxes in circuits can easily affect. In the absolute, digital systems are equally subject to noise, but the locus of information is in the basic energy state, not in small changes of that state. When the significant point is simply whether a circuit is on or off, it allows for a huge threshold before an intrusive fluctuation will become significant, making a circuit that is "on" appear to be "off" or vice versa.

To construct an example, consider a binary test for whether or not it is raining: looking out my apartment window to see if the sidewalk is wet or dry. This test is subject to noise — perhaps in this case we should call it "splash." During the summer window air-conditioners in the building adjacent condense water on hot, humid days, splotching the sidewalk. Also on the road on the other side there is a low spot where water collects from a leaky hydrant and occasionally passing cars splash it onto the sidewalk. Like the noise in the electrical system, extraneous wetness sometimes partially covers a dry pavement. This rarely confuses my binary test, however, because I establish a threshold — it is raining if the sidewalk is fully, uniformly wet and it is not raining if the sidewalk is dry, or partially splotched from random sources of water. Given the substantial threshold possible in a binary system, very, very rarely will electrical noise cause the misreading of a bit of information.

In sum, in comparison to analog coding, digital code registers values that are attributes of the thing being coded, not likenesses to it, and those values, once coded, will be remarkably resistant to error or degradation. These characteristics make digital code immensely useful in processes of communication and control.

Digitisation and Communication

Digital code records samples of phenomena, not analogies to them, and it does so by techniques that are remarkably stable and accurate. By themselves, these characteristics may not seem so extraordinary. But put in context, the context of human use, they have very significant effects on the computer as a communication system. Whatever the medium, in order to communicate people need to be able to produce and reproduce information, to store it, to transmit it, to select among it, and to process it intelligently in the course of action. These five areas determine the relative historic value of different communication techniques.

Reproduction, storage, transmission, selection, intelligent action: communication techniques that perform these functions well serve human needs well. Because digital coding registers samples of things and because it resists error and degradation, it has interesting effects in each of these five areas. These effects will determine how the computer as a system can contribute to our unfolding cultural history.

The difficulties in implementing multimedia are not primarily "technical," in the layman's sense of the term. Ordinarily we think that the technical problem lies in designing an apparatus to accomplish a novel purpose. In many areas, making the apparatus is relatively simple, and it can be done in numerous different ways. What is difficult is setting a controlling standard that will establish agreement on which one of the possible ways to design the apparatus will be the one put into common use. This is in part a question of technical standards — for instance, what sampling rates will be standard for digitally encoded sound or what screen resolution will be standard for digital high-definition television (HDTV)? But the problems of controlling standards goes far beyond the domain of technical standards — long established branches of law and language are at stake as well.

Thus, the production and reproduction of information is not simply a technical process. It is a process controlled by law and driven by incentives. Digital coding of information will affect these domains as well. For instance, copyright makes sense in a system in which people locate information in material objects — copying consists in expending the energy to implant the information in matter, preeminently by putting ink on a page.

Copying information that is located in matter is a laborious, error-prone process, subject to legal processes.

Recording and reproducing information that is located in energy has very different characteristics. It becomes extremely inexpensive, with the result that it can be done ad hoc by anyone who possesses easily available, inexpensive tools. Already, spontaneous reproduction through analog means, such as photocopying and audio and video tape, has put considerable stress on laws pertaining to the right to copy. The broadcast industries have had to develop novel ways to realise economic benefit from cultural works, ways that turn less on the right to copy and more on the right to use a work.

With digital coding the reproduction of material becomes even faster, cheaper, and vastly more accurate than it does with analog electronic media. Once something has been sampled and captured in digital code, the idea of a copy of that sample ceases to make much sense. The copy is not really a copy, but a second instance of the original. The computer radically changes the conditions bearing on the reproduction of information and ideas. Once the infrastructure is in place, the reproduction of materials has a negligible cost with respect to materials, work, or quality. In principle, in a digitally encoded culture, anyone can have instances of anything they wish without added cost to the system. It will require an elaborate process of technical, social, and legal development to achieve actualise such potentialities.

Digital coding will also transform the problem of storing information. Librarians concerned with the preservation of materials traditionally attend closely to the durability of paper and its possible substitutes. The key question they ask is: "How long will it last?" This makes a lot of sense as long as the information is located in matter. If the paper will quickly degrade, the cultural community will soon need to reprint its materials or reproduce them on some alternative material such as microfiche.

The shelf-life of all this is important as each cycle of reproduction is very costly, as well as an occasion for material to be lost and errors in reproduction to creep in. With digitally coded materials, shelf-life remains limited, but the costs of reproduction and the likelihood of errors arising from reproduction drastically declines. Hence, the keepers of the heritage need to rethink the standard principles of storage and preservation. Continuous reproduction can make the quest for durability unnecessary. Since reproduction is very cheap and very accurate, the problem is not one of finding the most enduring materials and keeping them as stable as possible. Rather the problem becomes one of regularly refreshing the energy-states in which the information is located and making sure that it is scattered in enough separate instances that a catastrophic failure in one instance would not obliterate the heritage.

Other, more novel problems of storage also arise. With respect to information located in material objects, we naturally store materials in institutions adapted to the attributes of the objects. Thus we use libraries for books and museums for paintings and artifacts. Much intellectual specialisation arises because people need specific skills to work effectively in these different collection of material resources. Insofar as we can record all these resources in digital code, we will store them in one, comprehensive system and we will thereby diminish in power many objective goads to intellectual specialisation.

As digital coding makes information easier to store with much diminished threat of loss, so too it improves our ability to transmit information. Transportation costs and limitations have long been a significant determinant of communication capacities. Through the twentieth century, techniques of coding information in energy have greatly reduced the costs and limits on its transmission.

With the substitution of digital for analog coding, these developments are extending far further as we enter the twenty-first century.

Analog systems using energy as the medium have developed two major principles: point-to-point circuit switching, as through the telephone, and the use of wide information channels in broadband transmissions, as through radio and television broadcasting. Digital systems are combining and unifying these two principles, allowing the links between point-to-point switched circuits to be wide information channels, creating a single transmission net of extraordinary flexibility and power.

We are already everyday users of the basic principles essential to these changes. My mother is eighty-eight and legally blind, but she can use a push-button phone with confidence and has a good head for phone numbers and thus she keeps up familial and social connections all over, in Mexico, in Canada, and around the United States. Each time she dials someone's number, she instructs the phone system to establish connections within its circuits to link her phone with that of the person she is calling. Phones code and decode voices from a very simple electrical signal that can be easily transmitted through complex switching systems and has a narrow band for coding information, one just sufficient for the low- fidelity reproduction of ordinary speech. How much traffic the phone system can bear depends on how many separate circuits it can switch together at any time and on how many separate transmissions its trunk lines can aggregate together in simultaneous calls. You'll get a busy signal if the system runs out of switches or transmission room.

Radio and television use much wider bandwidths, and they code them more intensely, with the result that their signals can be much more complex than those of the telephone. Thus radio can reproduce sound with much greater quality that the telephone, and the amount of information transmitted via television far exceeds that used in a phone conversation. The wider bandwidth, however, makes point-to-point switching in such transmissions more complicated to do without introducing noise into the signal, and without overwhelming the capacity of connecting circuits when many parallel transmissions are traveling on them simultaneously. Various properties of digital coding facilitate the combination of circuit switching with the information intensive transmissions that characterise broadband systems.

Both analog and digital systems make use of what we will call micro-time, the actuality of incredibly brief instants. For instance, radio waves fluctuate several million times per second and each fluctuation produces some of the information we hear. The higher the frequency, the more information the signal can contain, provided we can keep the receiver tuned to the proper spot upon the spectrum and provided we can minimise interference between signals and other sources of noise. Because the information bearing medium is a continuous wave, however, we find it much easier to propagate the information onto the medium at the rate it occurs at, and at which it is to be received. In contrast, when the information has been captured in digital code, it becomes much easier to make use of micro-time in more flexible ways: capture, transmission, and delivery can be separated.

The pace of capture depends on the pace of the phenomenon, what we call "real time." Transmission of the binary units, the bits encoding the phenomenon, can take place in different time — it can squeeze into each tenth of a second, or less, the information needed for one second of conversation, giving the circuit to other conversations for the remaining nine-tenths, or more, of each second. By this technique, and others like code compression and error correction, the capacity of a circuit carrying digital data can be greatly expanded.

Further, the transmission of analog data depends very closely on the particular characteristics of the transmitting medium. With the transmission of digital data, it does not matter what the transmitting medium is, provided that medium has been adapted to transmit digital code. Thus all the different electromagnetic transmission media in common use now easily transmit digital data.

More importantly, new media, useless for transmitting analog information, for instance, laser light in fiber optic cable, increasingly transmit digitised information with significant gains in speed and volume, at lowered cost, and with increased dependability. The frequencies of light waves are much higher than those of electromagnetic waves. Hence, we can pack information far more densely per unit of time into light for transmission over fiberoptic cables than we can with electricity over wires or electromagnetic signals in space. The usable bandwidth is much, much wider. The higher density allows much more intense timesharing of the circuit and the greater bandwidth means that in each instant a much larger load of information will be charging through the circuit. As a result, a system is emerging in which all forms of information — text, numerics, graphics, audio, video — can be transmitted, switched from point-to-point, as easily as we can with the phone.

Digital coding, thus, is making possible the use of one system to produce all forms of information, to reproduce anything in the system with low cost and little loss, to provide for its indefinite storage through this process of continuous reproduction, and to transmit any element of it to any user fast and cheaply. By themselves, these developments make oodles of good information easily accessible, threatening to overwhelm the user in a vast babel of bits. These three characteristics are of a piece with each other, setting limits on what intellectual resources a culture can provide its members. But they do not, alone, make for a well developed system of communication.

Selective retrieval, enabling people to get precisely the information they want and when they need it, has always been a key problem of culture and communication. How can you get from the culture the ideas and information that you want and need? And even more perplexing, how can the culture intimate to you and everyone else what possibilities of interest it does and does not offer in the infinity of circumstances surrounding us? Retrieval is a fundamental problem of all cultures, and it is becoming an even more pressing problem with digitally coded information. It is the fourth determinant of communication effectiveness in history and the widespread digitisation of information is transforming it as well.

Throughout history, major communication advances have brought with them new ways to retrieve information. The practice of citing books and articles by title and author, edition and page, rose to full significance in the era of print. The printed book, which could be distributed in many locations in identical versions, needed some logically effective technique of reference and recall, one that would work in many different places and many different times.

Prior to that people referred far more vaguely to an author and an argument or thesis, and to retrieve the actual text a scholar needed to know where a specific instance was physically located, with diverse works bound together for convenience. Today, people often handle their personal libraries in this pre-print fashion, jumbling certain books together say by size, or just shelving them as they come, able to find any particular one, not by a sense of logical order, but by having a feel for where it is by some sense of spatial juxtaposition. That works for small libraries, but it spells chaos for large collections of printed books. For those, people needed to develop far more systematic techniques of reference and recall.

With digitally coded information, the situation is much the same: people need to master new, more powerful retrieval routines to manage the cornucopia of information. These techniques relate to two different problems in the use of information — exchanging information and applying ideas. In both exchanging ideas and applying them to problems, people need to retrieve information selectively. Exchanging materials is somewhat similar to the phenomena of point-to-point switched circuits while applying them is related to finding a station or channel in broadcast communication. Exchange requires the precise identification of start and end points and application requires the substantive sifting through extensive materials to select out the precise components pertinent to the problem at hand. Since the problems and prospects in each domain are rather different, let us consider each briefly in turn.

Retrieval that involves sifting, selecting, and applying ideas presents different problems and opportunities. Our existing techniques for doing this involve time-consuming secondary processing of materials — indexing books, abstracting articles, cataloguing things under key words and subject headings, adding captions to pictures and tables, annotating works with cross- references and footnotes. Digital coding makes these practices more effective in three significant ways.

First it facilitates the processing by creating tools to help people to index, abstract, caption, and catalogue their culture. This presents us incremental gains. Second, it makes many traditional references, which had been unidirectional from one work to another, usefully bi-directional. Only where very special indexes have been laboriously developed can I go into a library and ask for a list of works that cite a passage that specially interests me. In a digital environment, the electronic reference that implements a note will point both ways, something that will make traditional references useful in powerful new ways. Third, traditional references implemented digitally will save users much time and energy, for following out a reference will be nearly instantaneous.

Currently it is often hard to maintain a train of thought in following a reference as one needs to go off to the library or bookstore, perhaps having to wait weeks for a work to arrive from a distance. Digitally coded links will be fast and transparent. Together, these three changes will significantly enhance traditional resources for the reflective retrieval of ideas and the application of them to our controlling purposes.

Memory, to be meaningful, must ultimately return to a sentient human mind — a library unread is not a culture preserved. In externalising memory into material objects, humans have not alienated memory from ourselves, but enhanced our capacity to remember by transferring parts of the task to objects that we make and manage. So too, in externalising intellectual activity, we do not entirely alienate it from ourselves. Instead we compensate for limitations, strengthen capacities for demanding operations, and enhance attention, precision, finesse, or speed.

To understand how the computer is accelerating the transfer of intelligence to external tools, it is important to realise that this is not a sudden novelty in our culture. We perceive the world with our senses and prepare it for thought: through most of history, people did this without the aid of instruments. That began to change some centuries ago. We can interpret the rise of modern science as the intellectual fruits of externalising capacities for perception into instruments of observation.

Clocks and chronometers permitted people to perceive time with ever greater precision. The telescope and microscope enhanced the human capacity to see distances and details. The thermometer lent accuracy to our capacity to perceive differences of hot and cold. Exact scales and rules and other measures, tuning forks, prisms, filters, balances, samples, gages, a wondrous panoply of instruments, allowed inquiring minds to develop the empirical base of observation upon which they built our stock of scientific understanding.

By working with digitally coded information, instrument designers are extending the power of perception greatly. The unmanned space-probes reporting on the solar system have perhaps been the most dramatic of these extensions, with wondrous photographs and other readings radioed back as masses of digital code. Not since the invention of the telescope has our ability to perceive the universe around us so leaped forward. But digital read-outs are all around us with the computer creeping into all sorts of mundane tools, enhancing our capacity to track and control their use.

For many decades car instrumentation, for instance, was very stable, consisting of a few analog gages that indicated the car's speed and possibly the RPM's of the engine, while additionally giving key hints about the state of the car's fuel, coolant, engine oil, and electrical system. That's fast changing now with digital sensors in new and old places giving a much more exact picture of the car's condition of operation, with an onboard computer relating readings to one another — "it's getting pretty close to empty" gives way to "range remaining fifteen miles." The computer will greatly extend the reach and accuracy of instrumentation as people apply it with increasing effects to small matters and large.

With the computer, people can externalise into their instruments more than their powers of perception. When Edison claimed that "genius is one percent inspiration and ninety-nine percent perspiration," he probably thought that the human capacity for both inspiration and perspiration were basically fixed, and by perspiration he had in mind the laborious calculations needed to test speculative insight, separating good from bad.

Digital systems do not do away with the need for perspiration, but they extend what we can accomplish with a given amount of it. Most forms of calculation, correlation, combination, and connection that people can make, computers can help them make better. They can expand our abilities to sort, order, rank, and select. Even this process of externalising powers of calculation is not entirely new historically, as one who has worked with a slide rule will realise, but it is being vastly increased. The consequences are likely to be very great.

Bibliography

Baskin, Wade, *Classics in education,* Philosophical Library 1966.

Blacker, David J., *Dying to teach : the educator's search for immortality,* Teachers College Press 1997

Bruner, Jerome S., *The culture of education,* Harvard University Press 1996

Bunting , Josiah, Robert Parkman, *An Education for Our Time,* Regnery 1998.

Comenius, Johann Amos, A.M.O. Dobbie (trans.), *Panorthosia, or, Universal reform,* Sheffield Academic Press 1993.

duke Cooney, William, Charles Cross, Barry, *Trunk From Plato to Piaget: The Greatest Educational Theorists from across the Centuries and around the World,* University Press of America 1993

Cremin, Lawrence Arthur, *Popular education and its discontents,* Harper & Row, 1990.

Cromer, Alan H Connected knowledge, *Science, philosophy, and education,* Oxford University Press, 1997

Egan, Kieran, "The educated mind: how cognitive tools shape our understanding", University of Chicago Press, 1997.

Gardner, Howard, *The disciplined mind: what all students should understand,* Simon & Schuster 1999.

Kneller, George F., *Movements of thought in modern education,* Collier MacMillan 1984.

Knight, George R., *Issues & alternatives in educational philosophy,* Andrews University Press 1998.

Locke, John, Ruth Weissbourd Grant, Nathan Tarcov (eds.), *Some thoughts concerning education,* Hackett Pub. Co.,1996

Melanchthon, Philipp, *Orations on philosophy and education,* Cambridge University Press 1999.

Noddings, Nel, *Philosophy of education,* Westview Press 1995.

Ornstein Allan C., Gerald L. Gutek, Chicago D. Levine, *Foundations of Education,* 6th ed. Houghton Mifflin 1996.

Ozmon, Howard, Samuel M. Craver, *Philosophical foundations of education,* Merrill 1995.

Pangle, Lorraine Smith, Thomas L. Pangle, *Learning of Liberty: Educational Ideas of the American Founders* University Press of Kansas 1995.

Power, Edward J., *A legacy of learning : a history of Western education,* Albany, N.Y.: State University of New York Press, 1991.

Reagan, Timothy G., *Non-Western educational traditions: alternative approaches to educational thought and practice,* L. Erlbaum Associates 1996.

Reed, Ronald F., Tony W. Johnson, *Philosophical documents in education,* Longman 1996.

Rorty, Amelie Oksenberg, *Philosophers on Education: Historical Perspectives,* Routledge 1998.

Theobald, Paul, *Teaching the Commons: Place, Pride, and the Renewal,* Westview Press 1997.

White, John Ponsford, *Education and the end of work: a new philosophy of work and learning,* Cassell 1997.

Winch, Christopher, John Gingell, *Key concepts in the philosophy of education,* Routledge 1999.

Woods, Ronald George, Robin Barrow, *An introduction to philosophy of education,* Methuen 1975.

Index